CONTEMPORARY SOCIAL RESE
General Editor: MARTIN BULMER

18
Quantity and Quality in Social Research

CONTEMPORARY SOCIAL RESEARCH SERIES

Quantity and Quality in Social Research

ALAN BRYMAN

Loughborough University

London and New York

First published 1988 by Unwin Hyman Ltd

Reprinted 1992, 1993
by Routledge
11 New Fetter Lane, London EC4P 4EE

Simultaneously published in the USA and Canada
by Routledge
29 West 35th Street, New York, NY 10001

Typeset in Times by Grove Graphics, Tring, Herts
Printed and bound in Great Britain by
Biddles Ltd, Guildford and King's Lynn

British Library Cataloguing in Publication Data
A catalogue record for this book is available from the British Library

Library of Congress Cataloging in Publication Data
A catalog record for this book is available from the Library of Congress

ISBN 0-415-07898-9

Contents

For Sue and Sarah — again

Preface

This book focuses upon the debate about quantitative and qualitative research which took root in the 1960s, although many of the central themes go back centuries. The basic terms of the debate have been felt in many of the disciplines which make up the social sciences, especially sociology, social psychology, education research, organization studies, and evaluation research. The discussions about the nature and relative virtues of quantitative and qualitative research reveal a mixture of philosophical issues and considerations of the virtues and vices of the methods of data collection with which each of these two research traditions is associated. In this book, I address the nature of quantitative and qualitative research, as generally perceived by the participants in the debate. The debate has tended to provide somewhat exaggerated portraits of the two traditions, so that one of the book's themes is the ways in which actual research practice may depart from these descriptions. I also examine the extent to which there is a clear connection between the practices of researchers working within each of the two traditions and underlying philosophical positions, as posited by the debate. The possibility of integrating quantitative and qualitative research is also examined.

The book has been written with undergraduates and postgraduates studying research methods in such fields as sociology, social pyschology, education, organization studies, social policy, and similar subjects in mind. I have drawn on research relating to a variety of topics and areas in the social sciences in order to enhance the book's general appeal.

I wish to thank thirteen generations of undergraduates who have taken my Research Methods course at Loughborough University. Many of the ideas in this book derive from this contact. The students' often blunt refusal to accept many of the extreme versions of the debate about quantitative and qualitative research sharpened my own appreciation of many of the issues. Martin Bulmer has been a supportive and extremely helpful editor. His comments and criticisms greatly assisted the formulation of the book's central themes. I am grateful to Michael Billig and Louis Cohen for their advice on a number of chapters. I also wish to thank Richard Jenkins for a personal communication relating to his research on Belfast youth. My wife, Sue, offered much stylistic advice, for which I am grateful. Of course, none of these individuals is to blame for any of the book's deficiencies, which are entirely of my own making. I also wish to thank both Sue and my daughter Sarah for their constant support during the writing of this book. I know that they have given up a great deal during the period of its preparation.

Alan Bryman,
Loughborough University

1

Introduction

The chief focus of this book is the debate about quantitative and qualitative research in the social sciences, in particular the relative merits and disadvantages of these two styles of inquiry. This is a controversy in which philosophical issues tend to be interwoven with discussions about the nature and capacities of different methods of research. Quantitative research is typically taken to be exemplified by the social survey and by experimental investigations. Qualitative research tends to be associated with participant observation and unstructured, in-depth interviewing. On the face of it, questions relating to the advantages and capacities of these two approaches and their associated techniques would seem to be technical ones, pertaining to their respective strengths and weaknesses in relation to particular research topics. In fact, philosophical issues figure very strongly and have much to do with a growing interest in the methods associated with a qualitative style of inquiry.

This state of affairs – the entanglement with philosophy and the interest in qualitative research – is of relatively recent origin. There has, of course, always been an awareness of the differences between the nature of, for example, the social survey and participant observation. However, the focus tended to be on the capacity of surveys to provide a framework in which the procedures associated with the scientific method could be followed, and the poor showing of participant observation in this regard. Consequently, qualitative methods such as participant observation tended to be regarded as relatively marginal in the context of the social scientist's armoury of data collection techniques.

The standard format of social research methods textbooks (particularly those published prior to the mid-1970s) exemplifies these tendencies. The typical methods text began with a number of chapters on the scientific method. This discussion formed a bedrock for examining the procedures associated with the survey and often with experiments. Because of its inability to conform to the canons of scientific method, a technique like participant observation was accorded scant attention. In Goode and Hatt's (1952) influential text, participant observation is consigned to a fairly cursory treatment in a chapter on 'Some problems in qualitative and case analysis' and another on 'Observation'; this contrasts sharply with the eight chapters dealing with aspects of survey procedures, three on scaling methods alone. The growing interest in the analysis of survey data, following the influence of writers like Lazarsfeld and Blalock, resulted very often in much greater attention being devoted to its associated procedures: Phillips (1966) and Nachmias and Nachmias (1976), for example, both wrote a whole section on data analysis, representing some one hundred pages in each; by contrast, participant observation can be found in a relatively short chapter on observational methods in which it is sandwiched between explications of structured observation (which is in fact typically deployed as a means of generating quantitative data). Even though writers often recognized the potential strengths of participant observation, the tendency was to view it somewhat deprecatingly as simply a procedure for developing hunches and hypotheses to be subsequently corroborated by the more rigorous survey, experiment or whatever.

> In general, techniques of participant observation are extremely useful in providing initial insights and hunches that can lead to more careful formulations of the problem and explicit hypotheses. But they are open to the charge that findings may be idiosyncratic and difficult to replicate. Therefore many social scientists prefer to think of participant observation as being useful at a certain stage in the research process rather than being an approach that yields a finished piece of research. (Blalock, 1970, pp. 45–6)

Such a statement carries a clear implication that the role of a qualitative technique such as participant observation is a very restricted one and that it does not possess the solidity of research designed within a framework more obviously redolent of the scientific method.

In the earlier generations of textbook there was a clear awareness of a difference between quantitative and qualitative research. This awareness can also be discerned in occasional attempts by researchers to compare and contrast the virtues and vices of participant observation and survey methods (e.g. Vidich and Shapiro, 1955; Becker and Geer, 1957). However, all of these discussions operated almost exclusively at the level of the technical adequacy of the techniques as such. What distinguishes the debate that gained ground in the 1970s was the systematic and self-conscious intrusion of broader philosophical issues into discussions about methods of research. The pivotal point for much of the controversy was the appropriateness of a *natural science model* to the social sciences. Whereas the writers of the earlier methods textbooks almost took for granted the desirability of following natural science procedures, the proponents of qualitative research argued that this was an inappropriate model for studying people. Much of the argument levelled against the orthodoxy of quantitative research derived from the growing awareness and influence of phenomenological ideas which gained a considerable following in the 1960s. It was argued that the application of a 'scientific' approach – in the form of surveys and experiments – fails to take into account the differences between people and the objects of the natural sciences. Research methods were required which reflected and capitalized upon the special character of people as objects of inquiry. A qualitative research strategy, in which participant observation and unstructured interviewing were seen as the central data gathering planks, was proposed since its practitioners would be able to get closer to the people they were investigating and be less inclined to impose inappropriate conceptual frameworks on them.

In other words, philosophical ideas gained prominence because a key ingredient is the question of the appropriateness of the canons of scientific method to the study of people. As indicated above, the growing interest in qualitative research (and the formation of a philosophical rationale for it) was a major impetus to this development. Increasingly, the terms 'quantitative research' and 'qualitative research' came to signify much more than ways of gathering data; they came to denote divergent assumptions about the nature and purposes of research in the social sciences. The fact that the terminology seems to imply that 'quantification' or its absence is the central issue is highly unfortunate, since the issues span much more widely than this implies. Indeed, a number of writers have proposed alternative terms. For example, Guba and Lincoln (1982) propose a contrast between rationalistic (i.e. quantitative) and naturalistic (i.e. qualitative) paradigms, while Evered and Louis (1981) use a contrast between 'inquiry from the outside' and 'inquiry from the inside'. Magoon (1977) and J. K. Smith (1983) refer to 'constructivist' and 'interpretive' approaches respectively in place of 'qualitative'. However, such alternative terms have not achieved a wide currency and the quantitative/qualitative divide tends to be the main focus.

It is difficult to say precisely at what point the debate became prominent. In the 1960s the discussion of the nature of participant observation by Bruyn (1966) and the delineation of an atttractive logic to the connection between theory and qualitative data by Glaser and Strauss (1967) did much to lay the groundwork. A volume edited by Filstead (1970) figured early in the foray.

Although it contained previously published papers, the fact that it was exclusively concerned with 'qualitative methodology' and that its introduction appeared to be pointing to a different approach to studying social life from that advocated by the practitioners of a scientific approach, heightened its impact. Hot on its heels came Lofland's (1971) little textbook on qualitative methods. By the end of the decade Schatzman and Strauss (1973), Fletcher (1974), Bogdan and Taylor (1975), Douglas (1976), Schwartz and Jacobs (1979) and others had written textbooks in which qualitative research figured strongly or exclusively. Journals devoted to publishing articles based on qualitative research began to appear and in 1979 the *Administrative Science Quarterly* − a bastion of quantitative research − published a special number devoted to qualitative research. Further, the debate has made incursions into a variety of territories: evaluation research, educational studies, organizational studies, social psychology, and other fields.

The interest in the debate may in part be attributed to the growing interest in T. S. Kuhn's (1970) work on the history of science. One aspect of this influential book is particularly pertinent, namely the idea of a 'paradigm' − a cluster of beliefs and dictates which for scientists in a particular discipline influence what should be studied, how research should be done, how results should be interpreted, and so on. The various social science disciplines were deemed to be 'pre-paradigmatic', meaning that there was no one overarching paradigm pertaining to each discipline; instead, it was suggested, there are a number of 'pre-paradigms' which compete for paradigmatic status. These ideas seemed to contribute to a greater sensitivity to the assumptions and methods associated with competing approaches to the social sciences. Further, many writers on the debate about quantitative and qualitative research refer to the two approaches as paradigms, while one can often detect among other writers a tendency to think in terms of the idea of paradigm even though the term itself is not used. However, the introduction of such issues into the language of the social sciences carries with it certain dangers, for, as one notable philosopher of science has remarked,

> Never before has the literature on the philosophy of science been invaded by so many creeps and incompetents. Kuhn encourages people who have no idea why a stone falls to the ground to talk with assurance about scientific method. (Feyerabend, 1975, p. 6)

On the face of it, the incursion of broader philosophical issues into the study of methods was a breath of fresh air. It implied that methodology is not an arid discipline replete solely with technical issues such as when to use a postal questionnaire, the structure of a Solomon Four-Group Design, or recognizing the dire effects of failure to control for suppressor variables. It could entertain the consideration of bigger issues.

What are 'quantitative research' and 'qualitative research'? In some treatments they are viewed as competing views about the ways in which social reality ought to be studied, and as such they are essentially divergent clusters of epistemological assumptions, that is, of what should pass as warrantable knowledge about the social world. For other writers, quantitative and qualitative research are simply denotations of different ways of conducting social investigations and which may be conceived of as being appropriate to different kinds of research question and even as capable of being integrated. When this second view is taken, they are more or less simply different approaches to data collection, so that preferences for one or the other or some hybrid approach are based on technical issues. In this view, the prime consideration is that of dovetailing the appropriate technique to a particular research question. Many writers, as the later chapters will reveal, vacillate between these two levels of analysis. To a very large extent, these two research traditions (be they indicative of epistemological or technical positions) can be thought of as divergent *genres*, especially in regard to their modes of presenting research findings and programmatic statements. Of course, they are more than merely literary devices; but it is difficult not to be struck by the different styles of exposition that practitioners of the two traditions espouse. The employment of a scientistic rhetoric − experiment, variables, control, etc. − in quantitative research imposes expectations on the reader about the sort of framework that is about to be encountered, what sorts of criteria of valid knowledge the author endorses, and so on. In short, such linguistic devices act as signals which forewarn the reader about the material to come. By contrast, the self-conscious endorsement by many qualitative researchers of styles of presentation and literary devices which entail a rejection of a scientific rhetoric can be seen as a countervailing genre. Through their rejection of a scientific idiom and their recourse to the style of qualitative research they signal their adoption of a different framework and expect their work to be read and judged within the confines of that framework.

A Comparison of Two Studies

Many of the points adumbrated thus far can be usefully illustrated by reference to two studies which exemplify the contrasting orientations which lie behind the quantitative and qualitative traditions in social research. Of course, the choice of studies is bound to be arbitrary, in that many other examples of reported pieces of research could have been selected as alternatives. The chosen studies are Hirschi's (1969) investigation of delinquency and Adler's (1985) research on drug dealers; these monographs may be taken as reasonably representative of the quantitative and qualitative traditions of social research respectively.

Hirschi's Study of the Causes of Delinquency

Hirschi's examination of delinquency fits squarely with what is usually taken to be a natural science approach to the study of social reality. This predilection is evident in an earlier work, in which he expressed his preference for quantitative research: 'because quantitative data can be analyzed statistically, it is possible to examine complicated theoretical problems, such as the relative importance of many causes of delinquency, far more powerfully than with the verbal analysis of qualitative data' (Hirschi and Selvin, [1967] 1973, p. xii). In *Causes of Delinquency*, Hirschi (1969) was concerned to test the relative validity of three contrasting theories of the etiology of delinquency; he was particularly interested in how well his own 'social control' theory – which posits that delinquent acts occur when 'an individual's bond to society is weak or broken' (p. 16) – held up to empirical testing. He used a social survey in order to achieve his aims. As 'subjects' he randomly selected a sample of 5,545 school children in an area of California near San Francisco. Great care was taken in the selection of the sample to ensure that it adequately represented the range of schools in the area, as well as the gender and race distribution of the children in the population. The bulk of the data was collected by a self-administered questionnaire which was completed by the students. In addition to questions relating to social background, the questionnaire comprised a great many questions designed to tap the extent to which children were committed or attached to the school, to the family, and to conventional lines of action, in order to test the social control theory which had been formulated. The questionnaire also contained questions designed to gauge the extent of each child's involvement in delinquent activities. Further data were gleaned from other sources, such as information on each child's performance in connection with academic achievement tests from school records.

Hirschi's basic orientation to the research process is clear: one needs to formulate some explicit propositions about the topic to be investigated and design the research in advance specifically in order to answer the research problem. There is a clear concern to be able to demonstrate that the sample is representative of a wider population of school children, though the question of the representativeness of the region in which the research is located is given scant attention. The questionnaire is taken to comprise a battery of questions which 'measure' the main concepts involved (e.g. attachment to society); each question (either on its own or in conjunction with other questions to form an index) is treated as a variable which can be related to other questions/variables in order to estimate relationships among the variables which are relevant to the theories being tested. For example, Hirschi presents a contingency table which shows a clear inverse relationship between an index of 'intimacy of communication between parent and child' (derived from answers to two questions) and the number of self-reported acts of delinquency (p. 91). But Hirschi is rarely content to leave his data analysis simply at the level of estimates of co-variation or correlation among the variables concerned. Much of the time he is concerned to extricate the causal relationships among his variables. Thus, at the end of a chapter on attachments to school, he writes: 'The causal chain runs from academic incompetence to poor school performance to disliking of school to rejection of the school's authority to the commission of delinquent acts' (p. 132). These causal paths are winkled out by multivariate analysis which allows the analyst to sort out the direct and indirect effects by controlling for intervening variables and the like.

In the end, Hirschi finds that none of the three theories of delinquency emerges totally unscathed from the empirical interrogation to which they were submitted. For example, the control theory seems to neglect the role of delinquent friends which his data suggest has considerable importance. Other writers have attempted to replicate aspects of Hirschi's research (e.g. Hindelgang, 1973).

Adler's Study of Upper-Level Drug Dealers

Adler (1985) and her husband took up residence in California in order to attend graduate school in sociology. They soon made friends with a close neighbour (Dave, a pseudonym), who, it transpired, was a drug dealer. He was not a small 'pusher' of drugs who was trying to provide funds for his own habit, but someone who dealt in vast quantities and who received huge sums of money in exchange, that is an 'upper-level' drug dealer. They were encouraged by their supervisor, Jack Douglas, a prominent contributor to qualitative research on deviance (Douglas, 1972; 1976), to infiltrate Dave's group of associates in order to carry out a study of such dealers, who are normally highly inaccessible. The nature of Adler's approach to data collection can be gleaned from the following passage:

With my husband as a research partner, I spent six years in the field (from 1974 to 1980) engaged in daily participant observation with members of this dealing and smuggling community. Although I did not deal, myself, I participated in many of their activities, partying with them, attending social gatherings, traveling with them, and watching them plan and execute their business activities . . . In addition to observing and conversing casually with these dealers and smugglers, I conducted in-depth, taped interviews, and cross-checked my observations and their accounts against further sources of data whenever possible. After leaving the field, I continued to conduct follow-up interviews during periodic visits to the community until 1983. (Adler, 1985, pp. 1–2)

Adler's broad orientation is to focus on the 'subjective understanding of how people live, feel, think, and act' (p. 2) and so 'to understand the world from their perspectives' (p. 11). She sees her work as 'an ethnographic description and analysis of a deviant social scene' (p. 2).

Adler's adoption of a perspective which emphasizes the way in which the people being studied understand and interpret their social reality is one of the most central motifs of the qualitative approach. Through this perspective Adler shows that the views of drug dealing that are often presented in the literature do not fully correspond to the dealers' own perceptions. For example, she argues that the suggestion that drug dealing is simply a form of occupation or business is incongruent with dealers' views; although drug dealing has some of the trappings of occupations in business firms, such as a rational organization, the dealers do not view what they do as just another occupation. Rather, she suggests that they are motivated by a quest for the fun and pleasure which are the products of involvement in the world of upper-level drug dealing. Adler portrays the drug dealers she studied as hedonistic: the copious drugs and their associated pleasures, the ability to afford vast numbers of material possessions, the availability of many sexual partners, considerable freedom and status, and so on, constitute the sources of their motivation. The general orientation of the dealers to the present and their ability to fulfil numerous desires for both experiences and possessions more or less immediately deters many from leaving the world of drug dealing while attracting many newcomers to it.

Adler's monograph is punctuated with many verbatim quotations from interviews and conversations which illustrate many of her points. For example, in characterizing the twin themes of hedonism and abundant money, she quotes a dealer:

'At the height of my dealing I was making at least 10 grand a month profit, even after all my partying. When you have too much money you always have to have something to spend it on. I used to run into the stores every day to find $50, $60 shirts to buy because I didn't know what else to do with the money, there was so much.' (Adler, 1985, p. 86)

Thus Adler's monograph combines a detailed description of the activities of upper-level drug dealers and an account of their hedonistic life-style and sub-culture. She sees her subjects as having chosen to enter this deviant world in order to gratify the pleasures they craved and argues that this aspect of entry into certain deviant milieux has received insufficient attention in the literature.

Here then are two highly contrasting studies. They are both about deviance (and purely by chance both were carried out in California) and reflect sociological concerns. But in style and approach to social research they are very different. Hirschi seeks to test the validity of theories; Adler seems to let her subjects form her focal concerns while retaining an awareness of the literature on deviance and drug use. Hirschi's sample is carefully chosen to reflect the characteristics of the population of school children in the region; Adler's 'sample' is determined by whom she meets and is put into contact with during the course of her field-work. Thus Hirschi's sample is pre-defined at the outset of his research and all of the children received roughly the same amount of attention in that they all fill out the same questionnaire; Adler's sample is constantly shifting and her research entails different degrees of association with each person. Hirschi's research is highly defined at the outset and his questionnaire reflects his concerns; Adler uses a much less standardized approach, relying on observations, conversations, and some informal interviewing. Hirschi's results and analysis are in the form of causal propositions; much of Adler's account is descriptive and is concerned with the dealers' perceptions of their life-style. Hirschi's results reflect the sorts of issue that he thought would be important to the study of delinquency at the outset of the research; Adler's findings reflect what her subjects deem to be important about their lives. The bulk of Hirschi's results is in the form of tables; Adler's results are in the form of quotations and detailed descriptions.

The list of contrasts could go further, but these are some of the chief elements. But what is the status of these two studies, and more particularly of the comparison between them, in terms of the question of whether quantitative and qualitative research reflect different philosophical positions? Perhaps we can fruitfully regard

Hirschi's work as reflecting a concern to follow the methods and procedures of the natural sciences, and that his concern with variables, causality, and so on, are symptoms of this predilection; Adler's research could then be viewed as indicative of an approach that deliberately eschews the natural science approach and prefers instead to ground investigations in people's own understandings of social reality, as perspectives like pheonomenology are taken to imply (see Chapter 3). Alternatively, we may prefer to see these two researchers as being concerned with different facets of deviant activity – Hirschi with causes, Adler with life-style – and as having tailored their methods of data collection and approaches to data analysis accordingly. Indeed, it is doubtful whether a group like Adler's drug dealers would have been accessible to methods that even remotely resembled Hirschi's because of the undercover nature of their operations and their considerable secretiveness. This second view suggests that quantitative and qualitative research are different ways of conducting research and that the choice between them should be made in terms of their appropriateness in answering particular research questions. According to the second view, the choice between quantitative and qualitative research is a technical decision. This contrast between epistemological and technical versions of the debate about quantitative and qualitative research will be a prominent theme in later chapters.

Plan of the Book

For the undergraduate and often the postgraduate too the terms of the debate about quantitative and qualitative research are often difficult to absorb. In Chapters 2 and 3, I map out the main characteristics of quantitative and qualitative research respectively, as well as what are taken to be their philosophical underpinnings. I will not go into excessive detail about the philosophical issues, but will try to show how they are supposed to have implications for research practice within each of the two traditions. In Chapter 4, I explore some of the problems in implementing the qualitative approach. This chapter allows the distinctiveness of the qualitative approach to be explored in greater detail. Chapter 5 outlines the contrast between quantitative and qualitative research and assesses the validity of some of the claims about the link between philosophical issues and research practice. Chapter 6 deals with the often encountered suggestion that we really ought to try to combine the relative strengths of the two approaches. In Chapter 7, I look at the problem of building up a total picture of research findings in fields in which both research traditions are pursued in conjunction.

2

The Nature of Quantitative Research

In this chapter, the fundamental characteristics of quantitative research will be explored. As suggested in the previous chapter, this research tradition is usually depicted as exhibiting many of the hallmarks of a natural science approach. One of the main purposes of this chapter will be to examine the degree to which the characteristics of quantitative research are a product of a natural science approach.

Quantitative research is associated with a number of different approaches to data collection. In sociology in particular, the social survey is one of the main methods of data collection which embodies the features of quantitative research to be explored below. The survey's capacity for generating quantifiable data on large numbers of people who are known to be representative of a wider population in order to test theories or hypotheses has been viewed by many practitioners as a means of capturing many of the ingredients of a science. Hirschi's (1969) research on delinquency, which was discussed in the previous chapter, exemplifies this approach well. Most survey research is based on an underlying research design which is called 'correlational' or 'cross-sectional'. This means that data are collected on a cross-section of people at a single point in time in order to discover the ways and degrees to which variables relate to each other.

The social survey approach contrasts with experimental designs, which constitute the main approach to data collection within the tradition of quantitative research in social psychology. In an experiment, there are at least two groups to which subjects have been randomly allocated: an experimental and a control group. The logic of experimental design is that the former group is exposed to an experimental stimulus (the independent variable) but the control group is not. Any observed differences between the two groups is deemed to be due to the independent variable alone, since the two groups are identical in all other aspects. Thus an investigator may be interested in whether autonomy or close control leads to more rapid task attainment. Experimental subjects will be randomly allocated to each of the two conditions, but the two groups will differ only in that one group will be allowed autonomy in how it accomplishes the assigned task, whereas the other group will receive clear instructions and be closely supervised. In all other respects (such as the nature of the task, the experimental setting, and so on) the experiences of the two groups will be identical, so that if there are any differences in time taken to accomplish the task, it can be assumed that this is due to the experimental treatment. The term 'control group' is a little misleading in that, as in this hypothetical study, it is not without an experimental treatment. Both groups are exposed to an experimental stimulus – either autonomy or close control.

Surveys and experiments are probably the main vehicles of quantitative research but three others are worthy of a brief mention. The analysis of previously collected data, like official statistics on crime, suicide, unemployment, health, and so on, can be subsumed within the tradition of quantitative research. Indeed, Durkheim's (1952) analysis of suicide statistics is often treated as an exemplar of research within this tradition (e.g. Keat and Urry, 1975). Secondly, structured observation, whereby the researcher records observations in accordance with a pre-determined schedule and quantifies the resulting data, displays many of the characteristics of quantitative research. It is often used in the examination of patterns of interaction such as studies of teacher–pupil interaction (Flanders, 1970) or in Blau's (1955) study of patterns of consultation among officials in a government bureaucracy. Finally, as Beardsworth (1980) has indicated, content analysis – the quantitative analysis of the communication content of media such as newspapers – shares many of the chief features of quantitative research.

Quantitative research is, then, a genre which uses a special language which appears to exhibit some similarity to the ways in which scientists talk about how they investigate the natural order – variables, control, measurement, experiment. This superficial imagery reflects the tendency for quantitative research to be underpinned by a natural science model, which means that the logic and procedures of the natural sciences are taken to provide an epistemological yardstick against which empirical research in the social sciences must be appraised before it can be treated as valid knowledge. As observed in the Introduction, the denotation of research within this tradition as 'quantitative research' is unfortunate, since it refers to more than the mere generation of quantitative information *tout court*. The epistemology upon which quantitative research is erected comprises a litany of preconditions for what is warrantable knowledge, and the mere presence of numbers is unlikely to be sufficient. Nor is it the emphasis on accumulating quantitative data by those working within the tradition that the critics of quantitative research find unacceptable. Indeed, many qualitative researchers − the main adversaries − recognize the potential benefits of some measurement (e.g. Silverman, 1984, 1985). Rather, it is the package of practices and assumptions that are part-and-parcel of quantitative research, which derive from the application of a natural science approach to the study of society, that occasions their distaste.

The foregoing discussion, of course, begs the question: why should students of society copy the approach of natural scientists whose subject matter appears so different? In part, the enormous success of the sciences this century in facilitating our understanding of the natural order has probably played a part. So too has the view of writers subscribing to the doctrine of positivism (about which more will be said below) that the natural sciences provide a standard against which knowledge should be gauged and that there is no logical reason why its procedures should not be equally applicable to the study of society. In addition, as social scientists have been looked to increasingly by governments and other agencies to provide policy-relevant research (or alternatively have sought to present themselves in this light), they have either been compelled to adopt a supposedly scientific approach or have sought to display an aura of scientific method in order to secure funding. The reasons are undoubtedly legion and since this is a somewhat speculative topic it is not proposed to dwell any further on it. Rather, it is more fruitful to examine the precise nature of the scientific method that forms the bedrock of quantitative research. In order to do this it is necessary to introduce the notion of *positivism*, which is invariably credited with providing the outline of the social scientist's understanding of what science entails, especially by the opponents of quantitative research (e.g. Walsh, 1972).

The Positivist Position

There are a number of problems with the term 'positivism', one of which can be readily discerned in the more recent writing on philosophical issues in relation to the social sciences. This problem is simply that in the context of the critique of quantitative research that built up in the 1960s, and which was carried forward into the subsequent decade, the attribution 'positivist' was used glibly and indiscriminately by many writers and in fact became a term of abuse. Nowadays writers on positivism bemoan this exploitation of the term and seek to distance themselves from the tendency to treat it as a pejorative designation (e.g. Giddens, 1974; Cohen, 1980;

Bryant, 1985). Thus in the eyes of many authors the term has become devalued as a description of a particular stance in relation to the pursuit of knowledge.

A further difficulty is that even among more sophisticated treatments of positivism a wide range of meanings is likely to be discerned. Different versions of positivism can be found; Halfpenny (1982) identifies twelve. Even when there is a rough overlap among authors on the basic meaning of the term, they rarely agree precisely on its essential components. Consequently, in the explication of positivism that follows can be found not a complete catalogue of the constituents which have been identified by various writers but an extraction of those which are most frequently cited.[1] The basic point about positivism is that it is a philosophy which both proclaims the suitability of the scientific method to all forms of knowledge and gives an account of what that method entails, divergent versions notwithstanding. Thus in following the widely held convention of regarding quantitative research as founded on positivism one is presumably subscribing to the view that the former reflects the aims and tenets of the latter. What then is positivism supposed to comprise?

(1) First and foremost, positivism entails a belief that the methods and procedures of the natural sciences are appropriate to the social sciences. This view involves a conviction that the fact that the objects of the social sciences – people – think, have feelings, communicate through language and otherwise, attribute meaning to their environment, and superficially appear to be uniquely different from one another in terms of their beliefs and personal characteristics – qualities not normally held to describe the objects of the natural scientist – is not an obstacle to the implementation of the scientific method. This position is often referred to as the principle of *methodological monism* or *methodological naturalism* (von Wright, 1971; Giedymin, 1975).

(2) Like the first constituent, this second one is rarely omitted from expositions of positivism. Positivism entails a belief that only those phenomena which are observable, in the sense of being amenable to the senses, can validly be warranted as knowledge. This means that phenomena which cannot be observed either directly through experience and observation or indirectly with the aid of instruments have no place. Such a position rules out any possibility of incorporating metaphysical notions of 'feelings' or 'subjective experience' into the realms of social scientific knowledge unless they can be rendered observable. This aspect of positivism is often referred to as the doctrine of

phenomenalism and sometimes as *empiricism*, although some writers would probably challenge the treatment of these two terms as synonyms.

(3) Many accounts of positivism suggest that scientific knowledge is arrived at through the accumulation of verified facts. These facts feed into the theoretical edifice pertaining to a particular domain of knowledge. Thus theory expresses and reflects the accumulated findings of empirical research. Such findings are often referred to as 'laws', that is, empirically established regularities. The notion of science, and in particular scientific theories, being a compendium of empirically established facts is often referred to as the doctrine of *inductivism*.

(4) Scientific theories are seen by positivists as providing a kind of backcloth to empirical research in the sense that hypotheses are derived from them – usually in the form of postulated causal connections between entities – which are then submitted to empirical test. This implies that science is *deductive*, in that it seeks to extract specific propositions from general accounts of reality. The logic involved might entail seeking to construct a scientific theory to explain the laws pertaining to a particular field; a hypothesis (or possibly more than one) is derived in order to enable the scientist to test the theory; if the hypothesis is rejected when submitted to rigorous empirical examination the theory must be revised.

(5) Positivism is also often taken to entail a particular stance in relation to *values*. This notion can be discerned in explications of positivism in two senses. The first is the more obvious sense of needing to purge the scientist of values which may impair his or her objectivity and so undermine the validity of knowledge. Clearly, within the domain of the social sciences, in which moral or political predispositions may exert a greater influence than in the natural sciences, this aspect of positivism has special relevance. The second aspect of positivism's posture on values is to draw a sharp distinction between scientific issues and statements on the one hand and normative ones on the other. Positivism denies the appropriateness of the sphere of the normative to its purview because normative statements cannot be verified in relation to experience. While positivists recognize that they can investigate the implications of a particular normative position, they cannot verify or falsify the position itself. In a sense, this standpoint is a special instance of the doctrine of phenomenalism, but it has been taken to have a particular relevance in the context of the social sciences (Keat, 1981), though it figures in more general treatments too (Kolakowski, 1972).

A number of liberties have been taken in this exposition: there is no single treatment of positivism which entails all of these principles and not all positivists (living or dead) would subscribe to all of them. Some points have been treated in a fairly cavalier manner in order to cut a swath through a very dense undergrowth of debate. The first two ingredients probably come closest to what most people mean by positivism and are also the ones which recur most strikingly in the various expositions of it.

There are a number of points about these tenets which are worth registering. Principles 2 and 4 together imply a belief that there is a sharp difference between theory and observation. Empirical verification is taken to entail devising observations which are independent of scientific theories and are hence neutral. Observations are viewed as uncontaminated by the scientist's theoretical or personal predilections. This contention has been severely criticized by many philosophers of science, who argue that observations are in fact 'theory-dependent'. Such a view is suggested by T. S. Kuhn's (1970) notion of a paradigm, which was briefly mentioned in the Introduction. A major implication of his account of the history of science is that, as one paradigm is supplanted by another, the image of the world held by ensuing scientists also changes, so that observations are interpreted within a different context. An example which gives a flavour of this line of reasoning can be cited:

> During the seventeenth century, when their research was guided by one or another effluvium theory, electricians repeatedly saw chaff particles rebound from, or fall off, the electrified bodies that had attracted them . . . Placed before the same apparatus, a modern observer would see electrostatic repulsion (rather than mechanical or gravitational rebounding). (T. S. Kuhn, 1970, p. 117)

Secondly, principles 3 and 4 in conjunction seem to imply that science is both an *in*ductive and *de*ductive activity. This view suggests a circular process whereby hypotheses are deduced from general theories and submitted to empirical test; the subsequent results are then absorbed into the general theories. This portrayal often underlies the accounts by social scientists of the way in which scientists proceed (see Wallace, 1969, and below). Thirdly, the importance accorded the rule of phenomenalism implies that observations are the final arbiters of theoretical disputes, and therefore generates a view which substantially relegates theoretical reasoning to a relatively minor role (Alexander, 1982). This tendency is further underlined by the doctrine of *operationalism*, which is generally associated with a positivist position and in particular can be viewed as a ramification of phenomenalism. Simply stated, operationalism seeks to remove the ambiguity in the concepts that are typically embedded in scientific theories by specifying the operations by which they are to be measured. Once concepts have been operationalized, we would conceive of them almost exclusively in terms of the procedures developed for their measurement. Further, the doctrine of operationalism implies that concepts for which operational definitions cannot be devised should have little or no place in the subsequent development of scientific theories in a particular field of inquiry. It is precisely this celebration of the domain of empirically observable and verifiable phenomena that has caused positivism to be the butt of much criticism.

This last point is strongly associated with a major problem in the positivist account of the nature of science, as perceived by a number of philosophers of science: namely, that it is quite simply wrong. In particular, philosophers of science like Harré (e.g. 1972) have argued that positivism fails to give adequate recognition to the role in many scientific theories of hypothetical entities which may not be directly observable. For example, such writers often draw attention to the frequent use by scientists of analogies and metaphors to facilitate their understanding of the causal mechanisms which underpin the phenomena being observed. Such rhetorical devices run counter to the positivist account of the *modus operandi* of the scientist, since they are frequently not amenable to observation.[2] The development of views such as these has done much to damage positivism's credibility as a valid account of the logic of the natural sciences. It seems likely that positivism is an accurate description of some scientific fields at certain junctures; for instance, certain aspects of physics seem to conform to the tenets of positivism, and it is no coincidence that the doctrine of operationalism was largely formulated within the context of that discipline (Bridgman, 1927).

If it is the case that positivism does not adequately describe the nature of the natural sciences, two related questions present themselves in the light of the chapter thus far. Why treat positivism as the central focus of a discussion of the nature of science, and why not give much more space to apparently more accurate accounts? In fact, although the positivist account has been questioned by some philosophers of science, it is misguided to believe that there is some absolutely definitive version of the nature of science. Philosophers of science disagree widely over what science comprises. Even when they share apparently similar positions, they are not necessarily in accord over certain issues.[3] As Halfpenny (1982, p. 118) has suggested, 'it is unlikely that the *whole* of scientific activity is characterized by those features that one philosophy of science identifies as central'. Further, the chief reason for dealing with the nature of positivism is that quantitative research has been heavily influenced by an account of scientific method which has typically been construed in positivist terms. In other words, quantitative research is conventionally *believed* to be positivist in conception and orientation. The authors of textbooks on social research methods give an account of the logic of quantitative research that bears a striking similarity to the positivist position (e.g. Goode and Hatt, 1952; Phillips, 1966). Further, the critics of quantitative research have invariably depicted it as inherently positivistic and have criticized its slavish endorsement of an approach which they deem inappropriate to the study of people (e.g. Filmer *et al.*, 1972). More recently, Guba (1985), who writes from the viewpoint of qualitative research, has noted the arguments against viewing the sciences as positivistic. He concludes that not only is positivism a poor way of going about the study of social reality; it is a poor account of the nature of science too.

However, the key points to note are that: science has invariably been believed to operate according to the tenets of positivism; quantitative researchers have typically sought to conform to the methods and procedures of the natural sciences and consequently have been considerably influenced by positivism; the critics of quantitative research have viewed it as seeking to follow the precepts of the scientific method and thereby positivism. The next step is to investigate more systematically the influence of positivism on quantitative research.

Positivism and Quantitative Research

Quantitative research is often conceptualized by its practitioners as having a logical structure in which theories determine the problems to which researchers address themselves in the form of hypotheses derived from general theories. These hypotheses are invariably assumed to take the form of expectations about likely causal connections between the concepts which are the constituent elements of the hypotheses. Because concepts in the social sciences are frequently believed to be abstract, there is seen to be a need to provide operational definitions whereby their degrees of variation and co-variation may be measured. Data are collected by a social survey, experiment, or possibly one of the other methods mentioned above. Once the survey or experimental data have been collected, they are then analysed so that the causal connection specified by the hypothesis can be verified or rejected. The resulting findings then feed back into, and are absorbed by, the theory that set the whole process going in the first place. This account is, of course, a somewhat idealized account of the research process offered by many writers and is particularly prevalent in textbooks on social research methods. It conceives of quantitative research as a rational, linear process. Some of positivism's main characteristics can be superficially observed: the emphasis on rendering theoretical terms observable, the presence of both induction and deduction, for example. Figure 2.1 captures some of the chief ingredients of the typical account of the quantitative research process.

However, although this view of the research process is commonly encountered in accounts of the logic of quantitative research, it has a number of defects. First and foremost, it almost certainly overstates the centrality of theory in much quantitative research. While Hirschi's (1969) investigation of juvenile delinquency was directly concerned with the testing of theory, by no means all quantitative research is theory-driven in this way. Of course, one needs to draw a distinction between grand theories and theories of the middle range. The latter term was devised by Merton (1967), who sought to bridge the apparently yawning gap between grand theories (e.g. functionalism, conflict theory) and low-level empirical findings. Since grand theories were so abstract they offered few clues as to how they might offer guides to empirical research; by contrast, much research in sociology seemed to offer little prospect of absorption into wider theoretical schemas. Middle-range theories were proposed to mediate these two levels of discourse by dealing with 'delimited aspects of social phenomena' (Merton, 1967, pp. 39–40). Thus one ends up with theories of juvenile delinquency, racial prejudice, bureaucracy in organizations, and so on. If it were the case that theory had the kind of priority that is implied by Figure 2.1, one might anticipate that there would be a connection between theoretical positions on the one hand and particular research traditions and their associated methods of investigation on the other. In fact, it is difficult to sustain such a connection. For example, Platt (1986) has examined the often expressed assumption that there is an affinity between functionalism and the social survey, and has found the contention wanting. She finds that noted functionalists do not seem to have been especially predisposed to the survey technique and that, vice versa, survey researchers have not necessarily been strongly influenced by functionalism. Platt draws these conclusions from an examination of the work of notable functionalists and survey researchers in American sociology, as well as from interviews with some particularly influential survey researchers.

However, the low level of input of theory into the quantitative research enterprise is not confined, as one might expect, to grand theory. The following writer, in his survey of American sociology, concludes that even 'small' theory (roughly the same as middle-range) rarely guides empirical research.

Figure 2.1 *The logical structure of the quantitative research process*

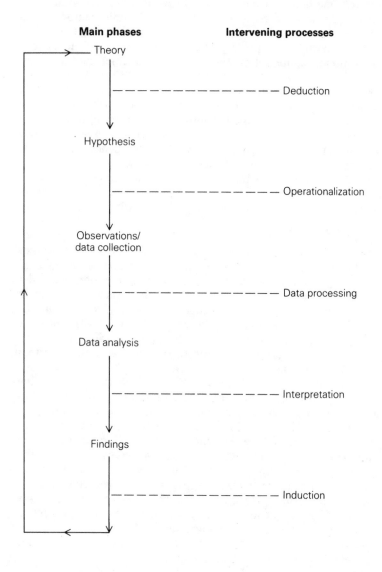

Probably the greater part of sociological activity does not explicitly use theory as the basis for research. Theory (large or small) is given lip service at best or is treated with hostility or disdain as unfounded, scientifically dangerous speculation. The role of theory is seen to follow inductively as its product or summary rather than preceding research as its subject or organiser. (Warshay, 1975, pp. 9–10)

Nor is the relatively low level of involvement of theory in the research process a special feature of sociology. Referring to the research process in psychology, Martin (1981, p. 142) writes that 'methods are often selected for reasons that have little to do with theoretical considerations'.

A further problem with this idealized model derives from its apparent linearity and orderliness. Quantitative research is invariably much more messy. It tends to involve false trails, blind alleys, serendipity and hunches to a much greater degree than the idealization implies. Nor does the idealized model take sufficient account of the importance of resource constraints on decisions about how research should be carried out. The idealized model implied by Figure 2.1 is better thought of as a depiction of the reconstructed, rationalized logic of the research process that is often enshrined in research reports. When researchers are asked to reflect upon the nature of their research, the image they project is of a much more untidy enterprise (e.g. Bell and Newby, 1977). Further evidence of the lack of a clearly ordered sequence of steps in quantitative research will emerge in the subsequent discussion.

The impact of a general commitment to the scientific method, and to positivism in particular, on quantitative research has been to create a cluster of preoccupations which can be gleaned from both reports of investigations and various writings on matters of method. The following discussion draws attention to some particularly prominent features.

Some Preoccupations in Quantitative Research

Concepts and Their Measurement

Figure 2.1 implies that one portion of the enterprise of quantitative research is the need to render observable the concepts which are rooted in the hypotheses derived from a prior theoretical scheme. While investigations displaying such a process exist, the problem that much quantitative research is relatively unconcerned with theory (to which attention has already been drawn) implies that it is a weak account of how concepts come into being and also how they come to be subject to a measurement process. In fact, concepts provide a central focus for much social science research but they are only loosely or tangentially related to theoretical considerations. Writing about quantitative research in American sociology, Warshay (1975) has argued that it tends to comprise the examination of concepts which are hardly at all derived from some prior theory. He refers to this tendency as 'conceptual empiricism', that is, 'the use of concepts rather than explicit theory as either the focus or outcome of research' (p. 10). The quantitative researcher tends to be concerned to relate these concepts to one another to investigate associations and to tease out causal processes. Thus the social world tends to be broken down into manageable packages: social class, racial prejudice, religiosity, leadership style, aggression, and so on. The body of research relating to a particular concept, or to connections between concepts, forms the backcloth and justification for carrying out an investigation into a particular topic relating to that concept. The literature review about previous research in relation to a particular concept or cluster of concepts, which is a standard precursor to the presentation of the results of the report of a piece of quantitative research, is often used as a substitute for a prior body of theory. Hypotheses, when constructed, are often not derived from a theory as such but from a body of literature relating to a concept. Bulmer and Burgess (1986, p. 256) are probably correct in their view that the concepts used by sociologists are 'embedded in theory', but such embeddedness is often loose rather than strongly rooted. Theoretical considerations are given lip-service rather than constituting major foci in their own right in much research. The emphasis on the concept as a focus for investigation is also evident in social psychology (Armistead, 1974, p. 12), or, as the authors of a major textbook on research methods for students of this discipline succinctly put it, 'To do any research we must be able to measure the concepts we wish to study' (Kidder and Judd, 1986, p. 40).

Concepts, then, are seen as a major focus – and in many instances the point of departure – for social research. The positivist leanings of quantitative research strongly reveal themselves in the insistence, which is patently clear in the quotation at the end of the previous paragraph, that they have to be rendered observable, i.e measured. This emphasis can be seen as the transportation into social research of the principle of phenomenalism and the doctrine of operationalism in particular. In fact, the strict doctrine of operationalism – that concepts should be viewed as synonymous with the measuring devices associated with them – has found few adherents. Some writers, like Dodd (1939) and Lundberg (1939), have endorsed such a view, but, in spite of the prominence that such authors are often accorded in philosophical treatments of the social sciences (e.g. Keat and Urry, 1975), their influence has been fairly marginal. There is, however, a diffuse commitment to the operationalist position which has broad support among quantitative researchers. This commitment takes the form of an avowed obligation to specify the meaning of particular concepts precisely and to develop sound measuring procedures which will stand for them.

According to many textbook accounts, as we reflect on the nature of the social world we come to recognize certain patterns of coherence. We recognize, in particular, that there are classes of objects which seem to exhibit a commonality. As we come to view a particular class of objects in this way, we want to say something about what it is that holds them together. To facilitate this exercise we give a name to this collectivity and we now have a concept. The problem, then, is to demonstrate whether the concept actually exists and to classify people, organizations, or whatever, in relation to it. This last phase is often referred to as the operationalization of the concept, that is, we want to measure it.[4] Thus we might discern from our general reflections that some people like their jobs, others dislike their work a great deal, still others seem indifferent. It would seem, then, that people vary markedly in relation to how they feel about their job. We come to think of these feelings as forming a collectivity and give it a name — job satisfaction. Here, then, is a concept. But as soon as we start to ask questions about job satisfaction — why do some people exhibit greater job satisfaction than others? — it is necessary to move towards an operational definition of the concept so that we can measure it and develop a precise yardstick for discerning its presence or absence in a person.

The measurement of concepts tends to be undertaken through the use of questionnaire devices or some form of structured observation, the latter being particularly prevalent in experimental research. In the view of many writers on research methods, the concepts used by social scientists are often fairly vague and/or abstract. Concepts like alienation, power, bureaucratization, and so on, are all very difficult to pin down. One of the best-known schemas for dealing with the translation of concepts into observable entities is Lazarsfeld's (1958) delineation of 'the flow from concepts to empirical indices'. He saw the flow as involving four stages in a sequence (see Figure 2.2). At the outset, as a consequence of our reflections in connection with a particular theoretical domain, we develop an *imagery* about a particular facet of that domain. It is then necessary to *specify* that imagery, which entails breaking it down into different components, often referred to as 'dimensions'. Thus job satisfaction may be broken down into: satisfaction with the work, satisfaction with pay and conditions,

Figure 2.2 *Lazarsfeld's scheme for measuring concepts*

STEPS IN PROCESS	IMAGERY →	CONCEPT → SPECIFICATION	SELECTION OF → INDICATORS	FORMATION OF INDICES
EXAMPLE IN TEXT (Aston Studies)	Notions of organization structure deriving from Weber, Classical Management Theory, etc.	Specialization, *Formalization*, Standardization, Centralization, Configuration	E.g. Formalization. Does the organization have: organization chart, written operating instructions, written job descriptions, written policies, etc.?	Indices (or more precisely scales and sub-scales) were developed out of the indicators used in respect of each of the 5 dimensions

satisfaction with peers and supervisors, and so on. Thirdly, it is necessary to develop *indicators* for each of these dimensions. This third step is the crux of the operational process: the development of a group of questions which can stand for each of the delineated dimensions. Thus for each dimension is developed questionnaire items which collectively act as signposts for that dimension. Finally, Lazarsfeld proposes the *formation of indices*, whereby the indicators are aggregated, either to form one overall index of job satisfaction or whatever, or to form an index of each of the constituent dimensions. Why use more than one indicator? Lazarsfeld reasoned that only a battery of questionnaire items would allow each dimension to be captured in its totality.

Examples of research which conform closely to Lazarsfeld's scheme are Seeman's (1967) measurement of the concept of alienation and Stark and Glock's (1968) work on religious commitment. So, too, are the 'Aston Studies', a programme of research into organization structure which derives its name from its association with the University of Aston in Birmingham.[5] In this research programme the 'subject' is not an individual as such but an organization. Following an examination of the literature on the shape and form of organizations, the imagery stage, the Aston researchers discerned five basic dimensions:

(1) specialization – the extent of the division of labour within an organization;
(2) formalization – the extent to which procedures and communications are recorded in formal documentation;
(3) standardization – the extent to which activities and roles are circumscribed by rules;
(4) centralization – the extent to which the locus of decision-making is at the apex of the organization;
(5) configuration – the shape of an organization's role structure.

It is also worth noting that the Aston researchers developed 'sub-dimensions' of each of the five primary dimensions. For example, specialization was taken to comprise functional specialization (i.e. specialization in terms of major functional areas, such as training) and role specialization (i.e. specialization within each functional specialism, such as operative training, clerical training, apprentice training, etc.). Empirical indicators were then developed for each dimension and sub-dimension. This was achieved through a very lengthy interview schedule whereby senior personnel in a sample of organizations were asked questions about their firm's activities. Answers to the individual questions were then aggregated to form scales relating to each dimension or sub-dimension. Thus, in order to measure functional specialization, respondents were asked whether their firm had at least one person who spent all of his or her time devoted to each of sixteen specialist areas. If at least one person was employed in training, there would be evidence of specialization for that one area. Each respondent was then asked the same question in respect of other functional areas like accounts, market research, sales and service, and so on. Each of these questions can be viewed as an indicator; they are then aggregated to form an overall index (or, more technically, a scale) of functional specialization. Similarly, in order to operationalize formalization, respondents were asked about such things as whether their firms used information booklets, job descriptions, written policies, and so on. The Aston programme reflects the concerns of quantitative research in both its preoccupation with the development of measurement devices for its central concepts and also in the sense that its chief conceptual focus – organization structure – was only loosely related to a wider body of theory, namely the writings on the functioning of bureaucracies by authors like Weber (1947). The basic steps in the approach of the Aston researchers to the operationalization of organization structure are presented in Figure 2.2.

The approach to the measurement of concepts used in the Aston Studies, and also recommended by Lazarsfeld, is rigorous and systematic. However, the practices associated with it are by no means as widespread as might be assumed from the frequent reference to it in the literature on social research procedure. The departure from the Lazarsfeld approach can be discerned in two areas. First, a great deal of social research is conducted in such a way that steps in the flow proposed by Lazarsfeld are bypassed. A battery of indicators of a particular concept is often developed with little if any consideration of the underlying dimensions to that concept. The failure to examine the possibility of there being constituent dimensions means that the battery of indicators is suggestive of only one strand of meaning that the concept reflects. Even more frequent is the use of just one or two indicators of a concept or its constituent dimensions. For example, many readers will be familiar with the notion of an 'instrumental orientation to work', which was a central focus of the research on the industrial attitudes and behaviour of affluent workers by Goldthorpe *et al.* (1968). This notion – which possibly can be thought of as a dimension of the concept 'orientation to work' – refers to an attachment to work in which matters of pay predominate in workers' thinking. This idea, which is the linchpin of this particular facet of the authors' work on affluent workers, was operationalized by means of two questions: one on respondents' reasons for staying in their firm, and another on their reasons for staying in their then present employment. Similarly, in order to find out how far their manual workers were 'privatized', Roberts *et al.* (1977) measured this concept by asking respondents to report the number of people at work and amongst their neighbours who were friends. In their research on the British clergy, Ranson, Bryman and Hinings (1977) measured their respondents' role definition by reference to a single question in which they were asked to rank seven 'tasks'. The point is that many researchers do not adhere to a lengthy procedure of operationalizing all of their key concepts in the manner proposed by writers like Lazarsfeld.

A second sense in which the 'flow from concepts to empirical indices' approach represents only a portion of quantitative research is that the linking of concepts and measurement is often much more inductive than the Lazarsfeld scheme implies. The widespread use of factor analysis in the social sciences exemplifies this point. Factor analysis seeks to delineate the underlying dimensions to a battery of questionnaire items. A classic use of this approach can be seen in the influential research on leadership developed by the Ohio State Leadership Studies.[6] The Ohio State researchers measured leader behaviour by administering to people in subordinate positions a battery of descriptions of leader behaviour which were supposed to pertain to their superiors. In one particularly notable study (Halpin and Winer, 1957), 130 questions (i.e. indicators) were administered to 300 members of US air crews. Each question was in the form of a description of a leader's behaviour, and respondents were asked to indicate the extent to which that description applied to their own superiors. A factor analysis was conducted to discern any 'bunching' in respondents' replies. Such bunching can be taken to be indicative of underlying dimensions of leader behaviour. The factor analysis revealed four dimensions, that is, groups of questionnaire items which tended to cling together. Of the four dimensions, two were particularly prominent: consideration and initiating structure. The former refers to the presence of mutual liking and camaraderie between leader and led; initiating structure refers to the leader's propensity to organize work tightly and clearly. Consideration is denoted by responses to questionnaire items like: does personal favours for crew members; is friendly and approachable. Initiating structure is represented by questionnaire items like: assigns crew members to particular tasks; makes his attitude clear to the crew. However, the designations, consideration and initiating structure, were arrived at after the factor analysis revealed the underlying dimensions. The researcher has to use his or her imagination to determine what the items which make up each dimension actually mean. This procedure entails examining what appears to be common to the items which make up each dimension. Thus, whereas the flow implied by Figure 2.2 suggests a move from dimensions to indicators, the factor analysis approach just described entails a progression from indicators to dimensions.

The topic of leadership provides another instance of inductive reasoning which might be called 'reverse operationalism'. Whereas Figures 2.1 and 2.2 imply that the researcher moves from theoretical terms like concepts to empirical indicators through the development of operational measures, the work of Fiedler (1967) seems to imply that the opposite of this procedure may occur. Fiedler developed a technique called the 'least preferred co-worker' (LPC) scale which involves asking people in positions of leadership to think of the person with whom they have least enjoyed working. They are then asked to evaluate their LPC in terms of a series of at least (the number varies) sixteen pairs of adjectival opposites, each pairing being on an eight-point scale. Examples are:

Pleasant	8	7	6	5	4	3	2	1	Unpleasant
Rejecting	1	2	3	4	5	6	7	8	Accepting

Fiedler found that leaders who described their LPC in favourable terms (e.g. pleasant, accepting) extracted better performance from their subordinates in some circumstances; in other circumstances, leaders whose depictions of their LPCs were unfavourable did better in this respect. Fiedler has consistently maintained that a leader's LPC score is indicative of his or her leadership style. Thus, the measure came first and then it was decided what the measure might be referring to. Further, at different times Fiedler has offered no fewer than four distinct ways of envisioning the leadership styles of leaders with different LPC scores.[7] In other words, for this measure there is very little in the way of a prior conceptual scheme which informs its meaning; the meaning has to be derived.

Because concepts and their measurement are so central to quantitative research, there is much concern about the technical requirements of operationalization. This concern is usually portrayed in textbooks and by writers on methods as a need to consider the validity and reliability of measures. The question of validity refers to the issue of how we can be sure that a measure really does reflect the concept to which it is supposed to be referring. Textbooks invariably routinely adumbrate the procedures that are available for establishing validity. For example, it is proposed that the researcher should seek to estimate a measure's concurrent validity, which means discerning how far the measure allows you to distinguish between people in terms of something else that is known about them. Thus if you were seeking to develop an index of job satisfaction you might examine respondents' absenteeism records to see if those who exhibit low levels of satisfaction are also more likely to be frequently away from work.

There is increasing concern among many writers that it is also necessary to test for the validity of a measure by using a different approach to measuring it (e.g. Campbell and Fiske, 1959). Frequently, examinations of validity point to the problems associated with simply assuming a fit between concepts and their measures. It is useful to return to the Aston Studies as a case in point. The Aston approach is not the only method used for operationalizing organization structure. Hall (1963, 1968) independently developed an alternative approach which used a similar characterization of the concept's dimensions (e.g. hierarchy of authority, division of labour, presence of rules, etc.) However, he used a different approach to the operationalization of these dimensions in that he administered a questionnaire to samples of members of a number of organizations. Thus, rather than adopting the Aston approach of using key informants who spoke for the organization, Hall drew his measures from the views of a broader constituency of people within each organization and then summed the scores. Azumi and McMillan (1973) and Pennings (1973) have combined both procedures within a single study and found a very poor correspondence between the apparently kindred dimensions of the Aston and Hall approaches.[8] However, in spite of the apparent concern about such issues, much quantitative research entails 'measurement by fiat' (Cicourel, 1964), whereby measures are simply asserted, and little, if anything, is done to demonstrate a correspondence between measures and their putative concepts. It is not difficult to see why there might be a disparity between the recommendations of textbooks and much research practice, for validity issues can easily become fairly major projects for researchers who may see such issues as excessive distractions.

The issue of reliability is concerned with the consistency of a measure. Consistency is taken to comprise two distinct questions. The first is internal consistency, which is really a matter for measures which are in the form of scales or indices, because it is concerned with the internal coherence of a scale − does it comprise one unitary idea or separate components? There is a veritable artillery of procedures and techniques which can be deployed to investigate this issue.[9] The second aspect of consistency is a measure's consistency over time, testing for which entails administering the measure more than once. It is probably the case that social scientists tend to be more concerned about the reliability than the validity of their measures. Textbooks tend to give the two issues equal attention, but researchers seem more inclined to report that reliability tests have been carried out. This creates the illusion that reliability is more important, and allows measures to be evaluated mainly in terms of this criterion. The real reason is probably that validity testing is highly time consuming and can easily turn into a major project in its own right.

The chief purpose in this section has been to point to the importance of concepts within the framework of quantitative research and to highlight how the preoccupation with their operationalization has led to a number of concerns such as validity and reliability. The very fact that there is much concern about these issues, particularly among writers on methodology, is evidence of the importance of concepts and their measurement. In passing, departures from the textbook approach to the measurement of concepts have been mentioned.

Causality

Quantitative research is often highly preoccupied with establishing the causal relationships between concepts. This concern can be viewed as a transposing of what are deemed to be the ways of the natural sciences to the study of society. As the author of one textbook on research methods has observed:

> One of the chief goals of the scientist, social or other, is to explain why things are the way they are. Typically, we do that by specifying the causes for the way things are: some things are caused by other things. (Babbie, 1979, p. 423)

Similarly, as a leading exponent of the analysis of survey data – James Davis – has put it: 'Social research aims to develop causal propositions supported by data and logic' (Davis, 1985, p. 10).

The frequent use of the terms 'independent variable' and 'dependent variable' by quantitative researchers is evidence of the widespread tendency to employ causal imagery in investigations. There is much discussion in the literature about the proper practices to be employed in order to be able to make robust claims about cause. Such discussion tends to revolve around the two main approaches to the generation of causality – those associated with experimental and cross-sectional social survey research designs.

The main aim of experimental designs is to maximize what Campbell (1957) calls 'internal validity', the extent to which the presumed cause really does have an impact on the presumed effect. Central to the exercise of establishing internal validity is the ability to rule out alternative explanations of a posited causal relationship. As indicated above, the presence of a control group, coupled with the use of random assignment to the experimental and control groups, means that experimental designs are particularly strong in this respect. Consequently, experimental designs are invariably depicted in textbooks on research methods as particularly effective in the context of establishing definitive causal connections. Such designs are particularly common in social psychology largely because of the very considerable store placed in that discipline on the establishment of causal relationships (Harré and Secord, 1972). Very often, such experimental research is depicted as a model of quantitative research precisely because of the ability of its practitioners to make strong claims about the internal validity of their findings (Hughes, 1976, p. 81). Within such a frame of reference, non-experimental research may appear to be inadequate, by virtue of the researcher's inability to manipulate aspects of the social environment and observe the effects of such intervention. Foremost among approaches to quantitative research which seems to be poorly equipped in this respect is the cross-sectional survey design.

In a survey, data are typically collected (by postal questionnaire, interview schedule, or whatever) from a sample of individuals at a single juncture. The data allow the researcher to establish whether there are associations among the various variables that are reflected in the questionnaire. The concern to establish causal connections between variables can be discerned in the widespread preoccupation among many survey researchers with the development of methods for imputing cause-and-effect relationships (e.g. Blalock, 1964; Davis, 1985), in spite of the fact that survey investigations are generally thought to be primarily geared to the establishment of simple associations and correlations among variables. The old maxim − correlation cannot imply cause − ostensibly implies that the social scientist's ability to establish causality from social survey research is severely limited. However, survey researchers have by no means been deterred and have developed a variety of procedures for the elucidation of causality by means of a *post hoc* reconstruction of the 'logic of causal order' (Davis, 1985) that lies behind the cluster of variables generated by a particular investigation.

In order to be able to establish causal relationships among variables in a cross-sectional study three conditions have to be met. First, it has to be established that there is a relationship among the variables concerned, that is, that they are not independent of each other. Well-known statistical techniques (e.g. chi-square, correlation coefficients) are available to assist with establishing the presence of a relationship. Secondly, the relationship must be non-spurious. This means that it is necessary to establish that an apparent relationship between two variables, x and y, is not being produced by the presence of a third variable which is antecedent and related to x and y. A researcher may find an inverse association between church attendance and delinquency, but has to ensure that a variable like age is not 'producing' this relationship − younger children are both more likely to attend church frequently and less likely to engage in delinquent acts, while older children attend less frequently and are more inclined to delinquency.

Thirdly, and perhaps most controversially, the data analyst must establish a temporal order to the assembly of variables in question. Since research designs like the cross-sectional survey entail the collection of data at a single point in time, this temporal order has to be imputed. To some extent this process implies an intuitive component in the analysis of such data. The establishment of a temporal order is not an arbitrary process: we frequently draw on our common-sense understanding of the life cycle of the individual in order to determine which variable is prior to another, e.g. formal schooling precedes divorce (Davis, 1985). While it may be objected that this approach treats life cycle stages as unproblematic − something which many social scientists have been seeking to question (Bryman *et al.*, 1987) − none the less it is useful as an interpretive device. Researchers using an experimental design do not face this problem, since the experimental treatment is a stimulus, the response to which is deemed to be the effect. Consequently, there is usually little doubt about questions of causal order. One of the best-known techniques used by survey researchers to unravel the relative importance of a cluster of variables as prospective causes of a dependent variable is path analysis, which is an extension of multiple regression analysis that allows the analyst to tease out the contribution of each causal factor while controlling for the others. A hypothetical instance of such a procedure in its skeletal form is provided in figure 2.3.

Many assumptions (albeit quite reasonable ones) are built into this causal model, such as the father's income precedes son's job, and son's job precedes son's income. However, a very real problem is that path analysis is agnostic in regard to equally plausible models. The Aston Studies provide a case in point. Researchers in the field of organization studies have been concerned to demonstrate which factors are most instrumental in determining the structure of organizations. While the Aston researchers tended to emphasize organizational size (Pugh and Hickson, 1976), others had found technology to be a crucial determinant (Woodward, 1965). When Hilton (1972) re-analysed the original data collected by the Aston researchers, he found that path analysis could sustain a number of different plausible *a priori* models of the causal interconnections among the three variables, viz. size, technology, and structure.[10] The problem here is that the temporal precedence of these variables is not readily determined by some kind of appeal to

Figure 2.3 *Hypothetical path diagram for the explanation of a male's income*

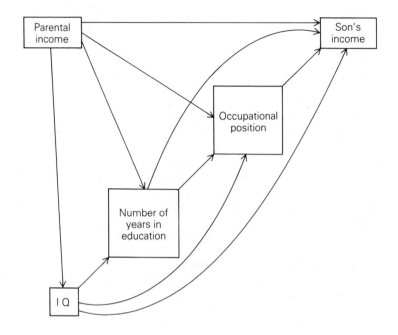

intuition – an organization's size may be thought of as both antecedent and subsequent to its internal structure, albeit at different junctures in its development. While 'reciprocal causality' is acknowledged as an inherent aspect of the relationships between certain pairs of variables, it does pose problems to researchers seeking to establish a time order to variables. In recognition of such difficulties, longitudinal designs are often proposed. For example, a researcher may observe a relationship between the extent to which leaders are participative and the job satisfaction of their subordinates; but which is temporally precedent? Does participativeness enhance job satisfaction, or do leaders allow greater participativeness to more satisfied subordinates? Questions such as this require a longitudinal approach, such as a panel design in which two or more waves of observations of the relevant variables are executed at different points in time. The fruits of research such as this often point to a complex pattern of interactions among the variables in question (Bryman, 1986). The main point is that there are many instances of patterns of relationships between groups of variables which derive from cross-sectional designs where temporal precedence is very difficult to determine and thereby so too is causality.

Questions of causality, then, greatly preoccupy the exponents of quantitative research. Since cross-sectional research designs pose far greater problems in respect to the establishment of causality than experimental ones, survey researchers have sought to develop approaches to data analysis which allow them to infer causal processes. The preoccupation with causality can be readily seen as a consequence of the tendency among quantitative researchers to seek to absorb the methods and assumptions of the natural scientist which have tended to be interpreted in positivist terms. This notion of causality has been called by Harré the 'regularity' or 'succession' view of cause (Harré, 1972; Harré and Secord, 1972). According to this view, causation is simply a matter of determining 'the regular sequence of one kind of event and another of the kind which usually follows' (Harré and Secord, 1972, p. 31). This way of thinking about causality can be discerned in Hirschi's (1969) depiction of a causal chain linking academic performance to delinquency, which was quoted in Chapter 1. Whether, in fact, this view adequately reflects the way in which scientists think about causality has been questioned by Harré and a number of other writers (e.g. Bhaskar, 1975; Sayer, 1984). According to this alternative view, often called the 'generative' approach to causality, science proceeds by describing the causal mechanisms which generate non-random patterns in the natural order. For example: 'Chemists discover reactions, and by describing the interplay and interchange of ions they explain them' (Harré and Secord, 1972, p. 70). Such mechanisms may be directly or indirectly observable, or they may have to be inferred, e.g. by reference to analogues which facilitate an understanding and explanation. This view of causality departs quite markedly from that which pervades quantitative research in which the succession of cause and effect is so paramount. While it is not the purpose of this chapter to enter into the debates about what scientists really do, as against what quantitative researchers *qua* positivists say they do, it is apparent that the approach to causality described in this section (the regularity view) is not necessarily an accurate account of the natural scientist's understanding.

Generalization

The quantitative researcher is invariably concerned to establish that the results of a particular investigation can be generalized beyond the confines of the research location. Among survey researchers this preoccupation manifests itself in a great deal of attention being paid to sampling issues and in particular the representativeness of samples. The widespread preference in textbooks and among many practitioners for random sampling is symptomatic of this concern. Essentially, the concern is to establish that findings can be legitimately generalized to a wider population of which the sample is representative. Further, statistical inference techniques (like chi-square), which are widely used by survey researchers, make sense only in the context of randomly selected samples which permit inferences to a population.

This preoccupation with establishing generality can probably be attributed to the quantitative researcher's tendency to mimic the methods and style of the natural scientist. By verifying generality, the quantitative researcher draws nearer to the law-like findings of the sciences. Perhaps for this reason, qualitative research, which is frequently based on the study of one or two single cases, is often disparaged by researchers in the quantitative tradition, for the cases may be unrepresentative and therefore of unknown generality. How does one know whether a slum in Boston (Whyte, 1943) is representative of all slums in the USA, and, if one is unsure, how can the fruits of such research be generalized beyond the confines of Boston? In the next chapter, the arguments against this view of the generalizability of case study research, which have been proffered by a number of writers (e.g. Mitchell, 1983; Yin, 1984), will be presented. However, it ought also to be noted that survey research often does not escape a similar accusation. While random sampling can establish within limits the generalizability of findings to the population from which the sample was derived, there may still be problems of establishing the generality of findings to other populations. National sample surveys are quite rare and more often than not researchers draw from particular regions or cities. These more localized populations may be selected on the basis of convenience (e.g. proximity to the researcher) or on the basis of strategic considerations. An example of the latter would be the selection of Luton as the test site for the embourgeoisement thesis because the investigators wanted a setting that was as favourable as possible to it (Goldthorpe *et al.*, 1968). An investigation of this same thesis (as well as other aspects of the changing class structure of the UK) was carried out in two districts of Liverpool by Roberts *et al.* (1977). The authors justified this more localized sample, as against a wider regional or national sample, on the grounds of local influences being held constant and 'reasons of convenience and cost' (p. 11). Hirschi's (1969) survey research on delinquency, although based on a random sample, was located in a single region − a county within the San Francisco–Oakland area of California. In other words, survey research findings may lack generality too, even when a random sample has been extracted. This possibility may prompt other researchers to establish generality. For example, the original research carried out under the banner of the Aston Studies entailed a random sample of West Midlands organizations (Pugh and Hickson, 1976); later the research was extended to a national sample and to other contexts like churches (Pugh and Hinings, 1976), as well as to other nations (Hickson and McMillan, 1981). However, it is quite unusual for a body of research to develop in this way in the social sciences, so the generality of much research is left undefined. Further, the extent to which the passage of time affects the generality of research findings is given scant attention, as Newby *et al.* (1985) have suggested in the context of research into social stratification in the UK.[11] It is also the case that even samples which are limited to a particular region do not use probability methods. In the field of organization studies, for example, Freeman (1986) has commented on the tendency to obtain samples opportunistically rather than according to random sampling procedures.

Researchers who employ experimental designs are preoccupied with problems of generalization too. This topic is often referred to as the problem of external validity, which denotes the extent to which findings (which may be internally valid) can be generalized beyond the experiment (Campbell, 1957). Assaults on external validity may derive from such factors as the contaminating effects of pre-testing experimental and control groups and from the unique effects of the experimental situation on subjects' behaviour. The latter difficulty is often subsumed under a general category of 'reactive effects' (e.g. Webb *et al.*, 1966). Laboratory experiments, which are especially prominent in social psychology, pose particular problems in regard to generalization and as a consequence greatly exercise their proponents. Two points seem to be particularly salient. First, the bulk of such research uses students as experimental subjects, who are unlikely to be representative of people as a whole because of their special socio-economic characteristics as well as their more limited range of experiences. Further, in many instances the subjects are volunteers, who differ from non-volunteers in a number of respects (Rosenthal and Rosnow, 1969). Secondly, the very artificial nature of the laboratory would seem adversely to affect the generalizability of findings. For example, laboratory experiments which are supposed to carry implications for the study of organizations may depart significantly from the context to which they are meant to apply – the experimental task may be very trivial compared to 'real' work, subjects are strangers, subjects' involvement is fleeting, and so on. Consequently, some social psychologists prefer field experiments, i.e. experiments within natural settings. On the face of it, such experiments would seem to solve the difficulties associated with research in the laboratory, but they bring other problems in their wake. The case for the greater generalizability of field experiments is often more apparent than real in that they often occasion a whole set of intractable reactive effects, which derive from the marked difference for subjects between their normal routine and the special conditions imposed by the experimental arrangements. Further, internal validity may be jeopardized since researchers in field settings often have to compromise over such features as random allocation to groups.

At the time of writing, the concerns among quantitative researchers who use experimental designs about the question of external validity show no signs of abating. A number of articles in *American Psychologist* (Berkowitz and Donnerstein, 1982; Dipboye and Flanagan, 1979; Mook, 1983) as well as the appearance of a volume specifically on the generalizability of laboratory experiments (Locke, 1986) – the contents of which point to a marked congruence between the findings of laboratory and field experiments in the study of organizational behaviour – provide a testament to the enduring concern of the issue of generalization. Mook (1983) provides a dissenting voice in arguing that laboratory experiments are not meant to be externally valid, only to discern whether a predicted effect can be made to occur. By and large, however, experimental and survey researchers are deeply concerned about the issue of generalization, albeit for different reasons.

Replication

The replication of established findings is often taken to be a characteristic of the natural sciences, a view which is often fuelled by scientists themselves:

> The essential basis for [physics'] success was the possibility of repeating the experiments. We can finally agree about their results because we have learned that experiments carried out under precisely the same conditions do actually lead to the same results. (Heisenberg, 1975, p. 55)

The belief in the importance of replication to scientists has led to a view among quantitative researchers that such activities should be an ingredient of the social sciences too. The prospective relevance of replication to the social scientist is often related to the focus of the preceding section – generalization. Replication can provide a means of checking the extent to which findings are applicable to other contexts. In addition, it is often seen as a means of checking the biases of the investigator. Few quantitative researchers subscribe to a view that research can be value-free; therefore, replication can act as a check on any excesses. As the authors of one textbook put it:

[T]he researcher's biases inevitably affect how observations are gathered and interpreted. The only way to avoid these biases is to replicate the research. Replication means that other researchers in other settings with different samples attempt to reproduce the research as closely as possible. (Kidder and Judd, 1986, p. 26)

One of the reasons why qualitative research is often criticized by quantitative researchers is precisely the difficulty of carrying out replications of its findings. Blalock's (1970) attitude towards participant observation, which was quoted in the Introduction, in which he criticizes the findings of such research as 'idiosyncratic and difficult to replicate', is an example of such a view from a major proponent of quantitative research.

In fact, replications are comparatively rare in the social sciences (and their prominence in the natural sciences is often exaggerated as well — Collins, 1985; Mulkay and Gilbert, 1986). Replication is often regarded as a somewhat unimaginative, low status activity among researchers. Why, then, is it so often regarded as an important facet of the quantitative research tradition? In all probability, it is not replication that is important so much as replic*ability*. It should be technically feasible for someone bent on replication to use precisely the same questionnaire in relation to a comparable sample (though probably in a different locale) as employed in an original study; or to set up an experiment using the same experimental conditions. The point is that research can be checked by using the same or roughly similar research design or instruments as in an earlier study. One of the reasons why qualitative research is often denigrated by exponents of quantitative research is that it has an intuitive component and is seen as a product of the idiosyncrasies of the researcher. It is therefore seen as difficult to replicate and hence untrustworthy.

Whether research is in fact replicated, then, does not seem to be the issue — otherwise one assumes that it would be a much more frequent activity among quantitative researchers. What seems to be a more critical issue is the ability to replicate, and it is this which is something of a preoccupation among researchers in the quantitative tradition. In this context, it is interesting to note that Heisenberg's quotation in connection with physics refers to the *possibility* of repeating experiments.

Individualism
Finally, quantitative research tends to treat the individual as the focus for empirical inquiry. Writing about what he calls 'instrumental positivism' (a term which is largely synonymous with

the idea of quantitative research as presented in this chapter, but more specifically to do with the survey tradition), Bryant (1985) has noted the tendency for the individual to be the centre of attention for researchers. In large part, this focus derives from the fact that survey instruments are administered to individuals as discrete objects of inquiry. Their responses are then aggregated to form overall measures for the sample. There is no requirement that individuals should know each other, only that their survey responses can be added up. Such an approach has often been referred to somewhat disparagingly as 'aggregate psychology' (e.g. Coleman, 1958), since it engenders a view of society as if it 'were only an aggregation of disparate individuals' (Blumer, 1948, p. 546). While writers like Coleman (1958) have recognized that this orientation is inappropriate to the study of patterns of relationships or interactions (for which different forms of sampling like snowball samples may be necessary), the emphasis within the survey tradition on random sampling and the administration of elegant research instruments to 'disparate individuals' has produced a pervasive individualism.

One manifestation of this tendency is the view that aspects of social units can be built up from the aggregation of individuals' survey responses. For example, in order to derive measures of the degree of bureaucratization (i.e. presence of rules, procedures, division of labour, impersonality, etc.), Hall (1968) administered a battery of questions designed to reflect its major dimensions to professionals working in a variety of organizational settings. In other words, aspects of organizational structure were built up for each of twenty-seven organizations by aggregating the replies of the individuals surveyed. In a later study in which the same author was involved (Hall *et al.*, 1977), measures of patterns of relationships among organizations (e.g. co-ordination, conflict, communication, form of contact) were derived from questionnaire items answered by employees in organizations concerned with 'problem youth'. Patterns of interaction within each of twelve US cities were the chief focus of investigation. This type of study stretches aggregate psychology beyond the familiar '70 per cent of *A*s think *p*, whereas only 12 per cent of *B*s think *p*' kind of finding, because it implies that it is possible to derive statements about social structures and processes from the responses of individuals to survey questions. Such social phenomena become simply the sum of the parts.

Psychology too exhibits a tendency to individualism. In a sense this is hardly surprising since it is typically depicted as the study of the individual. The emphasis on the individual seems to derive more from psychology's general orientation than from the methods it employs. But the stress has been questioned by some authors:

> In psychology generally, we must take account of the fact that remembering, reasoning and expressing emotions are part of the life of institutions, of structured self-regulating groups, such as armies, monasteries, schools, families, businesses and factories. (Harré, Clark and De Carlo, 1985, p. 6)

While Harré, Clark and De Carlo are making a somewhat different point about the individualistic focus of inquiry in psychology from that developed above in the context of survey research, their comment is none the less indicative of a theme that spans the two approaches.

There is an apparent irony in the suggestion that quantitative research is imbued with individualism, for one of the criticisms that has been levelled against it by critics influenced by the ideas associated with qualitative research (and phenomenology in particular − see next chapter) is that it tends to reify the social world. Such critics argued that the social world comes to be seen as separate from the individuals who are demonstrably instrumental in its creation. The neologism 'facticity' was used by some writers (e.g. Walsh, 1972) as a description of the image of the social order created by quantitative research, that is, a view of social reality as an external force detached from individuals. This representation was deemed to arise as a consequence of the treatment by quantitative researchers, by virtue of the influence of positivism on their approach, of social reality as if it were identical to the natural order. The social world, it was argued, is constituted by individuals and is therefore different from the natural order. Consequently, it would seem slightly perverse to describe quantitative research as suffused with individualism. In fact, the individualistic element in quantitative research is to do with its techniques of investigation (particularly those associated with the social survey) which use the individual as the source of data, largely independently of other individuals. A reified image of social reality, akin to that criticized by qualitative researchers, is built up from the 'disparate individuals' who provide the data. Thus, the image of society as an external object and the element of individualism go hand in hand.

Conclusion

Undoubtedly, this list of quantitative researchers' root preoccupations is not an exhaustive one, and possibly not all investigators whose work lies in this tradition would identify with each of them. Positivism reveals itself in quantitative research in particular in the emphasis on facts which are the products of observation, either direct or indirect. The stress on devising valid and reliable measurement procedures is especially redolent of positivism, particularly the tenet of phenomenalism. The connection between positivism and the other root preoccupations of quantitative research is more problematic, however. The emphasis on generalizability and replicability can be seen as indicative more of a generalized commitment to the procedures of the natural scientist than to positivism *per se*. The focus of attention on generalizability can be viewed as indicative of a diffuse proclivity for the generation of law-like findings *à la* natural sciences; while the issue of replicability can also be viewed as a more general commitment to the ways of the natural scientist, as well as indicative of the positivist unease about values and their possible intrusion in research. The individualism of much quantitative research can be considered a product of its technical procedures, though Bryant (1985), following Kolakowski (1972), comes close to viewing this level of analysis as a consequence of the positivist leanings of researchers within the quantitative tradition.[12] The question of the emphasis on causality is more complex, in that the establishment of causal statements is not a feature of positivism as such, but a component of most accounts of the natural sciences. What can be viewed as a consequence of positivism is the particular form that causal statements are supposed to take. Positivism has bequeathed a regularity view of the nature of causation to quantitative research, an account which has been challenged by some writers, as the section on this topic above explored. The regularity approach to causation can be viewed at least in part as a facet of positivism's preoccupation with the domain of the observable since it emphasizes that cause and effect may be directly demonstrated by establishing that one event precedes another. By contrast, the generative account of causality permits, even invites, causal explanations in terms of unobserved entities. The influence of positivism can also be discerned in its tendency to inductivism (in the form of the accumulation of research findings which theory simply absorbs) and a deductive account of the research process (such as the derivation of hypotheses from prior theoretical schemes). These two strands form a backdrop to the way in which quantitative researchers tend to perceive the logic of the research process, although the actual extent to which research is informed by theoretical considerations is a matter of some debate.

Quantitative research, then, can be seen as linked partly to positivism and partly to a diffuse and general commitment to the practices of the natural scientist. While all of the characteristics of what is conventionally taken to be positivism can be divined in quantitative research, not all of its preoccupations can be directly attributed to positivism. Rather, it seems more sensible to see some of them as a manifestation of a vague commitment to the ways of the natural sciences. It also seems that there may be aspects of the general approach of quantitative researchers which are not directly attributable to either positivism or to the practices of the natural sciences, for example, the aforementioned elevation of concepts as focal points of empirical inquiry. Thus, it may be that the tendency in some quarters to view quantitative research simply as positivist may not be an adequate precursor to allowing a fully fledged comprehension of its main facets. None the less, positivism and a broad commitment to mimicking the natural sciences is clearly in evidence, and it is precisely to this flirtation that the proponents of qualitative research have taken exception over the years. Their objections fuelled an alternative strategy for the examination of social reality, which provides the focus for the next chapter.

Notes

1   In arriving at this inventory, I have found the following especially helpful: Harré (1972), Kolakowski (1972), Giedymin (1975), Keat (1981), Alexander (1982), Halfpenny (1982), and Bryant (1985).

2   The philosophy of science being referred to here is the 'realist' approach which has found increasing favour among some philosophers and social scientists. Interested readers should consult Harré (1972), Harré and Secord (1972), Bhaskar (1975), Keat and Urry (1975), and Sayer (1984). The possibility of an alternative to positivism as a way of comprehending the nature of the natural sciences implies that one may be committed to a natural science approach without endorsing positivism. Nor do realism and positivism exhaust the full range of philosophies of science (Harré, 1972; Keat and Urry, 1975).

3   It is precisely for this reason that I have not dwelt too long on the philosophy of science issues. What is critical to the characterization of the nature of quantitative research is its clear espousal of a 'scientific' approach which bears many of the hallmarks of positivism. Further, as will be apparent from the discussion in later chapters, quantitative research has been criticized from the vantage point of qualitative research generally because of its scientific pretensions and the effects of such an orientation on the comprehension of social reality. The issue of whether positivism is an adequate account of the natural sciences has tended to figure much less directly in the various critiques offered by qualitative researchers.

4   A clear example of such an account of the origin of concepts can be found in Babbie (1979).

5   The main studies associated with this programme of research can be found in Pugh and Hickson (1976) and Pugh and Hinings (1976). Useful brief accounts which give a flavour of the approach of the Aston Studies can be found in Pugh *et al.* (1983, pp. 37–43) and Pugh (1988).

6 A summary of the main features of this programme of research may be found in Bryman (1986).

7 The most familiar account of the LPC scale is to depict high-scoring subjects as 'relationships oriented', low scorers as 'task-oriented'. However, it has also been used to distinguish between leaders in terms of their degrees of cognitive complexity. Alternative interpretations have been proffered by Fiedler and others. Bryman (1986) summarizes much of the research associated with the LPC scale.

8 For example, in the Azumi and McMillan (1973) study of thirty-eight Japanese factories, the Aston measure Functional Specialization achieved a correlation of $-.12$ with the 'equivalent' Hall measure, Division of Labour. At the very least, a positive correlation would have been anticipated. Pennings's research on twenty-three Canadian organizations noted similar discrepancies, albeit in respect to different dimensions and their respective measures.

9 Split-half correlation, average inter-item correlation, average item-total correlation, and Cronbach's alpha are the sorts of reliability gauges that I have in mind.

10 In fact, the Aston Studies tended, especially in the early days, to eschew the use of the word 'cause'. However, as Aldrich (1972, p. 27) has observed, the Aston researchers make 'statements that can only be interpreted causally'. Further, their data are as apparently amenable to path analysis as those deriving from any cross-sectional study.

11 The Aston Studies again furnish a fascinating instance of the influence of time. One of the best-known findings stemming from their investigations is that the larger an organisation, the more structured it is likely to be. Smaller organizations have less specialization and formalization than larger ones. When a replication of an earlier study was done by Inkson, Pugh and Hickson (1970), fourteen organizations were found in both the original and the second samples. This offered the opportunity of examining the data over a period of approximately six years. It was found that, while most of the fourteen firms were smaller at the time of the second study, twelve had higher scores for structure. In other words, although size was positively and highly correlated with structure, smaller size was accompanied by greater structure over time. This finding neatly illustrates the point that the passage of time can have an impact on the interpretations accorded an initial study (although this can be discerned only if a follow-up is carried out, which invariably does not occur). In addition, this example draws attention to the possibility that inferring a causal order from cross-sectional research may be highly misleading. It is clearly tempting to infer from a large positive correlation and from an intuitive logic that greater size engenders more structuring, but if over time *less* size and more structuring seem to go together, the hazards of inferring temporal precedence become strikingly apparent.

12 It was tempting to treat individualism as an ingredient in the general account of positivism explicated in this chapter. Kolakowski (1972, p. 13) treats the 'rule of nominalism' as a central component of positivism. This rule 'states that we may not assume that any insight

formulated in general terms can have any real referents other than individual concrete objects'. Bryant (1985) in particular emphasizes this aspect of positivism and views it in relation to 'instrumental positivism' in American sociology whereby 'it is always *individuals* who constitute the centre of attention' (p. 141, emphasis in original). However, the rule of nominalism tends not to be emphasized by many writers on positivism as one of its basic constituents. Further, it seems to me that much of the emphasis on the individual in quantitative research (i.e. instrumental positivism) derives from considerations of research technique rather than a commitment to the broader ontological position formulated by Kolakowski in the foregoing quotation.

3

The Nature of Qualitative Research

The methods of data collection with which qualitative research is associated have been employed by social scientists for many years. The best-known of these methods is participant observation, which entails the sustained immersion of the researcher among those whom he or she seeks to study with a view to generating a rounded, in-depth account of the group, organization, or whatever. The adoption of such a research strategy was specifically advocated by Malinowski soon after the turn of the century, with his plea for the social anthropologist to come down from the verandah and to mix with the natives. Indeed, the debt owed by participant observers and qualitative researchers in general to anthropology can be discerned in the widespread use of the term 'ethnography' to describe their approach (e.g. Hammersley and Atkinson, 1983), a term coined in the context of anthropology to denote 'literally, an anthropologist's "picture" of the way of life of some interacting human group' (Wolcott, 1975, p. 112). Some sociologists made use of participant observation in such classic studies as Whyte's (1943) research among street corner boys, Gans's (1962) investigation of an Italian-American community, Dalton's (1959) examination of the world of managers, and Roy's (1960) and Lupton's (1963) research on industrial workers.

The existence of such studies implies that qualitative research is not a new tradition, but one which has a history that precedes the surge of interest in its potential in the 1960s (referred to in Chapter 1). Indeed, some of the intellectual currents with which it is often associated (e.g. symbolic interactionism), and which are discussed below, precede the emergence of qualitative research as a conspicuous force in the social sciences. The factors which may have brought this subterranean tradition of qualitative research into the open include: the growing disillusionment with the products of the scientific approach (i.e. quantitative research), the promotion of self-reflection engendered by the interest shown in the writings of philosophers of science like T. S. Kuhn (1970), and the diffusion of ideas associated with phenomenology from the late 1960s. It is possible to see in the last of these three factors an intellectual current which both prompted an awareness of the deficiencies of the quantitative research orthodoxy and also provided a rationale for an emergent tradition of qualitative research. A number of synonymous terms have emerged as alternative labels for the qualitative approach, as delineated in the Introduction, but they all fundamentally refer to the same thing: an approach to the study of the social world which seeks to describe and analyse the culture and behaviour of humans and their groups from the point of view of those being studied.

While participant observation is probably the method of data collection with which qualitative research is most closely associated, it is by no means the only one. Unstructured interviewing, in which the researcher provides minimal guidance and allows considerable latitude for interviewees, is also a favoured technique. Most participant observers conduct at least a modicum of such interviewing, but some qualitative researchers use it more or less exclusively. The aims of such interviewing are quite different from the familiar survey approach. While some qualitative researchers make use of an interview schedule, others operate with a loose collection of themes which they want to cover. In both instances (as well as in the many examples in between these two types) the subject is given a much freer rein than in the survey interview. Consider the following account of interviewing in the context of a participant observation study of teachers:

> Inevitably the interviewee will 'ramble' and move away from the designated areas in the researcher's mind. 'Rambling' is nevertheless important and needs some investigation. The interviewee in rambling is moving onto areas which most interest him or her. The interviewer is losing some control over the interview, and yielding it to the client, but the pay-off is that the researcher reaches the data that is central to the client. I always go along with rambling for a while, but try to make a note about what is missed and cover it in the next interview. (Measor, 1985, p. 67)

This quotation demonstrates a number of points. The contrast with the survey interview is particularly striking, in that rambling would be regarded as a tiresome distraction from the main focus at hand. Rambling could not usually be dealt with by the analyst of survey data unless it were built into the research strategy in a standardized manner. Further, the interviewer's surrender of her control of the interview session would be anathema to the survey researcher, who is likely to view the interview schedule *inter alia* as a means of manipulating the topics to be addressed by the subject.

Measor's eschewal (possibly consciously) of the term 'subject' for the person being interviewed, and the alternative use of 'interviewee' and 'client', can be read as indicative of a desire for him or her not to be seen as someone who is simply the recipient of the researcher's promptings. Also, the notion of interviewing the teacher on another occasion to fill in the areas not covered in the initial session provides a further contrast with the survey context wherein interviews are almost invariably one-visit episodes; where they are not it is likely to be due to a failure to complete the interview in the time available. But the most critical departure in this account from the survey interview is the suggestion that rambling is interesting because it may reveal a matter of importance to the teacher; in the survey interview it is what is important to the researcher that is critical and so rambling would be seen as a nuisance in need of suppression. Instead, in the unstructured interview a phenomenon like rambling can be viewed as providing information because it reveals something about the interviewee's concerns. Unstructured interviewing in qualitative research, then, departs from survey interviewing not only in terms of format, but also in terms of its concern for the perspective of those being investigated.

The fact that unstructured interviewing is often used as an adjunct to participant observation (though it is frequently employed on its own as well) is indicative of the tendency for participant observers to bring into play a number of data gathering methods. Participant observers are rarely simply participant observers: they often conduct unstructured interviews, examine documentary materials, and even carry out structured interview and postal questionnaire surveys. One reason for the employment of a variety of techniques is that it allows inferences or 'leads' drawn from one data source to be corroborated or followed up by another. Woods (1979) carried out postal questionnaire surveys of parents and third-year students in the throes of making subject choices in the school in which he was acting as a participant observer. He felt that the questionnaires and the follow-up interviews he conducted helped to support the explanation of the subject-choice process which he was developing (Woods, 1986, pp. 117–18).

Secondly, participant observers may not be able to observe all relevant situations and processes. In his research on working class youth on a council estate in Belfast, Jenkins (1983, 1984) was primarily a participant observer, but needed to conduct both structured and unstructured interviews in order to glean information about firms' recruitment practices in the area:

In many of the situations I researched, for example the light engineering factory whose recruitment practices I looked at, I

simply was not *empowered* to observe directly much of what I
have written about. I could not *participate* in the making of
selection decisions at TransInternational Electronics. My
presence in such situations would have been inappropriate unless
I had been prepared in some fashion to associate my research
with the interests of the company. Even had I been happy enough
to do so, such an approach would have immediately closed off
other avenues of research to me. (Jenkins, 1984, p. 160, emphases in original)

This quotation nicely conveys the need to address another layer of
reality through an auxiliary method, as well as some of the dilemmas of identity and identification that many participant observers
face. The use of interviews and questionnaires may also enhance
the scope and breadth of the participant observation research.
While some of the information gleaned from such interviews may
be 'coded' and presented as quantitative data, many qualitative
researchers prefer to employ verbatim quotations from interviewees' replies in order to illustrate general points. Many
qualitative researchers feel uneasy about the quantitative treatment
of interview transcripts (see e.g. Crompton and Jones, 1988). To
some extent this unease can be attributed to the tendency for
qualitative research to be seen as standing for a number of intellectual commitments (which will be explicated later in this chapter)
with which quantification is not very compatible.

Even when participant observers are acting 'purely' as participant observers, there is immense variety in the kinds of activities
in which they are engaged. Gans (1967), reflecting on the various
activities in which he was engaged as a participant observer in his
research on a suburban community in the USA, observes:

These activities cast me in three types of research roles: *total
researcher, researcher participant*, and *total participant*. As a
total researcher I observed events in which I participated
minimally or not at all, for example, as a silent audience member
at public meetings. As a researcher-participant, I participated in
an event but as a researcher rather than as a resident, for example, at most social gatherings. As a total participant, I acted
spontaneously as a friend or neighbour and subsequently analyzed the activities in which I had so participated. (p. 440)

There is clearly a good deal of variety in the kinds of activities involved in performing the participant observer role *per se*. Indeed,
one of the major strengths of participant observation is that it is
not really a single method, but can embrace different ways of

gathering data and styles of observation. By contrast, survey and experimental research are much more uniform. Because there is a greater recognition of the inherent variability of participant observation as a method, many writers prefer terms like 'ethnography' (e.g. Hammersley and Atkinson, 1983; Woods, 1986) or 'field research' (e.g. Burgess, 1984) to denote the package of data collection practices in which participant observers typically engage. The term 'participant observation' can then be reserved for the more or less purely observational procedures carried out by ethnographers/field researchers, such as those cited by Gans in the foregoing quotation.[1] These semantic conventions will be followed in the remainder of this book.

In addition to participant observation and unstructured interviewing, the life history method is often depicted as a major method of qualitative research. This method entails the reconstruction of the lives of one or more individuals. The data sources are fairly varied, but diaries and autobiographies are two of the most prominent bases for generating life histories. Such materials may already exist for the qualitative researcher; or the researcher may solicit them. With the latter approach, the life history method becomes a highly protracted unstructured interview in which the researcher induces others to reflect at length about their lives and the changes and processes which underpin their experiences. One of the best-known examples of this technique is Lewis's (1961) study of the members of the Sánchez family and their experiences in a Mexican slum:

> In the course of our interviews I asked hundreds of questions of [the five members of the family] . . . While I used a directive approach in the interviews, I encouraged free association, and I was a good listener. I attempted to cover systematically a wide range of subjects: their earliest memories, their dreams, their hopes, fears, joys, and sufferings; their jobs; their relationship with friends, relatives, employers; their sex life; their concepts of justice, religion, and politics; their knowledge of geography and history; in short, their total view of the world. Many of my questions stimulated them to express themselves on subjects which they might otherwise never have thought of or volunteered information about. (p. xxi)

While there are signs that there is a burgeoning of interest in the life history approach, some fifty or sixty years after Thomas and Znaniecki's (1918–20) declared enthusiasm for the method, it is little used by qualitative researchers.[2]

Finally, the group discussion is a method which is finding

increasing favour among some qualitative researchers (e.g. Woods, 1979; Griffin, 1985a). Essentially, it is a form of unstructured interview but with more than one subject. Griffin (1985a, 1985b) used this method as part of a qualitative research project on the transition from school to work for a number of young women. Group discussions were pursued in tandem with observation and conventional unstructured interviews. The group discussions 'were loosely structured around a series of key topics and questions to allow for a degree of flexibility' (Griffin, 1985b, p. 101). They focused on the women's experiences of school, friends, leisure, and family life, and their expectations of work. These discussions have the advantage of bringing to the surface the differences among the participants and the contradictions within and between their replies. When used by qualitative researchers the group discussion technique is almost always one among a number of methods of data collection.

The Intellectual Underpinnings of Qualitative Research

In the same way that quantitative research is often depicted as deriving from a natural science (and in particular positivist) understanding of how knowledge about the social world should be generated, qualitative research is also viewed as being predicated upon a prior set of assumptions about the study of social reality. The following statement illustrates this view:

> When we speak of 'quantitative' or 'qualitative' methodologies, we are in the final analysis speaking of an interrelated set of assumptions about the social world which are philosophical, ideological, and epistemological. They encompass more than simply data gathering techniques. (Rist, 1977, p. 62)

Guba and Lincoln (1982) refer to quantitative and qualitative research as resting on divergent paradigms, and hence assumptions, about the proper study of social life. According to such formulations, qualitative research derives from a different cluster of intellectual commitments from quantitative research. Consequently, crucial epistemological differences between the two approaches mean that they operate with divergent principles regarding what is knowledge about the social world and how it can legitimately be produced. The main intellectual undercurrents which tend to be viewed as providing qualitative research with its distinct epistemology are: phenomenology, symbolic interactionism, *verstehen*, naturalism, and ethogenics. The backgrounds to these intellectual positions will be explicated below, but it should be noted that the boundaries between them are often not absolute, in that they exhibit considerable overlap.

Phenomenology
The study of phenomenology is a vast field which can be addressed here only in a highly summarized form and with specific relevance to the topic of qualitative research. Writing in the early twentieth century, Husserl[3] proposed a programme for the study of the universal structures of people's apprehension of the world. Recognizing that our subjective experience of the world is filtered through an unquestioning acceptance of its form and content (what he called 'the natural attitude'), Husserl advocated that the observer needs to bracket this dense thicket of prior understandings in order to grasp subjective experience in its pure, uncontaminated form. This bracketing of the immediate comprehension of the world is referred to as the 'phenomenological reduction'. Phenomenological ideas had little influence on the social sciences until the writings of Alfred Schutz (a major interpreter of the work of Husserl and other phenomenologists after the Second World War) came to notice following their translation from German in the 1960s. In one of his major works, Schutz (1967) was concerned to extend Weber's notion of *verstehen* (see discussion below) making use of Husserl's phenomenology. This preoccupation led him to view the constructs that people use in order to render the world meaningful and intelligible to them as the key focus of a phenomenologically grounded social science. Conterminously, he was concerned to provide a framework for the rebuttal of the growing incursion of positivism in the social sciences in the 1940s and 1950s. These two major themes in his writing come together in this often quoted, evocative passage:

> The world of nature as explored by the natural scientist does not 'mean' anything to molecules, atoms and electrons. But the observational field of the social scientist − social reality − has a specific meaning and relevance structure for the beings living, acting, and thinking within it. By a series of common-sense constructs they have pre-selected and pre-interpreted this world which they experience as the reality of their daily lives. It is these thought objects of theirs which determine their behaviour by motivating it. The thought objects constructed by the social scientist, in order to grasp this social reality, have to be founded upon the thought objects constructed by the common-sense thinking of men, living their daily life within the social world. (Schutz, 1962, p. 59)

Two themes in this quotation exemplify the phenomenological approach to the social sciences and recur in the methodological writings of many qualitative researchers. First, the subject matter of the social sciences − people and their social reality − is fundamentally different from the subject matter of the natural sciences. This view entails a pointed rejection of the positivist position that the differences between the natural and the social orders do not present any problems to the application of scientific methods to the study of society. Secondly, any attempt to understand social reality must be grounded in people's experience of that social reality. This reality has already been interpreted by its adherents and so the social scientist must grasp individuals' interpretive devices which provide the motivational background to their actions. Failure to recognize and encapsulate the meaningful nature of everyday experience runs the risk of losing touch with social reality and imposing instead 'a fictional non-existing world constructed by the scientific observer' (Schutz, 1964, p. 8). Schutz realized that the natural attitude of everyday life is a relatively unreflective stance toward everyday life, so that when social scientists seek to interpret this mundane reality they are in effect 'intellectualizing' what is to the social actor unproblematic. Thus, Schutz suggests, the social scientist is in the business of creating 'second order constructs' of social actors' comprehension of social reality. But these second order constructs must retain a basic allegiance to the actors' own conceptions of the social world − their 'typifications', to use Schutz's nomenclature. In short, social action must be examined by the social scientist in terms of the actor's own interpretation of his or her action and its motivational background.

While there is a good deal more to phenomenology and Schutz's particular version of it than this summary can do justice to, the essential themes have been captured. There is some debate about the extent to which the incorporation of some of these themes into sociology and other social sciences has led to a genuinely phenomenological approach. For example, Heap and Roth (1973) have argued that many writers who describe their own or others' work as phenomenological are using the term in a metaphorical rather than in a bona fide manner. They suggest that the writings of social scientists who claim to be working within the phenomenological tradition rarely embrace its full extent and complexity. Schutz was aware that the application of phenomenological ideas to the study of the social world may run into difficulties. He argued that the real phenomenological approach has to be abandoned in the study of the social world, since we always start out by accepting the existence of that world (Schutz, 1967, p. 97). This gives rise to doubt as to whether the phenomenological reduction is a feasible first step in the analysis of social reality.

The metaphorical, or in any event loose, depiction of styles of research and thinking as 'phenomenological' can be discerned in the writings of various proponents of qualitative research. 'Phenomenology' often seems to denote little more than a commitment to attending to actors' points of view and the meanings they attribute to their behaviour. The following passage is fairly representative of this viewpoint:

> The phenomenologist views human behaviour . . . as a product of how people interpret their world. The task of the phenomenologist, and, for us, the qualitative methodologists, is to capture this *process* of interpretation . . . In order to grasp the meanings of a person's behaviour, *the phenomenologist attempts to see things from that person's point of view.* (Bogdan and Taylor, 1975, pp. 13–14, emphases in original)

Accordingly, the dubbing of a particular piece of research or the philosophical basis of qualitative research as 'phenomenological' very often has to be interpreted as being indicative of little more than a commitment to the actor's perspective. In many cases, the attribution 'phenomenological' is used as a rationale for taking this perspective.

One of the chief routes by which phenomenological ideas made inroads into the social sciences was through *ethnomethodology*, a term coined by Garfinkel (1967) to denote an approach to the study of social reality which takes people's practical reasoning and the ways in which they make the social world sensible to themselves as the central focus. Ethnomethodologists were very influenced by Schutz's writings, although other intellectual influences (e.g. Talcott Parsons) were also acknowledged. Ethnomethodologists also produced examples of qualitative research, in which they made substantial use of participant observation, unstructured interviewing, and the like. In the early years of its development, ethnomethodology spawned ethnographic studies undertaken in a variety of milieux which resemble traditional ethnographic research quite strongly, e.g. Bittner's (1967) study of the police, Sudnow (1967) on the dying in hospital, and Cicourel's (1968) examination of the operation of juvenile justice. At a later stage, an alternative approach to ethnomethodological research was formulated in the form of 'conversation analysis' which, as the term implies, draws on full transcripts and recordings of conversations in natural situations, which are presented in an unadultered form to the reader, along with the researcher's own interpretation of the flow of events.[4] The proponents of conversational analysis see their approach as more in keeping with the phenomenological emphasis on the subject's perspective than conventional ethnography, since the reader is able to draw his or her own inferences regarding the meaning of the data to actors. More latterly, research drawing on this general orientation has been called 'constitutive ethnography' (e.g. Mehan, 1978). The conversational style of ethnomethodological research can be viewed as a form of qualitative research. However, the tendency to view developments in ethnomethodology as contributing to the growth of interest in qualitative research (e.g. Bogdan and Taylor, 1975; Schwartz and Jacobs, 1979) seems to derive partly from ethnomethodologists' general perspective on social life (with their emphasis on how people see the accomplishment of social order) and partly from ethnomethodology's ethnographic phase. Consequently, the impact of phenomenological ideas on qualitative research can be viewed as a direct route, as Schutz's writings received greater and greater attention, and as a slightly circuitous journey via ethnomethodology.

Symbolic Interactionism
Unlike phenomenology, symbolic interactionism is an explicitly social science approach to the study of social life. While it has its own philosophical forebears (e.g. pragmatism), the development of symbolic interactionism has largely been undertaken under the aegis of the social sciences. It has been a predominantly American tradition (at least in its early years), with the bulk of the early classic statements being written in the first four decades of this century. Symbolic interactionists view social life as an unfolding process in which the individual interprets his or her environment and acts on the basis of that interpretation. Thus a stimulus to act is depicted as undergoing a process of interpretation before a response (an act) is forthcoming. Two central concepts to this tradition — the definition of the situation and the social self — give a flavour of the approach as well as capture some focal themes. The notion of the definition of the situation is central to W. I. Thomas's famous dictum: 'If men define situations as real, they are real in their consequences.' According to Thomas, before the individual acts 'there is always a stage of examination and deliberation' (1931, p. 41) which informs the direction of the act. The idea of the definition of the situation has proved to be a powerful tool in facilitating an understanding of the bases of action, as well as providing an awareness of the implications of varying definitions for people's behaviour. The idea of the social self draws attention to the individual as a complex mixture of biological instincts and internalized social constraints. These two facets of the self are captured in the distinction between respectively the 'I' and the 'Me' which was forged by G. H. Mead (1934), probably the most influential of the early symbolic interactionist thinkers. The 'Me'

contains our views of ourselves as others see us, an idea neatly captured in Cooley's (1902) notion of the 'looking-glass self'. Whereas the 'I' comprises the untrammelled urges of the individual, the 'Me' is a source of reflection about how we should act in particular situations in the light of how our behaviour will be seen by others. We see ourselves as others see us and in adopting this stance we are reflecting on the tenability of a particular line of action, as viewed by others.

These two central motifs have two ingredients in common: process and interpretation. The self is depicted as a process in that it is the outcome of the dialectic between the 'I' and the 'Me'. Further, action and interaction are viewed as part of a process, in that we do not 'simply' act, but we act on the basis of how we define the situation at hand and how we think others will view our actions. Thus, interaction entails a continuous process of mutual interpretation of the nature of situations and how we believe our actions will be received. This general representation of social life has been evident in the writings of Herbert Blumer (e.g. 1969), who was a student of Mead's and who has been a major interpreter of his writings and their relevance for the social sciences. He depicts symbolic interactionism as resting on three premises:

> The first premise is that human beings act toward things on the basis of the meanings the things have for them . . . The second is that the meaning of such things is derived from, or arises out of, the social interaction that one has with one's fellows. The third premise is that these meanings are handled in, and modified through, an interpretative process used by the person in dealing with the things he encounters. (Blumer, 1969, p. 2)

It is probably the third premise that has been most influential in the eyes of many qualitative researchers, for it directs attention to the need to examine actors' interpretations. According to Blumer (1962, p. 188) 'the position of symbolic interaction requires the student to catch the process of interpretation through which [actors] construct their actions'.

This emphasis on the need to focus on the meanings and interpretations of actors has tended to be taken to imply a need for participant observation. In an examination of the ways in which the methodological implications of symbolic interactionism have been interpreted by its practitioners, Rock (1979, p. 178), for example, has described participant observation as its 'pivotal strategy'. Certainly, this is a common view: many of the school ethnographies which were spawned in the 1970s − some of which will be mentioned in later sections of this chapter − make clear their debts to symbolic interactionism. One example will suffice:

The theoretical framework of this study [of a comprehensive school] is based broadly on symbolic interactionism . . . In focusing upon the meanings that participants attribute to social situations I used the 'definition of the situation' . . . This allowed me to examine how situations are defined and how the definitions are interpreted by different groups and individuals . . . The school is therefore seen as a social creation which arises out of the processes of definition, redefinition, and interpretation that continuously occur among teachers, between teachers and pupils and among pupils. (Burgess, 1983, p. 3)

However, there are grounds for questioning the widely accepted linkage between symbolic interactionism and participant observation. Blumer (1969, p. 41) mentioned other methods as consistent with symbolic interactionism, including individual and group interviews, letters and diaries, and listening to conversations. Some of the classic studies within the tradition (e.g. Becker *et al.*, 1961) did not rely exclusively on participant observation. The aforementioned school ethnographies, like Burgess's study, invariably buttressed participant observation with other methods of data collection, especially interviews. None the less, the most critical methodological implication of Blumer's writings was to orientate the researcher's attention to actors' perspectives, interpretations and meanings, irrespective of whether this emphasis implied the use of participant observation or other methods of data collection.

Blumer's interpretation of the methodological implications of symbolic interactionism has not been shared by all writers within the tradition. At the University of Iowa, M. H. Kuhn developed a programme of research for the empirical investigation of concepts associated with symbolic interactionism which was closer to the natural science approach encountered in Chapter 2. He developed the 'Twenty Statements Test' to measure self-attitudes, which he saw as enabling him to operationalize a sub-set of Mead's ideas (M. H. Kuhn, 1964). Further, there has been some discussion about whether Blumer has correctly interpreted the methodological ramifications of Mead's writings; McPhail and Rexroat (1979) and Blumer (1980) have clashed over the question of whether Mead's epistemology was closer to the natural science model than Blumer has typically allowed. However, the critical issue is that symbolic interactionism has invariably been taken to conform to the emphasis on gaining access to people's interpretational schemes, along the lines depicted by Blumer.

Verstehen
Max Weber's idea of *verstehen* is often taken as one of the intellec-

tual precursors of the qualitative research approach (e.g. Filstead, 1970, p. 4). The term means 'to understand' in German. Writing in the early twentieth century, Weber placed 'understanding' at the forefront of his own view of what sociology entailed: 'Sociology . . . is a science which attempts the interpretive understanding of social action in order to arrive at a causal explanation of its course and effects' (Weber, 1947, p. 90). Weber recognized two forms of understanding: 'direct observational understanding of the subjective meaning of a given act' (p. 94) and 'explanatory' or 'motivational' understanding in which 'the particular act has been placed in an understandable sequence of action, the understanding of which can be treated as an explanation of the actual course of behaviour' (p. 95). The former implies that we understand, for example, that a particular kind of facial expression is indicative of anger; explanatory understanding occurs when we probe the motive for the outburst of anger.

Weber's writings on this subject are part of a predominantly European tradition which sought to establish that the study of society requires a different kind of understanding from that of the natural sciences. As such 'motivational' understanding entails a very different kind of understanding from that of the scientist seeking to understand the meaning of a causal law. There is some debate about the precise meanings of the terms Weber employed, but more particularly there has been considerable discussion about the role of *verstehen*. Abel (1948), for example, sought to confine it to a relatively subordinate role of generating hunches, because the analyst can never be certain that he or she has hit upon the correct interpretation of social action.

The suggestion that Weber's *verstehen* is a major influence on qualitative research has been partially challenged by Platt (1985). Drawing on interviews and analyses of references, she points out that early qualitative researchers of the 1920s and 1930s seem to have been unaware of the concept; those of the 1940s and 1950s (like Whyte, Gans, Becker, Hughes, and Strauss, who will all be encountered later in this and the next chapter) were either unaware of Weber's *verstehen* or did not regard it as relevant to their concerns as participant observers. Platt goes on to argue that the reason for the apparent affinity between Weber's writings on understanding and the needs and interests of early qualitative researchers was that they had access to alternative theorists whose work converged considerably with Weber – in particular symbolic interactionists like Cooley and Thomas.

However, for more recent writers, Weber's writings on *verstehen* seem to be used as one of a number of intellectual precursors of qualitative research, in addition to phenomenology and symbolic interactionism. To a certain degree, its citation along with the other intellectual precursors is used to confer a cachet on qualitative research, that is, as a source of legitimation for a tradition which, as suggested in Chapter 1, has been a poorly regarded underdog when compared to the widespread acceptance of quantitative research.

Naturalism

The theme of naturalism in qualitative research is in part a separate philosophical foundation, and in part a sub-theme within the three previously mentioned intellectual undercurrents, most notably symbolic interactionism. In the previous chapter, 'naturalism' was one of a number of terms used to describe the belief in the applicability of the natural science model to the study of social reality. However, Matza (1969), following Randall (1944), has pointed to another meaning of naturalism which is almost the exact opposite of the identification of the term with the natural sciences. This second sense of the term implies that the researcher should treat the phenomena being studied as naturally as possible, that is, he or she should seek to minimize the adulteration of the setting under investigation as far as possible. Thus according to Matza, people engage in activities that have meaning to them and they also create their own social realities; therefore,

> a view which conceives man as object, methods that probe human behavior without concerning themselves with the meaning of behavior, cannot be regarded as naturalist . . . because they have molested in advance the phenomenon to be studied. Naturalism . . . claims fidelity to the empirical world. (Matza, 1969, p. 8)

According to this view, naturalism is 'the philosophical view that strives to remain true to the nature of the phenomenon under study' (Matza, 1969, p. 5).

Blumer (1969, p. 27), writing from the perspective of symbolic interactionism, has also argued that methods for studying social life 'must be assessed in terms of whether they respect the nature of the empirical world under study'. As writers like Lofland (1967) have noted, this conception of naturalism is not unlike the approach to the study of flora and fauna that botany and zoology exhibit, whereby such phenomena are observed in their natural settings. Naturalism, in this sense, departs from the practices of quantitative researchers, who are depicted as imposing their own conceptual schemes on the social world and using research instruments (e.g. experiments, survey interviews) which interrupt and disturb the naturalness of that world.

'Naturalism' subsumes two interrelated themes: a distaste for artificial methods of research which are seen as providing distorted pictures of social reality, and a concern to reveal the social world in a manner consistent with the image of that world which its participants carry around with them. The theme of naturalism has been particularly evident in the study of deviance. For example, Matza (1969) contrasts the 'correctional' stance of much criminology, whereby crime is depicted as a pathological phenomenon to be purged, with a growing tendency to 'appreciate' deviance. The correctional stance entails a concern for the factors which contribute to crime so that it might be controlled; appreciation is concerned to understand and empathize with deviants. This theme is evident in the following recommendation for

> the study of career criminals *au naturel*, in the field, the study of such criminals as they go about their work and play . . . Successful field research depends on the investigator's trained abilities to look at people, listen to them, think and feel with them, talk with them rather than at them. It does *not* depend fundamentally on some impersonal apparatus such as a . . . tape recorder or questionnaire, that is interposed between the investigator and the investigated. (Polsky, 1969, pp. 120, 124)

Adler (1985, p. 28) endorsed this view when writing about her qualitative research on upper-level drug dealers: 'By studying criminals in their natural habitat I was able to see them in the full variability and complexity of their surrounding subculture.' Naturalism is one of the intellectual undercurrents to qualitative research in that it proposes that the study of social phenomena should involve the researcher getting close to his or her subjects and not imposing the technical paraphernalia of quantitative research on them.

Ethogenics
Within social psychology, a recent intellectual spur to qualitative research has been the 'ethogenic' approach associated with Harré (1974, 1979, 1986; Harré and Secord, 1972). The approach is a ramification of his incisive critique of the application of positivist ideas in social psychology. Harré objects to the use of experiments in this discipline, arguing that they create a mechanistic conception of people who are viewed as simply responding to experimentally induced stimuli. One of the central planks of Harré's epistemological position is that positivism does not adequately describe the nature of scientific activity; rather science proceeds by constructing hypotheses about observed regularities. The scientist seeks

to construct hunches about the mechanisms which generate such regularities, i.e. he or she seeks to explain them. As indicated in Chapter 2, these hypotheses entail imagining mechanisms which generate observed patterns. This conception of scientific activity (which he calls 'realism') is then used as a blueprint for a genuinely scientific social psychology. The ensuing approach – ethogenics – aims to provide a framework for the examination of the genesis of human social actions.

A central feature of the ethogenic approach is the understanding of episodes in social life. 'Episodes' are sequences of interlocking acts by individuals. It is the task of ethogenics to elucidate the underlying structures of such episodes by investigating the meanings actors bring to the constituent acts. This approach is viewed by Harré and his co-workers as the analogue of the scientist's stance in relation to the natural order. A central methodological ingredient of ethogenics is the analysis of people's accounts of their actions within identified episodes; along with ethnographic research, the analysis of accounts 'is required to formulate hypotheses about the belief system which is being used by actors in generating typical episodes' (Harré, 1986, p. 103). In grasping the belief systems which underlie social episodes, the rules and conventions of social life from the subject's perspective can be derived. The understanding and analysis of such phenomena facilitate the construction of theories about the resources upon which actors draw when acting. It is the socially shared knowledge upon which actors draw that is the particular province of ethogenics.

One of the main pieces of research to emerge from the ethogenic approach is a study of disorder in classrooms and on football terraces by Marsh, Rosser and Harré (1978). The approach to data collection took the form of observation in both contexts coupled with intensive interviews designed to elicit accounts. Marsh *et al.* argue that trouble in schools and football hooliganism are frequently depicted as meaningless. By contrast, when examining disorder in classrooms, the authors

> are concerned to explore the interpretation and genesis of disorder and violence in the schoolroom from the point of view of pupils. We are concerned with disorder as it is seen by our participants and as it is represented in their accounts. There is no way of telling how many of the episodes described are elaborations designed to impress, or how far they are accurate descriptions of action sequences on which both teachers and pupils would agree. Our interest . . . lies in the principles employed by the pupils themselves to fit the actions they describe into a meaningful framework. (Marsh, Rosser and Harré, 1978, p. 30)

The material collected on both schools and football terraces reveals that the apparently disordered events that often occur in these milieux 'can be seen as conforming to a very distinct and orderly system of roles, rules and shared meanings' (p. 97); in other words, people's accounts of particular episodes and the observation of their acts (as components of episodes) reveal a structure in the midst of apparent disorder.

The ethogenic approach is a further epistemological position which is associated with qualitative research. Unlike much writing about qualitative research (such as some works which have been inspired by the phenomenological position), the ethogenic approach is perceived by its advocates as providing a *scientific* framework for the analysis of social action. The growth of interest in qualitative research is often viewed as indicative of a reaction against the application of a natural scientific model to the study of society. It is clear from Harré's work that it is specifically the imposition of a positivist notion of science that the proponents of ethogenics object to, rather than a scientific approach as such.

The Characteristics of Qualitative Research

It should already be apparent that qualitative research, in both its underlying philosophical allegiances and its approach to the investigation of social reality, differs from the quantitative style of research. In Chapter 5 the contrasts between them will be the main focus. The present section will elucidate some of the chief characteristics of qualitative research.

'Seeing through the eyes of . . .'

The most fundamental characteristic of qualitative research is its express commitment to viewing events, action, norms, values, etc. from the perspective of the people who are being studied. There is a clear connection between this undertaking and the underlying philosophical positions outlined in the previous section. The strategy of taking the subject's perspective is often expressed in terms of seeing through the eyes of the people you are studying. Such an approach clearly involves a preparedness to empathize (though not necessarily to sympathize) with those being studied, but it also entails a capacity to penetrate the frames of meaning with which they operate. The latter may open up a need to comprehend a specialized vernacular, or even a new language, as is typically the case for the social anthropologist. In order to gain the necessary vantage point from which empathy may be feasible, sustained periods of involvement are required. While this predilection would seem to imply long periods of participant observation, as noted above, other methods, most notably in-depth, unstructured interviewing, are also employed.

There may often be the problem for the researcher of knowing through whose eyes he or she is supposed to be seeing. School ethnographers have to be sensitive to the different perceptions of teachers, parents and pupils. Diversity of perspective *within* these three groups may also be expected. In his ethnographic study of a secondary school, Woods (1979) was able to draw out the different ways in which various groupings made sense of the institution and their own positions within it. For example, the process of subject choice revealed a contrast between the predominant perspective of working class pupils − one of relative indifference − and their middle class peers, in which a marked concern for careers and prospects was revealed. Similarly, Jenkins's (1983) research on working class youth in Belfast revealed three different groupings − 'lads', 'ordinary kids' and 'citizens' respectively on a rough-to-respectable continuum − with divergent frames of reference for looking at the worlds of school, leisure, work, and the like. In other words, the injunction to take the perspective of the people you are studying may mean needing to attend to a multiplicity of world-views. This commitment may cause the ethnographer a number of difficulties, which derive from his or her age or gender. For example, participant observation with children is likely to be a difficult undertaking for the school ethnographer, so that interviews may have to be used in order to gain access to their world-views. Woods (1979) derived much of his understanding of teachers' perspectives through participant observation, but relied on unstructured interviews with pupils and parents (because of the inaccessibility of the latter). Jenkins (1983) recognized the problem of a male carrying out participant observation with girls and relied more extensively on interviews for access to their interpretations of their social environments.

It is not easy for ethnographers to sustain the constant recourse to seeing through the eyes of their subjects. Indeed, taken literally the injunction would seem to imply that researchers would be totally subservient to the people they study for all facets of the enterprise of ethnography − it would even have a prerogative over what should be researched. In fact, most ethnographers operate with their own foci of interest, albeit with a commitment to retain a fidelity to the subject's viewpoint. It is worth returning to the passage from Measor (1985) quoted above on p. 46. She reflects the concern of the qualitative researcher to see events from the interviewee's perspective in that 'rambling' is not to be suppressed as it may reveal matters of importance to the individual. But equally her reference to making 'a note about what is missed' implies that the researcher has a focus which the interview has not adequately covered, and so a further session is deemed to be necessary. Further, confessions by ethnographers of their field-work lacunae occasionally point to an awareness that they are not always able to recognize everything that is important to their subjects. Hammersley (1984) has written that he now realizes that his omission of an examination of the reorganization of the school he was studying was an error. He had failed to recognize that the reorganization was important to the people he was studying. Hammersley attributes his failure to attend to the issue of reorganization to his theoretical and political leanings at the time of the research.

This facet of qualitative research – its avowed aim of seeing through the eyes of the people studied – is a *keynote* of the tradition. However, there is a hint in this discussion that it is an orientation which entails certain difficulties, which will be examined in greater detail in the next chapter.

Description
There is a clear recognition among most ethnographers that one of the main purposes of their research style is to provide detailed descriptions of the social settings they investigate. Adler (1985), for example, portrayed her research on drug dealers as 'an ethnographic description and analysis of a deviant social scene' (p. 2). Qualitative researchers advocate that such description should be at the very least consistent with the perspectives of the participants in that social setting. This emphasis on description entails attending to mundane detail; the apparently superficial trivia and minutiae of everyday life are worthy of examination because of their capacity to help us to understand what is going on in a particular context and to provide clues and pointers to other layers of reality. Qualitative researchers often display a certain defensiveness in recognizing the descriptive slant to much of their work. For example, Rist (1984, p. 161) has written: 'Asking the question, "What is going on here?" is at once disarmingly simple and incredibly complex.' This statement contains an element of defensiveness, because the scientific ethos that pervades much thinking in the social sciences sees analysis and explanation as the real stuff of research; consequently, mere description is often demeaned and portrayed as lacking intellectual integrity.

Qualitative researchers invariably seek to go beyond pure description and to provide analyses of the environments they examine. None the less, there tends to be a substantial attention to detail in such research. Burgess's (1983) ethnographic study of a comprehensive school reveals in great detail such topics as: the physical and social structure of the school, the curriculum, patterns of relationships among the teachers, and the headmaster's conception of the school. One of the main reasons for the ethnographer's endorsement of such descriptive detail is to allow a backdrop whereby events and situations can be viewed within a social context. For example, Burgess (1983, p. 238) writes: 'By focusing on the teachers in houses and departments it was possible to see the way in which different versions of the school were being presented to the school.' An awareness of the social structure of the school – houses and departments – provided a framework for the understanding of the different perspectives teachers offered on the school and its aims. Thus an important contribution of descriptive detail for the ethnographer is to the mapping out of a context for the understanding of subjects' interpretations of what is going on and for the researcher to produce analyses and explanations which do justice to the milieux in which his or her observations and interviews are conducted. This theme is the focus of the next section.

Contextualism

As the previous section has prefigured, qualitative research exhibits a preference for contextualism in its commitment to understanding events, behaviour, etc. in their context. It is almost inseparable from another theme in qualitative research, namely *holism* which entails an undertaking to examine social entities – schools, tribes, firms, slums, delinquent groups, communities, or whatever – as wholes to be explicated and understood in their entirety. The implications of the themes of contextualism and holism, particularly in connection with the others delineated thus far, engender a style of research in which the meanings that people ascribe to their own and others' behaviour have to be set in the context of the values, practices, and underlying structures of the appropriate entity (be it a school or slum) as well as the multiple perceptions that pervade that entity.

An extended example allows these different keynotes of the qualitative research approach to be revealed. The example draws on Cohen's (1978) discussion of his approach to studying people's sense of 'community' in the Shetland island of Whalsay. First, Cohen argues that it is crucial to have understood the chief categories of referent used by the islanders – kinship, neighbouring, and fishing crew – in order to appreciate the bases of their allegiances to different segments of the community. This scheme is in effect a 'cognitive map' which provides a foundation for the understanding of social relationships. Further, Cohen's failure to recognize at a sufficiently early stage the significance of the fishing crew as a basis for allegiance led to a premature (from his point of view) identification with a particular boat when he went on a trip with it, thereby making other boats less accessible to him. Thus the patterns of social relationships needed to be understood within the framework of the prior depiction of the context in which they are grounded. Secondly, Cohen points to the preparation of peat as a lengthy, technical procedure with numerous stages. There is much scrutinizing of the practices relating to each stage and any departure from the orthodox method is the source of much discussion and argument. In fact, Cohen eventually found out that the peat would burn irrespective of how it was treated. Consequently:

one comes to understand that the argument and disputation which goes on about the 'right way to do it' has very little to do with peat at all. It has to do with who is engaged in the debate − that is, who can be shown to be correct and who can be shown to be wrong; who can present himself as the guardian of traditionally-hallowed knowledge and skills and who can be shown to be lacking them . . . Casting the peats, then, is a mundane task; yet one which is only properly understood within the context of the whole culture. (Cohen, 1978, p. 15)

The emphasis here is on the need to interpret what is going on in terms of an understanding of the whole society and the meaning it has for the participants. The basic message that qualitative researchers convey is that whatever the sphere in which data are being collected, we can understand events only when they are situated in the wider social and historical context.

Process

There is an implicit longitudinal element built into much qualitative research, which is both a symptom and cause of an undertaking to view social life in processual, rather than static terms. Participant observers have been very attuned to the notion of viewing social life as involving interlocking series of events and so tend to place a much greater emphasis on the changes that the processes which provide its bedrock are responsible for inducing. The emphasis on process can be seen as a response to the qualitative researcher's concern to reflect the reality of everyday life which, they tend to argue, takes the form of streams of interconnecting events. Further, qualitative researchers argue that this is precisely how people experience social reality, so that the inclination to emphasize process is in part a product of the qualitative researcher's commitment to participants' perspectives. The general image that qualitative research conveys about the social order is one of interconnection and change. This emphasis has been attractive to students of policy, for example, since such research can be much more concerned with the process of implementation rather than solely with its outputs (Finch, 1986). Thus a qualitative research approach would emphasize the various responses of both those who implement and those who are affected, the interpretations they invoke of the policy initiative, how they respond to each other's views, how perspectives change, and so on.

Similarly, in his participant observation study of a comprehensive school, Ball (1981) was interested in the way in which a major innovation − the introduction of mixed-ability groupings − was implemented. Ball documents not only the sequence of events that this innovation comprised, but also the variety of responses of the teachers. He found that

> In the absence of an agreed or imposed 'mandate' for change, the teachers at Beachside were free to attribute their own categories of meaning to the innovation . . . Furthermore, the absence of a mandate for change also meant that the teachers were not obliged to change their teaching methods. Indeed, in some respects constraints inherent in the culture and ethos of the school militated against drastic changes in the organization of learning in the classroom. (Ball, 1981, p. 237)

Thus Ball concludes from his investigation of the meanings attributed to the change to mixed ability groupings that there was substantial variation in teachers' perspectives on it and that the extent of the impact of the change on their teaching practices may have been less pronounced than might otherwise have been anticipated. From the teacher's point of view, Ball shows, change is not a radical departure from a pre-existing state, but a gradual drifting away, and it is from this latter stance that he or she sees change as having occurred. Ball's analysis of the innovation entails treating it as a process whereby the change is introduced, then interpreted by teachers, and the implications of these interpretations for teaching practices are then examined. The final sentence in the above quotation also serves as a reminder of the qualitative researcher's inclination towards a contextual understanding, whereby the teachers' interpretations of the change are grounded in the context of the school's ethos.

Flexibility and Lack of Structure

Qualitative researchers' adherence to viewing social phenomena through the eyes of their subjects has led to a wariness regarding the imposition of prior and possibly inappropriate frames of reference on the people they study. Consequently, they tend to favour a research strategy which is relatively open and unstructured, rather than one which has decided in advance precisely what ought to be investigated and how it should be done. It is also often argued that an open research strategy enhances the opportunity of coming across entirely unexpected issues which may be of interest to the ethnographer. Participant observation particularly lends itself to this orientation because the researcher is immersed in a social context and can defer analysis until fully acquainted with it.

The foregoing discussion would seem to imply that qualitative researchers do not even have a 'problem' that they seek to investigate at the outset of their investigations. In fact, they vary quite considerably in this respect. Some researchers seem to have very loose notions of what they are intending to investigate once they have negotiated access to a research site. For example, writing about his ethnographic study of 'fiddling' in a bakery, Ditton (1977, p. 11) affirms that his research 'was not set up to answer any empirical questions'. His decision to concentrate on fiddling was not made until a considerable proportion of the research had already been conducted. Adler (1985) conceived of an ethnographic study of drug dealers only after she and her husband had moved to California to attend a graduate school course in sociology and had come into contact with dealers through a neighbour. By contrast, some ethnographers have somewhat more precise notions of their focus of study at the outset. Bloor (1978) conducted an observational study (including data from conversations) of ENT (ear, nose and throat) clinics, because he 'was concerned to establish whether or not geographical differences in the incidence of adenotonscillectomy among children could be attributed to . . . differences between ENT specialists in different geographical areas in their routine assessments' (Bloor, 1978, p. 545). While not quite as specific as Bloor in this last statement, Ball (1981) describes his study of comprehensive schooling as aiming to examine 'the dynamics of selection, socialization and change . . . as well as the playing out of social structural and cultural forces in the school' (p. xv).

Irrespective of whether the research problem is closely defined, qualitative researchers tend to the view that the predominantly open approach which they adopt in the examination of social phenomena allows them access to unexpectedly important topics which may not have been visible to them had they foreclosed the domain of study by a structured, and hence potentially rigid, strategy. It is even possible for the researcher to discover that a particular focus is irrelevant. In his study of Whalsay, Cohen (1978) had intended to look at the ways in which changes in the technological and economic infrastructure of fishing may have affected skippers' authority. He was also concerned with the ways skippers had responded to changes in the bases of their authority. However, after the start of the field-work Cohen found that the problem he had formulated was 'empirically irrelevant' and considers that the factors which conspired to render his research problem unproblematic were of greater importance. In particular, he argues that when he viewed the problem within the context of the community's pattern of social relations and culture the issue of skippers' authority could not be sensibly extracted from its wider milieu. What is of particular interest here is the qualitative researcher's ability to recognize the irrelevance of his research question from within the framework of the community (the contextualist emphasis) *and* the ability to change direction in the formulation of his problem.

Theory and Concepts

In line with their preference for a research strategy which does not impose a potentially alien framework on their subjects, qualitative researchers frequently reject the formulation of theories and concepts in advance of beginning their field-work. In particular, they view the imposition of a pre-ordained theoretical framework as deleterious because it may excessively constrain the researcher and also may exhibit a poor fit with participants' perspectives. By and large, qualitative researchers favour an approach in which the formulation and testing of theories and concepts proceeds in tandem with data collection. This issue will be the focus of a more detailed discussion in Chapter 4. In the meantime, a fairly general treatment of the connection between concepts and research is supplied.

Blumer's (1954) writing on concepts is widely cited and accepted in broad terms by many qualitative researchers. He argued strenuously against treating concepts in terms of fixed empirical referents which are then applied to the real world. This is the basic procedure of much quantitative research, which sets up precise operational definitions against which reality may be gauged. Against such an approach he proposed treating social scientific concepts as *sensitizing concepts* which provide 'a general sense of reference and guidance in approaching empirical instances' (p. 7). This approach to the connection of concepts and data means that a concept provides a set of general signposts for the researcher in his or her contact with a field of study. While the concept may become increasingly refined, it does not become reified such that it loses contact with the real world. One concomitant of this approach is that the qualitative researcher is attuned to the variety of forms that the concept may subsume. As such, a sensitizing concept retains close contact with the complexity of social reality, rather than trying to bolt it on to fixed, preformulated images. In a study of power in a medical school in the USA, Bucher (1970, p. 26) preferred 'to postpone sharp definitions of my terms and concentrate on the empirical situation in the expectation that definitions appropriate to my setting will emerge from analysis of the data'. This procedure allowed the author to draw out the different forms and bases of power within the school and to look at its operation in both formally designated offices and beyond. The general understanding of concepts, then, seems to imply that they are both inputs and outputs in relation to the research enterprise; that is, they provide a general frame of reference at the outset and are also refined by the researcher during the field-work period.

The general approach of qualitative researchers to concepts and theories is to be mistrustful of their specification prior to the start of the research enterprise. This is not to say that a method like participant observation is incapable of testing theories and allowing concepts to be operationally defined at the outset of a qualitative study. Becker (1958) proposed an approach to participant observation in which the testing of theories was a prominent ingredient, in order to infuse it with (as he put it) a more 'scientific' flavour. Thus participant observation may not be entirely incompatible with the kind of approach detailed in Figure 2.1 in the context of quantitative research, but qualitative researchers have tended to perceive it as ideal for the extraction of actors' rather than social scientists' prior conceptual schemes. Further, the disillusionment with the underlying principles of quantitative research, which has already been alluded to, almost certainly has militated against the enlistment of participant observation for such purposes by researchers working within the qualitative tradition.

Conclusion

Whereas quantitative research was described in the previous chapter as drawing the bulk of its intellectual inspiration from a natural science approach, and from certain tenets of positivism in particular, qualitative research derives from, and has been stimulated by, traditions which are distinctively different from such an orientation. The connection between the intellectual traditions delineated above and the chief characteristics of qualitative research is most evident in relation to the commitment to seeing through the eyes of the people being studied. All five of the intellectual currents discussed reveal this general concern. Indeed, some writers (e.g. Deutscher, 1973) see all perspectives which take the actor's point of view as the empirical point of departure as 'phenomenological'. The emphasis on description is in large part a product of the tendency in these perspectives to adopt a naturalistic approach which retains fidelity to the real world. The stress on contextual and holistic understanding can be attributed to a preference for grounding accounts of social reality in subjects' perceptions of their environment: the symbolic interactionist emphasis on the definition of the situation, for example, illustrates this tendency. Symbolic interactionism is also responsible for the accent on process in that its exponents tend to view social life as a series of interlinked events, mediated by people's interpretive devices. The tendency for conceptual and theoretical reasoning to be seen as something which either occurs *en passant* or towards the end of the research enterprise can be attributed to the qualitative researcher's distrust of stances which may fail to do justice to the subject's orientation to the social world.

Interest in qualitative research has gained increasing momentum since the late 1960s. Yet qualitative research as such predates this period. While the extent to which the work of the Chicago School of sociology in the 1920s and 1930s can be interpreted as qualitative research (in the sense in which the term is currently used) has been questioned, it has none the less been viewed as an early example of such research (Platt, 1983). Since then, the work of writers like Whyte and Gans has provided notable examples of qualitative research before the burgeoning of interest in the 1960s. Further, the notion of *verstehen* and the perspective of symbolic interactionism have long been familiar to social scientists. Why then does one find a fairly sudden increase in interest in qualitative research if some of the intellectual traditions on which it is supposed to rest and the methods with which it is associated predate the 1960s? Two factors are particularly noteworthy. First, it is possible to detect considerable disillusionment with the fruits of quantitative research among the early writers on qualitative research. These writers invariably explored the major features of qualitative research in contradistinction to those of quantitative research. The second factor is the growing awareness of phenomenology, and more particularly Schutz's version of it, which occurred in the 1960s. This work seemed simultaneously to offer the epistemological basis for a critique of quantitative research and a novel approach in its own right. One the one hand, the growth of phenomenology acted as a spur to congruent perspectives like symbolic interactionism and *verstehen*; on the other hand, it spawned interest in methods like participant observation and unstructured interviewing, which seemed to allow the phenomenological approach to be set in motion.

Notes

1 Participant observation should not be confused with 'pure' observation. This technique involves the researcher observing others, but with no participation. It has been used by L. Lofland (1973) in her studies of urban life, although she buttressed her observations with interviews. Many participant observers use pure observation some of the time, but the relative absence of involvement with the subjects of the research has meant that pure observation is rarely used alone by qualitative researchers because it is unlikely to allow access to the world-views of those being studied.

2 However, there are signs of increasing interest in the use of the life history method (see Plummer, 1983).

3 A useful summary of some major phenomenological ideas can be found in Husserl (1927), which also provides a flavour of his style.

4 On conversational analysis and its relationship with the ethnographic phase of ethnomethodology, see Atkinson and Drew (1979).

4

Problems in Qualitative Research

With the basic features of qualitative research having been explicated, a number of problems in the implementation of
qualitative research will be addressed. Three central facets of
qualitative research are examined: the ability of the investigator to
see through other people's eyes and to interpret events from their
point of view; the relationship between theory and research in the
qualitative tradition; and the extent to which qualitative research
deriving from case studies can be generalized. Each of these topics
is central to the issue of the extent to which qualitative research
constitutes an approach to the study of social reality that is distinctively different from the quantitative approach.

The Problem of Interpretation

There can be little doubt that the commitment to explicating the subject's interpretation of social reality is a (one might even say 'the') *sine
qua non* of qualitative research. Each of the philosophical positions
which underpins such research displays a devotion to participants'
perspectives, and it would be very difficult to find an exposition of
qualitative research in which the theme does not figure strongly.[1]
Many qualitative researchers are highly explicit about their focus on
their subjects' interpretations of social reality. Birkstead (1976)
specifically examined academic performance at school from the
perspective of schoolboys, because he felt that existing research had
dwelt excessively on schools' conceptions of performance. He conducted participant observation with a group of boys both in and outside school. He chose this method because he needed to elicit

> how people construe their environment. I was not interested in
> testing hypotheses but in finding out about other people's point
> of view . . . I was interested in the concepts and categories of the
> adolescents. I could not assume from the start that 'school' would
> be a significant category to them, nor, if it were, what it would
> mean. (Birkstead, 1976, pp. 65, 66)

By adopting his boys' conceptual frameworks, Birkstead argues that he was able to establish that school was not an organizing principle in their lives. Further, contrary to much common-sense and sociological wisdom, failure at school is not generalized to life outside the school gates. It is seen by the boys as specific to the school context.

But how feasible is it to perceive as others perceive? The assumption that an interpretive approach to the study of social action is feasible often goes unexamined, to the extent that one might transform Cicourel's (1964) well-known phrase 'measurement by fiat' into 'interpretation by fiat' in order to capture the often uncontested belief in its viability. This is not to say that qualitative researchers are insensitive to the problems of interpretation. Indeed, they occasionally point to their own frailties in this respect. Ball (1984) has noted that his participant observation study of a comprehensive school tended to focus on the academic side of the school, and correspondingly may not have accorded sufficient significance to pastoral and extra-curricular work. Yet these sides of school life may be highly significant to both teachers and pupils, as Ball recognizes. Ball's justification for giving less emphasis to these non-academic facets of school life is interesting:

> Access to a world of fleeting, overlapping, contradictory, murky, incoherent realities demands selective attention from the fieldworker. For everything that is noticed a multitude of other things go unseen, for everything that is written down a multitude of other things are forgotten. Great parts of the real world experienced by the participant observer, probably the greater part, is *selected out*. (Ball, 1984, p. 78, emphasis in original)

Ball's disinclination to accord as much attention to the non-academic side of the school, albeit for such practical reasons, may be problematic because of the considerable importance of these activities for the participants. This raises some questions about the feasibility of taking the subjects' perspective, if indeed ethnographers have to partition their own perceptions in this manner.

In any case, ethnographers rarely adopt a stance of being 'sponges' whereby they simply absorb subjects' interpretations. Very often they exhibit a focus of interest, though usually couched in fairly broad terms, which may not be part of their subjects' viewpoint. Ball's (1981) concern was to examine 'how one can study the social mechanisms operating within a school and employ such knowledge to explain the disappointing performance of working-class pupils' (p. xv). By taking a stance which focuses upon the interpretations by pupils of the school, their position within it, their notions of success, and the like, Ball was able to address the social processes which underpin this pattern of differential achievement. But the problem of differential achievement as such is not one which stems from his subjects but from a prior set of concerns. Ironically, the impetus for the examination of the social processes which underpin the link between social class and school performance in earlier ethnographic studies of schools by writers like D. H. Hargreaves (1967) and Lacey (1970), in whose wake Ball's study follows, almost certainly derives from quantitative research which established a correlation between these two variables (e.g. Halsey, Floud and Martin, 1956).

The point of the preceding discussion is not to imply a deficiency within qualitative research; indeed, it would be a very strange subject which simply projected subjects' perspectives without any analysis or wider orientation. What has proved to be disquieting to some commentators, both within and outside the qualitative approach, is whether researchers really can provide accounts from the perspective of those whom they study and how we can evaluate the validity of their interpretations of those perspectives. This concern can be discerned in a critique of British school ethnographies by McNamara (1980). For example, he examines a brief transcript from Keddie (1971) of a conversation between a teacher and two boys about a wolf child. At one point, in response to a question by the teacher, one of the boys establishes that the wolf child's experience of being kept in a chicken coop made him 'go backwards'. The boy then asks 'How do you unlearn?', to which the teacher replies, 'Well, you simply forget'. This response is interpreted by Keddie as devised to render the question unproblematic. But how do we know that this is what the teacher intended? The teacher

> may have wished to 'close' the conversation because he wanted to keep the lesson moving or because he was running out of time, he may have decided to avoid discussing the point because it was the subject of next week's lesson, or he may have felt the child was trying to sidetrack him. (McNamara, 1980, p. 119)

In other words, we may question why one interpretation has been plumped for rather than any other, and whether it is genuinely one which is consistent with the teacher's perspective.

Such concerns also surface when we are confronted with the spectacle of divergences of opinion between two ethnographers of the same social context. If the aim is to see through the eyes of those whom one studies, the expectation of some consistency of findings is not unreasonable. Unfortunately, re-studies of a particular community or whatever by different observers are rather rare. Also, most examples seem to have occurred under the umbrella of social anthropology. Possibly, the best known of these cases is Lewis's (1951) re-study of a Mexican village, Tepoztlán, which in the years 1926–7 had been studied by Redfield (1930). The latter found the village to be harmonious, well integrated, and free of divisions, and its inhabitants were seen as contented. Lewis's re-study seventeen years later portrays a village in which conflict, divisions, individualism and a 'pervading quality of fear, envy, and distrust in interpersonal relations' (Lewis, 1951, p. 429) were rife. One explanation for such contrasting accounts is the passage of time, but interestingly Redfield did not seem to accept this as a major factor:

> Lewis is especially interested in the problems of economic need and of personal disharmony and unhappiness, topics which I did not investigate . . . I think we must recognise that the personal and cultural values of the investigator influence the content of the description of the community. (Redfield, 1955, p. 136)

As he goes on to say, Redfield was concerned to answer the question 'What do these people enjoy?', whereas Lewis's was 'What do these people suffer from?'

This kind of clash has recurred more recently and in a highly public arena in the context of Freeman's (1983) critique of Margaret Mead's (1928) attempt to provide support for the view that nurture is a more crucial determinant of human behaviour than nature, on the basis of an anthropological study of child-rearing in Samoa. She depicted adolescents in Samoa as not suffering from the storm and stress of their American counterparts. She attributed this contrast to the free-and-easy, non-authoritarian style of upbringing Samoan children enjoy; also the relative absence of sexual repression and low levels of rape, crime and suicide seemed to be indicative for Mead of a consensual, well-integrated society. Freeman first went to Samoa some twenty years after Mead and revisited it on a number of other occasions. His conclusions were quite different in that he perceived Samoans to be much more aggressive, much stricter in regard to the socialization of the young and sexual mores, more competitive, and more inclined to suffer stress in adolescence than Mead allowed. This clash of views has been hotly debated within anthropology. While attention has been drawn to technical problems in relation to the comparison of the two accounts (differences in time and also place, in that Freeman's research was conducted in a different village on a different island of the Samoan archipelago), it is clear that differences in interpretation are in evidence, as in the case of the Redfield–Lewis clash. In the case of the differences between Mead and Freeman, it is made more interesting by the presence of other Samoan ethnographers in the debate, notably Holmes (1983, 1984), who in the early 1950s conducted a re-study of Mead's original research but, unlike Freeman, in the same village. Holmes concluded that in large part Mead's original findings were correct, and he has repeatedly affirmed this view in the face of Freeman's (1983, p. 103) accusation that his conclusions were in error. Thus we are presented with considerable variety in the perceptions by social anthropologists regarding the basic facts of Samoan life as perceived by the Samoans themselves.

In much the same way that Redfield argues that different assumptions and interpretations lie at the heart of the differences between his findings and those of Lewis, the hub of Freeman's critique is that Mead was excessively influenced by cultural, as against biological, theories about human behaviour. This manner of addressing the divergent findings can be viewed in terms of the old saw that research cannot be undertaken in a totally objective manner, devoid of presuppositions (Bittner, 1973). However, the researcher's biases are not the only source of difficulties in this context. Gartrell (1979) reports that within twelve months of the completion of a spell of field-work among the Nyiha of southwestern Tanzania, Slater (1976) conducted ethnographic research in the same area. Unlike the Redfield–Lewis and Mead–Freeman episodes, the span of time separating the two blocks of research was minimal. Although Gartrell agrees with Slater about many aspects of Nyiha society, their overall views of the people differ. Slater portrays the Nyiha people as 'like zombies', reticent, suspicious of others, inward, apathetic, hostile, and as exhibiting little individuality. Gartrell's view of these same people is almost the exact opposite of Slater's negative view. Gartrell found them to be warm, vital, generous and open. One possible reason for these sharp differences lies in a technical issue: they did not conduct their field-work in precisely the same region, so that the divergent findings may be a function of differences in the areas studied. More interesting from the point of view of the present discussion is Gartrell's suggestion that she and Slater experienced different field situations. For example, Slater was a lone woman researcher, whereas Gartrell was not at the time a trained anthropologist and was accompanying her husband – a geologist – who was working in the area. This simple difference, coupled with other facets of their behaviour on which they differed (e.g. Slater drove a Land Rover which was probably considered unusual for a woman, whereas Gartrell did not), may have meant that Gartrell harmonized better with Nyiha notions of sex appropriate behaviour (i.e. women should be submissive and dominated by men) and hence may account for the more reserved attitude which Slater encountered. Further, Slater's interpreter, who acted as an informant, was a highly educated but arrogant and condescending man, who may have inhibited the Nyiha people with whom Slater came into contact. This suggestion tallies with other anthropologists' experiences of the influence that key informants can exert on ethnographic research (e.g. Berreman, 1962). These reflections suggest that the practicalities of ethnographic research, in addition to the personal predispositions of the investigator, may have an impact upon the nature and direction of ethnographers' findings when they seek to look through the eyes of their subjects.

These episodes are at once fascinating and disconcerting. Such re-studies are relatively rare and yet when they do occur they seem to occasion considerable division and anxiety. Further, these incidents invite us to question the feasibility of seeing through others' eyes if observers themselves are so heavily implicated in what is found. Such sharp disparities should not be expected if ethnographers indeed base their accounts on native understandings and interpretations. One reason why there is some uneasiness about the issue of interpretation is that we, as readers of an ethnography, cannot readily decide for ourselves whether researchers have genuinely put themselves in a strategic position to enter the world-view of their subjects, whether they have adequately understood that world-view, and whether their interpretations of actions and events are congruent with their subjects' understandings. There is a tendency towards an anecdotal approach to the use of 'data' in relation to conclusions or explanations in qualitative research. Brief conversations, snippets from unstructured interviews, or examples of a particular activity are used to provide evidence for a particular contention. There are grounds for disquiet in that the representativeness or generality of these fragments is rarely addressed. Further, field notes or extended transcripts are rarely available; these would be very helpful in order to allow the reader to formulate his or her own hunches about the perspective of the people who have been studied and how adequately the ethnographer has interpreted people's behaviour in the light of the explication of their systems of meaning. The reader is rarely given a vantage point from which the formulation of alternative accounts is possible. Interestingly, one of the reasons why McNamara, in his aforementioned disagreement with Keddie's interpretation of a classroom incident, was able to propose alternative formulations of what the teacher meant may be because he was referring to a particularly long verbatim passage.

Similar concerns have been voiced by writers with roots in the ethnomethodological tradition (e.g. McDermott, Gospodinoff and Aron, 1978; Mehan, 1978; Hester, 1985), though they are not exclusive to writers of this persuasion (e.g. Pahl, 1984, p. 13). Mehan (1978), for example, proposes the term 'constitutive ethnography' to denote studies in which the apparently objective and routine features of social structures in everyday life are treated as practical accomplishments. Thus, in the context of classroom research, the focus of Mehan's concern, the ways in which the apparent 'social facts' of school life like students' intelligence or school organization are accomplished during social interaction is the fundamental issue. But constitutive ethnography is also concerned to preserve the social world that is being investigated as data for others to interpret:

> constitutive studies stress the importance of retrievable data . . . For constitutive ethnographers, exhaustive data treatment is a necessary check against the tendency to seek only evidence that supports the researchers' orienting hypotheses or domain assumptions . . . Constitutive studies therefore attempt an exhaustive analysis of behaviour in the flow of events. (Mehan, 1978, pp. 36–7)

The result is an intricate and detailed description of patterns of interaction, sequences of events, conversations, and so on, which allow alternative interpretations of what is happening and how participants understand their circumstances.

An alternative approach to the problem of interpretation is 'respondent validation', whereby the ethnographer submits a version of his or her findings to the subjects themselves. This procedure can be done in a number of ways. Buchanan, Boddy, and McCalman (1988) report that in their studies of firms they provide 'sanitized' transcripts of interviews (i.e. from which false starts, grunts, repetitions, etc. have been purged) in order to check information. Bloor (1978), in his observational study of ENT clinics, wrote reports for each consultant on his or her assessment practices. In some instances his account was confirmed, while other consultants raised some points. Sometimes, these queries turned out to be misunderstandings; where the differences were more fundamental, he returned to his notes. Ball (1984) approached respondent validation in a number of ways in his study of Beachside School: he handed copies of papers or chapters to his informants; he held two seminars at the school at which draft chapters were made available; and gave a copy of his thesis to the headmaster who circulated it to heads of department. There is an intuitive appeal to such procedures, but they do present problems. They may invite censorship, as occurred on one occasion to Buchanan *et al.* They may incite defensive reactions, as Ball found; so too did Abrams (1984), whose respondent validation project in connection with his research on informal care in the community 'turned into a series of furious arguments, wrangles and recriminations', which he attributed to the results being incompatible with 'the self-image of the respondents' (p. 8). Bloor was clearly uneasy about his respondent validation exercise in that, when he was confronted with alternative interpretations (his own and those of consultants) of the disposal of particular ENT cases, he buttressed the exercise with interviews or the examination of hypothetical cases.

A more fundamental difficulty with respondent validation is the nature of the linkage between the ethnographer's data (i.e. interpretations of his or her subjects' world-views) and the elaboration of those data for presentation to an academic audience. Buchanan *et al.*, Bloor, and Abrams presented data to their respondents with little or no elaboration; Ball, in making available chapters from his book, was including some of his elucidation for a social scientific audience. In either case, the ethnographer has to recognize that the respondent validation exercise still leaves the translation of his or her subjects' interpretations for the academic audience as a problematic stage. It is not clear from Ball's exercise how far the teachers were able to make a contribution to this translation stage. Willis (1977) presented the early drafts of his Marxist study of the world of working class youth and elicited some of their views at a group discussion. It is apparent that the translated sections did not mean a great deal to them, whereas, as one of his subjects put it, 'The bits about us were simple enough' (p. 195). Similarly, Strathern (1987) conducted a respondent validation exercise in the context of her ethnographic study of an Essex village and became aware of the 'discontinuity between indigenous understandings and the analytical concepts which frame the ethnography itself' (p. 18). As anthropologists like Geertz (1973) recognize, ethnographers are engaged in interpretations of other people's interpretations. It is unlikely that respondent validation will greatly facilitate the ethnographer's second-order interpretations of subjects' first-order interpretations.

Indeed, anthropologists seem to have gone much further than sociologists in recognizing the range of ways in which they themselves are implicated in the writing of ethnography. For example, Wagner has written:

An anthropologist *experiences*, in one way or another, the sub-

ject of his study; he does so through the world of his own meanings, and then uses this meaningful experience to communicate
an understanding to those of his own culture. He can only communicate this understanding if his account makes sense in terms
of his culture. (Wagner, 1981, p. 3)

In other words, the researcher, the discipline, the culture to be
translated, and the culture into which it is translated form an interwoven amalgam of elements. Thus the presentation of the natives'
point of view can be viewed as comprising three components: the
way in which the natives view the world; the ethnographer's interpretation of how they view the world; and the ethnographer's construction of his or her interpretation of the natives' view of the
world for the ethnographer's own intellectual and cultural community. Respondent validation may be of assistance with the
second element, but not with the third.

In recent years, anthropologists have come to examine the
literary devices ethnographers use in order both to convey an alien
culture to their audience and to obtain a mandate to speak with
authority about that culture (e.g. Clifford and Marcus, 1986). Such
reflections prompt a questioning of the bland assertion that an account based on native interpretations and understandings is being
presented, since to a very significant degree the account is an
ethnographic invention. Crapanzano (1986) has argued that,
although anthropologists invariably acknowledge the tentativeness
of their interpretations of the world-views of their subjects, they
simultaneously convey to the reader a sense of having cracked the
social and cultural systems they address. Further, Clifford (1986)
has observed that, following Freeman's critique of Mead's account
of Samoa, one 'is left with a stark contrast: Mead's attractive, sex-
ually liberated, calm Pacific world, and now Freeman's Samoa of
seething tensions, strict controls, and violent outbursts' (p. 103).
As Clifford observes, Freeman (on the last page of his book)
appears to view the contrast as between an Apollonian emphasis on
cultural balance and harmony in Mead's work and a Dionysian
stress on impulse and emotion in his own study. The problem with
this contrast, Clifford suggests, is that one must question a refuta-
tion that can so neatly be slotted into a recurring Western opposi-
tion of elements. The implication is that Freeman's Western mode
of thought may have influenced his perception of the broader
implications of the contrast between his own and Mead's research
and consequently may have influenced the writing of the ensuing
monograph.

Nor should it be assumed that such reflections apply only to the
problems of anthropologists having to come to terms with, and

rendering for others in the discipline, an alien culture. These three basic ingredients are inherent in any attempt to provide an interpretation of other people's interpretations for a social scientific audience.[2]

Theory and Research

Qualitative researchers tend to espouse an approach in which theory and empirical investigation are interwoven. The delineation of theoretical ideas is usually viewed as a phase that occurs during or at the end of field-work, rather than being a precursor to it. The prior specification of a theory tends to be disfavoured because of the possibility of introducing a premature closure on the issues to be investigated, as well as the possibility of the theoretical constructs departing excessively from the views of participants in a social setting.

One of the most frequently cited approaches to the qualitative researcher's view of the linkage between theory and investigation is *analytic induction*, a term which was coined by Znaniecki (1934). The basic sequence of procedures is outlined in Table 4.1, which follows Robinson's (1951) delineation of stages. One of the best-known examples of a piece of research which embodies the basic steps of analytic induction is Lindesmith's (1968) study of opiate addiction. Accordingly, some of the elementary phases in Lindesmith's reasoning are presented side by side with the chief steps in analytic induction.

Lindesmith's example is often cited because he clearly seeks to provide a theoretical explanation of a problem, whereas many apparent examples of analytic induction seem to be much more exploratory. Bloor's (1978) study of ENT specialists' decision-making practices regarding whether to recommend an adeno-tonsillectomy is a case in point. He depicts seven stages to his procedure, which he describes as having similarities with analytic induction:

(1) Each case of each specialist was tentatively classified in terms of the 'disposal category' (e.g. whether to recommend removal of tonsils or antibiotics).
(2) Bloor then attempted to glean the common features of all cases which were subsumed under a particular category.
(3) Deviant cases were examined to determine whether either the list of common features could be expanded or the categorization of cases could be modified to embrace these departures from the general pattern.
(4) He then searched for features of cases which were unique to

Table 4.1 *Steps in analytic induction and the example of Lindesmith's study of opiate addiction*

Chief Steps[1]	*Lindesmith's (1968)[2] Procedure*
1. Rough definition of the problem	1. Opiate addiction as focus
2. Hypothetical explanation of problem	2. '[T]hat individuals who do not know what drug they are receiving do not become addicted and . . . that they become addicted when they know what they are getting and have taken it long enough to experience withdrawal distress when they stop' (p. 7)
3. Examination of case(s) to determine fit with hypothesis	3. 'One of the first addicts to be interviewed, a doctor, had received morphine for several weeks; he was aware of that fact, but he did not become addicted at that time' (p. 7)
4. If lack of fit, either (a) hypothesis is reformulated or (b) problem re-defined to exclude negative case	4. Hypothesis re-formulated: '[P]ersons become addicts when they recognize or perceive the significance of withdrawal distress which they are experiencing, and that if they do not recognize withdrawal distress, they do not become addicts . . .' (p. 8)
5. Hypothesis is deemed to be confirmed after a small number of cases has been examined; negative cases require further re-formulation	5. '[C]ases were found in which individuals had experienced and understood withdrawal distress, though not in the severest form, did not use the drug to alleviate the distress and never became addicts' (p. 8)
6. Procedure continues until no further negative cases have been encountered and a universal relationship has been established	6. 'The final revision of the hypothesis involved a shift in emphasis from the individual's recognition of withdrawal distress to his use of the drug to alleviate the distress after his insight has occurred' (p. 8)

1 After Robinson (1951).
2 Originally published in 1947.

the disposal categories of each specialist and those that overlapped. The overlapping case features were deemed to be 'necessary rather than sufficient for the achievement of a particular disposal' (Bloor, 1978, p. 546).

(5) For each disposal category, Bloor then extracted the underlying decision-rules which prompted the specialist to determine that a particular case should be subsumed under that category.

(6) For each decision rule, the relevant cases were then re-examined to discern 'the search procedures associated with that decision rule' (p. 546).

(7) These steps were repeated for all disposal categories of all specialists.

This general approach seems to be somewhat more exploratory than Lindesmith's strategy, in that an explicit hypothesis is not formulated in the manner of stage 2 in Table 4.1. This is not to say that Bloor's research is devoid of an explanatory ingredient; his general problem was to explain the geographical distribution of adeno-tonsillectomy in terms of possible variations in specialists' routine assessments of ENT cases. It is exploratory in that the aspects of such assessments which impinge on disposals do not appear to be specified.

As Bloor recognizes, his approach to analytic induction departs from the model (as in Table 4.1), because he did not interrupt the research process as a deviant case appeared in order to re-appraise his theoretical constructs; the analysis was conducted after the data had been collected. Either way, analytic induction is a highly stringent approach to the analysis of data in that the occurrence of a single negative case is sufficient to send the researcher off to reformulate the problem.

Another way in which the relationship between theory and data in qualitative research is often formulated is in terms of *grounded theory*, an approach which draws on some of the basic ingredients of analytic induction. The idea of grounded theory was first formulated by Glaser and Strauss (1967) as a means of generating theory which is embedded in data. Turner (1981) has usefully compiled a sequential series of stages which provide the chief components of grounded theory:

(1) After some exposure to the field setting and some collection of data, the researcher starts to develop 'categories' which illuminate and fit the data well.

(2) The categories are then 'saturated', meaning that further instances of the categories are gathered until the researcher is

confident about the relevance and range of the categories for the research setting. There is a recognition in the idea of 'saturation' that further search for appropriate instances may become a superfluous exercise.

(3) The researcher then seeks to abstract a more general formulation of the category, as well as specifying the criteria for inclusion in that category.

(4) These more general definitions then act as a guide for the researcher, as well as stimulating further theoretical reflection. This stage may prompt the researcher to think of further instances which may be subsumed under the more general definition of the category.

(5) The researcher should be sensitive to the connections between the emerging general categories and other milieux in which the categories may be relevant. For example, can categories relating to the dying in hospital (Glaser and Strauss's main research focus) be extended to encapsulate other social settings?

(6) The researcher may become increasingly aware of the connections between categories developed in the previous stage, and will seek to develop hypotheses about such links.

(7) The researcher should then seek to establish the conditions in which these connections pertain.

(8) At this point, the researcher should explore the implications of the emerging theoretical framework for other, pre-existing theoretical schemes which are relevant to the substantive area.

(9) The researcher may then seek to test the emerging relationships among categories under extreme conditions to test the validity of the posited connections.

Thus for Glaser and Strauss, theories are derived from the field-work process, refined and tested during field-work, and gradually elaborated into higher levels of abstraction towards the end of the data collection phase.

This approach has some appeal to the qualitative researcher: it allows theory to emerge from the data, so that it does not lose touch with its empirical referent; it provides a framework for the qualitative researcher to cope with the unstructured complexity of social reality and so render it manageable; and it allows the development of theories and categories which are meaningful to the subjects of the research, an important virtue if an investigation is meant to have a practical pay-off. By contrast, Bulmer (1979) has questioned whether the researcher is genuinely capable of suspending his or her awareness of relevant theories and concepts until a relatively late stage in the process. Quite apart from the question of whether it is desirable to defer theoretical reflection, the notion that one may conduct research in a theory-neutral way is open to some doubt. Further, there may be considerable practical difficulties associated with field-work conducted within a grounded theory approach. For example, Hammersley (1984), drawing on his experience of conducting a school ethnography, has suggested that when field-work entails tape recording of conversations, interviews, lessons, and the like, the time needed to transcribe such materials may render the grounded theory framework, of a constant interweaving of categories and data, almost impossible to accomplish. One might also question whether what the grounded theory approach provides really is theory. Much of the discussion of the approach and its associated procedures seems to concentrate on the generation of categories rather than theory as such.

In spite of the frequency with which Glaser and Strauss and the idea of grounded theory are cited in the literature, there are comparatively few instances of its application along the lines developed above. The term is often used as a way of conveying the notion of an approach to the generation of theory which is derived from a predominately qualitative research base. Much qualitative research relies on the elucidation of a theoretical framework subsequent to (rather than during) the data collection phase. The idea of grounded theory is often used as a way of justifying the use of a qualitative research approach, i.e. so that such work can be confirmed as respectable. For example, Turner (1988) has pointed out that Glaser and Strauss intended their book to be cited as a methodological text when submitting proposals for qualitative research to funding bodies and others, and adds that he has found their work useful in this regard as well.

In fact, one of the accusations that is periodically levelled at qualitative researchers is that they are disinclined to instil theoretical elements into their research. Rock (1973) has drawn attention to the disinclination of many sociologists of deviance to depart analytically from the meaning systems they glean from the groups they study. Any attempt to shift away from their subjects' constructs and interpretive devices is seen as running the risk of reifying and thereby losing touch with the real world. This concern over the possible loss of the integrity of the phenomena being investigated can be attributed, at least in part, to the avowal of naturalism which has been particularly conspicuous among sociologists of deviance. Rock regards this preoccupation with faithful accounts of deviant groups and their sub-cultures to be a form of 'phenomenalism' (see Chapter 2) and sees it as a barrier to the field's development, since 'Any intellectual analysis entails some abstraction and some movement away from the "purely" phenomenal' (p. 20). In addition to the emphasis on naturalism that pervades much research in this field is the predilection for contextualist understanding, whereby the understanding of events and activities has to be grounded in the specific milieu being examined. This tendency inhibits comparison with other contexts and thereby discourages theoretical development.

The tendency towards atheoretical investigations among qualitative researchers has also been noted among commentators on school ethnographies (e.g. Delamont, 1981; Hammersley, 1985). There has been a slight 'softening' among some qualitative researchers in their attitudes to the testing of theories. For example, Hammersley, Scarth and Webb (1985) advocate a 'comparative' approach, whereby research sites are strategically chosen to allow theories to be tested. In their case, they were interested in the implications of external assessment in secondary schools on both teaching and learning. Two schools were chosen: one traditional school with a strong emphasis on examinations; the other a progressive community school with a less pronounced accent on examinations. The authors wanted to investigate the contention, drawn from other studies of schools, that 'external examinations lead to lecturing and note-taking on the part of secondary-school teachers and to rote-learning and instrumental attitudes among their pupils' (Hammersley, Scarth and Webb, 1985, p. 58). The authors had intended to adopt a longitudinal design, following pupils as they moved from third- through to fifth-year streams, but largely abandoned this strategy since it proved to be impracticable. In its place was substituted a cross-sectional design; for example in one of the schools they were able to compare pupils in the same years doing both externally examined and coursework-based courses. Just prior to this change of direction, they also formulated a theory about the possible reasons for the posited effects of external examinations, which emphasized the nature of the tasks set under the two different conditions. In fact, many of their hunches proved incorrect. What is striking about such an approach is that it is quite highly structured, partly because, as the authors indicate, they needed some way of coping with the mass of data which were coming their way. Indeed, the basic design has many of the hallmarks of an experimental approach, in that contrasting groups are taken to expose key differences between them. The general strategy was highly flexible, involving numerous changes of direction, a characteristic which sharply distinguishes it from the experimental method.

The dilemmas for those working within the qualitative tradition are very clear. The elaboration and application of theory prior to, or even at a relatively early stage of, a qualitative study may prejudice the researcher's ability to see through the eyes of his or her subjects. Theory may constrain researchers excessively and blind them not only to the views of participants but also to the unusual and unanticipated facets of a strand of social reality. Moreover, these unanticipated aspects of social life may be important to the participants. Indeed, there are grounds for suggesting that analytic induction, with its stipulated requirement of formulating (at least) a general idea of the problem at the outset, suffers in this way, as does the 'comparative' approach of Hammersley, Scarth and Webb (1985). Grounded theory appears to be more forgiving in that the relatively late incursion of theoretical considerations into a study informed by this approach is consistent with the qualitative researcher's inclination to defer the conceptual elaboration of data. However, how one deals with the oncoming flood of data, or how one holds theoretical considerations in abeyance, or how one chooses a research site in the first place, constitute practical difficulties for such an approach. Further, there is still a fair amount of qualitative research which seems to have little connection with theoretical concerns or which alternatively takes the form of '*post factum* interpretation', a term which Gans (1962, p. 347) used to describe his own research of an Italian-American slum area in Boston.

It is also striking that the discussions in this section have largely been directed to fairly low-level theories, although the aim of grounded theory, for example, is the progressive elaboration of a substantive theory into formal theory. Writers sometimes express a commitment to fairly grand theoretical positions, like symbolic interactionism (e.g. Woods, 1979; Burgess, 1983), or to Marxism (e.g. Willis, 1977). Adherence to such positions usually implies deploying them both as a means of deciding what should be examined and how the data should be interpreted. The aforementioned dilemmas recur in this context too, for adherence to the theoretical position may lead to the accusation of circularity or to bias.[3] Thus, while there is a groundswell of opinion which favours a growing sensitivity to theoretical issues in qualitative research, the tension of such a standpoint in juxtaposition with the preoccupation with the unadulterated exploration of participants' views of the social world is very evident.

Case Studies and the Problem of Generalization

Much of the research discussed thus far derives from studies in a single setting, be it a school, community, gang, firm, or whatever. Indeed, some writers treat 'qualitative research' and 'case study research' as more or less synonymous terms (e.g. Rist, 1984,

p. 160). For many people, this reliance on a single case poses a problem of how far it is possible to generalize the results of such research. Many qualitative researchers themselves display an unease about the extent to which their findings are capable of generalization beyond the confines of the particular case. Research which relies on unstructured interviews within the qualitative tradition may be slightly less vulnerable to the charge of limited generality, since respondents are often drawn from a variety of social and geographical milieux. By contrast, investigations in which participant observation figures strongly seem to be more liable to the charge of having looked at a single locale and therefore of creating findings of unknown generality. How do we know, it is often asked, how representative case study findings are of all members of the population from which the case was selected? How representative are the findings drawn from the study of a particular school (e.g. Woods, 1979; Ball, 1981; Burgess, 1983)? The concern that findings may be untypical is understandable when a subject is keen to develop a modicum of empirical generalization and possibly to make a contribution to wider theoretical developments. Further, as Bulmer (1986) has observed, the qualitative researcher's ability to have an impact on social policy through the use of a case study can be diminished by a belief that the findings may be idiosyncratic.

It is possible to conceive of a number of solutions to these problems. First, the qualitative researcher may study more than one case. For example, Skolnick (1966) conducted the bulk of his participant observation of police officers in one US city, Westville. In addition, he writes: 'For the sake of broad comparison, two weeks were also spent in Eastville, a city of comparable size, nonwhite population, industry and commerce' (p. 23). This extra case allowed Skolnick to place his observations in Westville in perspective and to develop a number of contrasts between the two forces, such as their different ways of using informers (p. 136). Lupton (1963) was a participant observer in two firms in order to pursue his research on output regulation among manual workers. Interestingly, he chose a second case because his initial firm, much to his surprise, did not exhibit output regulation to any marked degree. His serendipitous strategy of comparing two case studies enabled him to extract numerous suggestions about the factors which are likely to promote output regulation.

A second possible approach to the case study generalization problem is through the examination of a number of cases by more than one researcher, whereby the overall investigation assumes the framework of 'team research', such as that found in much quantitative research. There is a tendency to think of qualitative research, and participant observation in particular, as the work of one investigator confronting the mysteries of the field alone, or possibly with a wife who acts as an (unpaid) assistant (e.g. Gans, 1962). Team field research can take one of two main forms. There are examples of teams which have jointly investigated one setting, particularly well-known examples of which are studies of student culture in a medical school (Becker *et al.*, 1961) and student life in a university (Becker, Geer and Hughes, 1968) in the USA, both under the direction of Everett Hughes. The main justification for such research is that a team is likely to be better able to embrace a variety of different facets of the host institution. The greater breadth of coverage that team research of this kind is capable of producing is a considerable advantage, but does not depart from the general problem of being limited to a single case.

It is where team field research investigates more than one case that further possibilities would appear to be opened up in relation to the problem of generalization. Douglas (1976), who has been a particularly prominent advocate of such investigations, has argued that team field research projects also benefit from team members providing mutual support, being able to check and compare each other's findings, and so on. The field of education has provided a context for such research in the UK on a number of occasions. For example, the 'Observation Research and Classroom Learning Evaluation' (ORACLE) project discussed by Galton and Delamont (1985) entailed a multisite case study approach, which included elements which approximated to more conventional ethnography. The team comprised some thirteen full-time or part-time researchers. The ethnographic component was particularly in evidence in the studies of the transfer of pupils between schools in three local authorities. Each school was studied by more than one researcher so that it was possible to produce accounts of each case which were the product of two or more researchers. When research of this kind is undertaken the team leaders are confronted with the considerable difficulty of ensuring that the cases conform to certain common themes. This problem may mean that the field-work is considerably more structured than is typically discerned in the approach of the lone enthnographer, hence the dubbing of much team field research as 'structured ethnography' (Smith and Robbins, 1982). Very often multisite team field research comprises a considerable component of quantitative research; the ORACLE research employed structured interview and observation schedules and personality tests. Clearly, the need to impose a degree of common purpose and approach on teams of observers may entail the surrendering of some of the flexibility which is one of the strengths of ethnography.

A third approach to the problem of case study generalization is to seek a case which is 'typical' of a certain cluster of characteristics

(Woods, 1979, p. 268); other researchers can then examine comparable cases which belong to other clusters of characteristics. This procedure is one way of approaching the summation of case studies so that generalizations may be extracted as evidence is accumulated (Kennedy, 1979). A corollary of this course is the 'deviant' case, which is of interest because it is known to differ on an important characteristic from other like cases. The study by Lipset, Trow, and Coleman (1956) of the International Typographical Union in the USA is an example, in that the union was chosen because it was known to exhibit a democratic style of internal government (unlike other unions) and therefore provided a rare opportunity for the examination of the forces which promote democracy. However, the more general point — the accumulation of evidence by comparative case studies — is not without its problems, in spite of a superficial attraction. Foremost among these difficulties is the problem of ensuring that differences in findings between case studies carried out by two observers can be solely attributed to differences associated with the case studies themselves. The fact that the research may have been conducted at different times may well have something to do with the observed differences. Further, in much qualitative research the importance of the ethnographer as a conduit for the generation of data should not be ignored. Whyte acknowledged this point in his study of a street corner group in a Boston slum: 'To some extent my approach must be unique to myself, to the particular situation, and to the state of knowledge when I began research' (Whyte, 1981, p. 280). In the earlier discussion of the problems of possibly divergent interpretations by observers of the same social context, the difficulty of disentangling the various factors which may have produced the differences was mentioned. These difficulties also could be anticipated in team research when different observers take responsibility for research sites.

There are grounds for thinking that the 'problem' of case study generalization entails a misunderstanding of the aims of such research. In particular, this misconception arises from a tendency to approach a case study as if it were a sample of one drawn from a wider universe of such cases. There are at least two reasons for considering this view to be misguided. First, within a case study a wide range of different people and activities are invariably examined so that the contrast with survey samples is not as acute as it appears at first glance, especially when the widespread tendency for survey researchers to draw samples from localities rather than on a national basis is borne in mind. Secondly, the issue should be couched in terms of the generalizability of cases to theoretical propositions rather than to populations or universes (Mitchell, 1983; Yin, 1984). Case study data become important when the researcher seeks to integrate them with a theoretical context. The 'grounded theory' approach of Glaser and Strauss (1967) exemplifies this reasoning: a 'substantive theory', based on the care of the dying in a hospital, suggests that the greater the social loss of a dying patient, i.e. nurses' estimation of the degree of impact that the patient's death will have on his or her family or occupation, the better is his care and the more likely nurses are to concoct rationales to explain away the death. This is then translated into a formal hypothesis: 'The higher the social value of a person the less delay he experiences in receiving services from experts' (Glaser and Strauss, 1967, p. 42). The issue of whether the particular hospital studied is 'typical' is not the critical issue; what is important is whether the experiences of dying patients are typical of the broad class of phenomena (the differential social evaluation of persons and its effect on the delivery of services) to which the theory refers. Subsequent research would then focus on the validity of the proposition in other milieux (e.g. doctors' surgeries). However, it also needs to be recognized that the disinclination of many qualitative researchers to seek out in this way the essential properties of everyday life and to devise theories in relation to them may mean that such formulations are more programmatic than they are depictions of how case study research proceeds.

Conclusion

In this chapter three issues have been singled out as areas of concern for the qualitative researcher. Each represents a significant problem in the implementation of the qualitative approach. The issue of interpretation is the keynote of qualitative research, but the foregoing discussion suggests that the idea of looking through the eyes of one's subjects should not be regarded as an unproblematic practice. The discussion of the connection between theory and research indicates that analytic induction and grounded theory have provided qualitative researchers with possible frameworks for attending to theoretical issues, but that these approaches to theory are often honoured more in the breach than in the observance. There is considerable ambivalence about the nature and role of theory among qualitative researchers. There is a growing view that qualitative research ought to be more consciously driven by theoretical concerns, in contrast to the belief (with which qualitative research is more usually associated) that theoretical reflection ought to be delayed until a later stage in the research process. Ironically, the 'front loading' of theory in qualitative research brings it much closer to the model of the quantitative research process outlined in Figure 2.1. Finally, the suggestion that the reliance on case studies in much qualitative research detracts from the investigator's ability to generalize his or her findings has been critically addressed. In drawing attention to the importance of theoretical reasoning as the crux of the issue of case study generalization, the question of the relationship between theory and research again raises its head.

Notes

1 The injunction to empathize and to see through the eyes of one's subjects can cause the qualitative researcher problems in certain domains. Billig (1977) has written about the difficulties associated with qualitative research on fascists; in particular, he argues that adopting a posture of disinterest or of sympathetic understanding is inappropriate in such research. Robbins, Anthony and Curtis (1973) have drawn attention to the difficulties of maintaining a stance of empathy without sympathy when studying religious groups like the 'Jesus Freaks', who define their view of the world as exclusively true.

2 Readers interested in the considerable attention being given by anthropologists to the tentativeness of their accounts of other cultures and to the devices they use to convey a sense of ethnographic authority should consult Clifford and Marcus (1986) and Marcus and Fischer (1986).

3 An example is Marcus's (1986) criticism of Willis's (1977) ethnographic research on working class lads. Marcus argues that Willis selected nonconformist boys and was uninterested in why some boys are nonconformist while others are not. Further, Marcus suggests that it is inappropriate to draw inferences about the operation of capitalism from such a sample.

5

The Debate about Quantitative and Qualitative Research

In this chapter, the main contrasting features of quantitative and qualitative research will be etched out. Much of the discussion in the literature on these two research traditions has created a somewhat exaggerated picture of their differences. These discussions reflect a tendency to treat quantitative and qualitative research as though they are mutually antagonistic ideal types of the research process. This tendency can be clearly discerned in some of the programmatic statements relating to qualitative research (e.g. J. Lofland, 1971; Bogdan and Taylor, 1975). While there *are* differences between the two research traditions, as the first section of this chapter will explicate, there are also a number of points at which the differences are not as rigid as the programmatic statements often imply. Consequently, in addressing some of the contrasting features in quantitative and qualitative research, some areas of similarity will also be appraised. The discussion will then proceed to an assessment of the degree to which epistemological issues lie at the heart of the contrast, or whether it is more a matter of different styles of data collection and analysis *tout court*. This issue has implications for the extent to which quantitative and qualitative research are deemed to be capable of integration (the focus of Chapter 6). It also has implications for the question of the extent to which quantitative and qualitative research constitute divergent models of the research process, since it has been the suggestion that they represent distinct epistemologies that has played a major role in the exaggeration of their differences. Finally, the question of whether these two research traditions share some common problems is examined.

Contrasting Features in Quantitative and Qualitative Research

Some of the main contrasting dimensions of quantitative and qualitative research have been either explicitly or implicitly explored in the previous chapters. This section will draw out these dif-

Table 5.1   *Some differences between Quantitative and Qualitative Research*

		Quantitative	Qualitative
(1)	Role of qualitative research	preparatory	means to exploration of actors' interpretations
(2)	Relationship between researcher and subject	distant	close
(3)	Researcher's stance in relation to subject	outsider	insider
(4)	Relationship between theory/concepts and research	confirmation	emergent
(5)	Research strategy	structured	unstructured
(6)	Scope of findings	nomothetic	ideographic
(7)	Image of social reality	static and external to actor	processual and socially constructed by actor
(8)	Nature of data	hard, reliable	rich, deep

ferences more directly. Table 5.1 lists eight important dimensions on which the two research traditions diverge. The subsequent discussion explores these themes in some greater detail.

View of the Role of Qualitative Research
Quantitative researchers rarely totally deny the utility of qualitative research, but have tended to view it as an essentially exploratory way of conducting social investigations. Consequently, they have typically seen it as useful at the preparatory stage of a research project, a view which is clearly discernible in Blalock's (1970) attitude to participant observation which was quoted in Chapter 1. Precisely because of its exploratory and unstructured approach, qualitative research is often depicted as useful as a means of throwing up hunches and hypotheses which can be tested more rigorously by quantitative research. Such a view treats qualitative research as a somewhat second rate activity in implying that qualitative data

cannot stand in their own right because they need to be verified. The proponents of qualitative research see it as an end in itself, in particular because of its capacity to expose actors' meanings and interpretations, which is a central requirement of the approach and of its presumptive intellectual underpinnings which were discussed in Chapter 3. However, it is possible to detect a degree of unease among some qualitative researchers about the extent to which their findings can stand alone. Gans (1962, p. 350), at the end of his participant observation study of an Italian-American slum, exemplified this diffidence in proclaiming that his research 'is a *reconnaissance* − an initial exploration of a community to provide an overview', and went on to say: 'Many of the hypotheses reported here can eventually be tested against the results of more systematic social science research.' Interestingly, in the second edition of the book which derived from this research, Gans (1982, p. 414) has indicated that he would get rid of this 'apologetic conclusion' if he were able to rewrite the book. He argues that the reason for this apologetic style was that at the time social scientists were strongly influenced by a belief in the appropriateness of the scientific method. By implication, Gans seems to be suggesting that the assertiveness of qualitative researchers coupled with the growing disillusionment with quantitative research have created a different climate, whereby investigations of the kind he undertook are increasingly regarded as ends in themselves.

Relationship between Researcher and Subject

In quantitative research the researcher's contact with the people being studied is fairly fleeting or even nonexistent. While the data collection phase often extends over many months, the contact with each individual is usually brief. In longitudinal surveys or in before-and-after experiments, the investigator returns to his or her subjects, but the degree of contact is still fairly short-lived. Indeed, the use of some methods associated with quantitative research may require no contact with subjects at all, except in an indirect sense; postal questionnaire surveys, laboratory experiments in which the researcher simply observes while others conduct the experiment (e.g. Milgram, 1963), and many forms of unobtrusive, structured observation (Webb *et al.*, 1966) involve virtually no contact between researcher and subject. Even in interview surveys, the main investigator may have little or no contact with respondents since hired staff frequently carry out many (and sometimes all) of the interviews.

By contrast, qualitative research entails much more sustained contact, especially when participant observation is the central method. The degree to which there is sustained contact within a

particular study will vary a good deal; Gans (1962) had some contact with 100 to 150 West Enders but only twenty of these were in-
tense. The need for the fostering of such relationships is a product
of the qualitative researcher's need to see the world through his or
her subjects' eyes, since the researcher would be unable to gain any
leverage on this level of analysis from a distance. Unstructured interviewing typically entails less sustained researcher–subject relationships than participant observation, but is invariably longer
than survey interviews. In any case, the wide-ranging nature of the
unstructured interview invariably necessitates a fairly close relationship between researcher and subject, which re-visits (which are
relatively rare in survey interviewing) may intensify.

This contrast between the two research traditions can be illustrated through the work of Hirschi (1969) and Adler (1985). In
the former case, self-administered questionnaires were the chief
source of data. The questionnaires were administered to the
children by their schools, so that Hirschi's contact with his subjects
was minimal. By contrast, Adler had contact over a period of six
years with some of the drug dealers she was investigating.

The Researcher's Stance in Relation to the Subject
The quantitative researcher adopts the posture of an outsider looking in on the social world. He or she applies a pre-ordained
framework on the subjects being investigated and is involved as
little as possible in that world. This posture is the analogue of the
detached scientific observer. Hirschi was chiefly concerned to test
a theory of delinquency, and adopted a stance towards his subjects
which entailed limited contact with them. They were merely fodder
for the examination of his concerns, and not people with their own
views and perspectives in relation to delinquent behaviour, school,
and the other elements of Hirschi's research.

Among qualitative researchers there is a strong urge to 'get close' to
the subjects being investigated – to be an insider. For qualitative
researchers, it is only by getting close to their subjects and becoming
an insider that they can view the world as a participant in that setting.
Thus, Hirschi's outsider stance can be contrasted with Adler's view:
'the only way I could get close enough to [upper-level drug dealers and
smugglers] to discover what they were doing and to understand the
world from their perspectives (Blumer, 1969) was to take a membership role in the setting' (Adler, 1985, p. 11). The insider standpoint may
have its costs, the most frequently mentioned of which is the problem
of 'going native', whereby the researcher loses his or her awareness of
being a researcher and is seduced by the participants' perspective.
Oakley (1984, p. 128), drawing on her research on becoming a mother,
describes the experience of going native as follows:

at three forty-five after two hours of a busy antenatal clinic I too would sigh with the doctors as we jointly peeped into the corridor and saw, still waiting, another row of abdomens . . . Or at two in the morning I wanted someone to get in there quickly and do a forceps delivery so I could (like them) go home to bed.

The experience of going native was not entirely negative in that it enabled her to understand the pressures obstetricians are under. In any event, qualitative researchers are likely to see such drawbacks (if indeed they acknowledge them as such) as unavoidable consequences of a standpoint which is needed to gain access to their subjects' views. It is also apparent that the possibility of going native, with its implication of a loss of detachment, is to a significant degree incongruent with the image of impartial scientist which many quantitative researchers espouse.

Relationship between Theory/Concepts and Research

The model of quantitative research presented in Figure 2.1 implies that theories and concepts are the starting point for investigations carried out within its framework. Thus Hirschi in the Preface to *Causes of Delinquency* wrote: 'In this book I attempt to state and test a theory of delinquency.' By contrast, qualitative researchers often reject the idea of using theory as a precursor to an investigation (except perhaps as a means of providing an initial orientation to the situation as in 'grounded theory') since it may not reflect subjects' views about what is going on and what is important. Consequently, as one advocate of qualitative research has put it, 'It is marked by a concern with the discovery of theory rather than the verification of theory' (Filstead, 1979, p. 38). Thus Adler's (1985) chief theoretical contribution − the notion of upper-level drug dealing as a component of a hedonistic life-style rather than an occupation − was an outcome of her research rather than a precursor to it.

In fact, the extent to which quantitative research is explicitly guided by theory has been questioned of many commentators. Instead, theoretical reasoning often occurs towards the end of the research process (Cicourel, 1982, pp. 19–20). Indeed, quantitative research is often much more exploratory and unpredictable in outcome than its description by the advocates of qualitative research seems to imply. An example of the misleading nature of the view that quantitive research is devoid of surprise is the study of the International Typographical Union in the USA by Lipset, Trow, and Coleman (1956), which involved a mixture of qualitative research and survey data. The latter were compiled in order to examine *inter alia* the relationship between union shop size and members' political involvement. However,

This analysis did not merely test hypotheses already held before the survey was conducted. Rather, the earlier hypotheses pointed to a fruitful line of enquiry, but many of the ideas and insights regarding the bearing of shop size on union politics emerged only in the course of the analysis of the survey data. (Lipset, 1964, pp. 116–17)

Lipset (1964, pp. 111–12) also provides a number of other examples of the way in which his survey data were a source of surprise. Similarly, Pugh (1988), writing about the Aston research which was discussed in Chapter 2, has commented on his disappointment that the effect of organization size on structure was so pervasive, an observation which can be interpreted as indicative of a certain element of surprise.

Quantitative research is often depicted as a routine practice whereby theories and their integral concepts are simply operationalized with a view to verifying their validity (see, for example, Filstead's remark on this issue in the passage cited on p. 97). Ironically, some qualitative research is showing an explicit concern with theory, not solely as something which emerges from the data, but also as a phase in the research process which is formulated at the outset (Woods, 1986, pp. 156–61). Some of the school ethnographies cited in Chapters 3 and 4 show signs of a movement in this direction. Consequently, the contrast between quantitative and qualitative research in terms of verification of theory against preferring theory to emerge from the data is not as clear-cut as is sometimes implied.

Research Strategy

Quantitative research tends to adopt a structured approach to the study of society. To a large extent, this tendency is a product of the methods with which it is associated; both surveys and experiments require that the issues to be focused upon be decided at the outset. In the previous section, the point was made that there is the possibility of an element of surprise in survey research which is frequently underestimated. However, it is evident that such investigations require that the variables be mapped out and introduced into the survey instruments. Survey research is structured in the sense that sampling and questionnaire construction are conducted prior to the start of data collection and then imposed on the sample members. Similarly, in experimental designs, independent and dependent variables, experimental and control groups are all part of the preparatory stage. In both cases, once the research has been designed the broad shape of the findings can be discerned, that is, before one person has been interviewed or one experimental subject has received a treatment. An examination of Hirschi's (1969) questionnaire reveals that he was fully aware of the material that needed to be collected in order to test the theories of delinquency which were to be examined.

By contrast, qualitative research tends to be more open. Many ethnographers advocate that the delineation of a research focus be deferred as long as possible (e.g. Cohen, 1978). Consequently, many qualitative researchers refer to a sensation of being overwhelmed during their early days in the field, since everything they observe is potentially 'data'. Whyte (1984), for example, sees ethnographic research as deriving much of its strength from its flexibility, which allows new leads to be followed up or additional data to be gathered in response to changes in ideas. But he also notes a limitation of such flexibility since 'you may find so many interesting things to study that you are at a loss to delimit the scope of your project and focus on specific problems' (Whyte, 1984, p. 225). Barrett (1976) has shown how his use of a prior theoretical framework (and a structured research strategy which derived from this framework), which was used to guide his anthropological research on the factors associated with the economic success of a village in Nigeria, caused him to misconstrue his data. Initially, his theoretical focus had led him to believe that his data implied that the communal economic organization of the village, rather than religion, was the main contributor to its success. Almost two years after the completion of his thesis which was based on this fieldwork, Barrett felt impelled to accord religion a stronger role, following some critical comments he had received on his explanation. However, Barrett has since revised his explanation yet again to provide what he believes to be the most accurate explanation of the village's success. This explanation differs radically from its predecessors in that it goes far beyond the simple juxtaposition of religion and communal organization and emphasizes the emergence of development as a paramount goal within the village. But Barrett's main point is that he was able to arrive at this more accurate account only when he had cast off the shackles of his prior theoretical framework. Such an experience underscores the strength of the qualitative researcher's preference for postponing theoretical reflection, albeit at the possible cost (noted by Whyte) of being overwhelmed by data. It also suggests that it may be disadvantageous to ethnographers to structure their strategies in advance.

Also, the role of luck may be more apparent in such research, where being in the right place at the right time may significantly affect the direction of the research (Bryman, 1988), or alternatively may give access to a potential research site (Buchanan, Boddy, and McCalman, 1988). For example, Bresnen (1988) refers to a lucky encounter in the pub soon after he had started his research on a construction project. Most of the site management team were present, but two senior managers had gone home. It became apparent that there was a considerable gap in attitudes between senior and junior management, which prompted Bresnen to develop a new line of questioning following on from this unexpected lead. One of the undoubted strengths which qualitative research affords the practitioner, by virtue of its unstructured nature, is precisely this capacity to encounter the unexpected and possibly to change direction.

Scope of Findings

It is common to conceive of the quantitative/qualitative dichotomy in terms of respective commitments to *nomothetic* and *ideographic* modes of reasoning (Halfpenny, 1979). This distinction effectively refers to the scope of the findings which derive from a piece of research. A nomothetic approach seeks to establish general law-like findings which can be deemed to hold irrespective of time and place; an ideographic approach locates its findings in specific time-periods and locales. The former mode is taken to be indicative of the scientific approach, whereas ideographic reasoning is often more closely associated with the historian's method. By taking random, and hence representative, samples, survey research is taken to exhibit a nomothetic approach because of the investigator's ability to infer findings to larger populations. Thus, Hirschi (1969) took great pains to ensure that the data on the children he studied would be representative of the wider population of school children through a stratified random sampling procedure which took account of such population characteristics as race, sex, and school attended.

By contrast, the qualitative researcher frequently conducts research in a specific milieu (a case study) whose representativeness is unknown and probably unknowable, so that the generalizability of such findings is also unknown. Adler's (1985) subjects were acquired in an apparently much less rigorous manner than Hirschi's children. Her initial contacts were accidental and were her source of further contacts. Moreover, these subjects were mainly located in a limited geographical area, so that their broader representativeness may be questioned. Qualitative researchers often exhibit some unease over this point. Liebow (1967) conducted participant observation in relation to 'two dozen Negro men who share a corner in Washington's Second Precinct' (p. 11) and goes on to note:

> To what extent this descriptive and interpretive material is applicable to Negro streetcorner men elsewhere in the city or in other

cities, or to lower-class men generally in this or any other society, is a matter for further and later study. (Liebow, 1967, p. 14)

The discussion about generalization in quantitative research in Chapter 2 suggests that the extent to which investigations within this tradition are nomothetic is often exaggerated. Surveys are often not based on random samples and, even when they are, they refer to highly restricted populations. For example, writing about the field of organization studies, Freeman (1986, p. 300) has observed: 'They rarely work with samples that are representative of even the restricted types of organizations they choose to study.' The fact that Hirschi's sample derives from a geographically restricted area – a county in the San Francisco–Oakland metropolitan area – is given much less attention in his book than his attempts to select a random sample of that region's population of school children. Further, the consistency of findings over time is rarely given much attention. Experimental research also suffers from a number of deficiencies in regard to the generalizability of findings stemming from such designs. Moreover, as the discussion in Chapter 4 on case study research implies, qualitative researchers are building up strategies for enhancing the generalizability of their research. Consequently, caution is necessary in treating the two research traditions as being strictly associated with nomothetic and ideographic findings.

Image of Social Reality
Quantitative research conveys a view of social reality which is static in that it tends to neglect the impact and role of change in social life. Surveys examine co-variation among variables at a particular juncture; experimental research usually entails the exploration of a restricted range of variables within a restricted time period. While both styles of research examine connections between variables, the proponents of qualitative research argue that quantitative research rarely examines the processes which link them (e.g. Blumer, 1956). They also charge that the 'independent' and 'dependent' variables fail to take into account the flow of events in which these variables are located. Quantitative researchers might argue that they do take such factors into account. For example, the notion of an 'intervening' variable, which is both a product of the independent variable and an influence on the dependent variable, might be interpreted as a device which examines intervening processes (Rosenberg, 1968). However, the suggestion is still open to the accusation that intervening processes are ignored (e.g. between the independent and intervening variables) and that the nexus of factors within which such chains of causality are grounded is rarely examined. For example, the causal chain in Hirschi (1969), quoted

in the Introduction, suggests that academic incompetence is causally related to delinquency via a sequential series of intervening variables (poor school performance, dislike of school and rejection of school's authority). It might legitimately be argued that the processes which account for the intermediate connections (e.g. rejection of school's authority and delinquent acts) are unexplored.

The qualitative researcher is in a better position to view the linkages between events and activities and to explore people's interpretations of the factors which produce such connections. This stance affords the qualitative researcher a much greater opportunity to study processes in social life. Adler's (1985) ethnographic research was concerned to demonstrate the nature of the 'career progressions' of the dealers and smugglers with whom she was in contact. She shows how dealers enter and climb to the top of these 'occupations' and how they and their experiences change with their ascendancy into upper-level activities. Similarly, Adler and Adler (1985) used participant observation and unstructured interviewing to study basketball players at an American university in order to examine the relationship between athletic participation and academic performance among college athletes. They note that the bulk of the literature implies that participation in college sports is associated with poor academic performance, although some studies are not consistent with this finding. Adler and Adler confirmed the negative relationship between athletic participation and school performance but show that most athletes come to college with a commitment to doing well in their academic studies. However, they encounter a number of experiences which conspire to deflate their academic motivation: athletic experiences (e.g. the time spent in training, playing and recovering), social experiences (e.g. the domination of their lives by interaction with other athletes) and classroom experiences (e.g. adverse attitudes towards them indicated by their professors) have a deleterious effect on their interest in academic work. Both of these studies inject a sense of process and transformation in social life which quantitative research can rarely address.

In addition to their respective tendencies to convey static and processual views of social life, quantitative and qualitative research differ in their view of the mutual relationship between the individual and social reality. There is a tendency for quantitative researchers to view social reality as external to actors and as a constraint on them, which can be attributed to the preference for treating the social order as though it were the same as the objects of the natural scientist. By contrast, the influence of perspectives like phenomenology, symbolic interactionism, and naturalism led qualitative researchers to suggest that 'we cannot take for granted, as the natural scientist does, the availability of a preconstituted world of phenomena for investigation' but must 'examine the processes by which the social world is constructed' (Walsh, 1972, p. 19). Thus, whereas quantitative research tends to invoke a perspective which implies that social reality is static and beyond the actor, the image deriving from qualitative research gives a sense of that same reality in processual terms and as socially constructed. This point can be illustrated by reference to the study of organization structure. Quantitative research on this topic, like the Aston Studies (Pugh and Hickson, 1976; Pugh, 1988), depicted organization structure as something which is determined by forces such as an organization's size or its technology. In turn, organization structure was seen as affecting the behaviour and orientations of its members (Pugh and Payne, 1977; Pugh, 1988). This approach seems to view organization structure as external and as a constraint on the actor, and differs from the qualitative research on a psychiatric hospital by Strauss *et al.* (1963) which suggests that the organization's structure was a 'negotiated order'. This latter study suggests that the behaviour of the hospital's members was largely unaffected by a formal structure of rules and role prescriptions; instead, the various groupings within the hospital produced their own structure, which they negotiated and which was in a constant state of renegotiation.

Nature of the Data

The data emanating from quantitative studies are often depicted as hard, rigorous, and reliable. These adjectives suggest that such data exhibit considerable precision, have been collected by systematic procedures and may be readily checked by another investigator. These positive attributes are often taken to mean that quantitative data are more persuasive and hence more likely to gain the support of policy-makers. Okely (1987), for example, has described how she was under great pressure from her employers at a research centre, in which she was to conduct research on gypsies, to use survey methods, because they believed that such research provided the only means of influencing policy-makers. She writes: 'At the outset the declared ideal was to be a report "with a statistical table on every page" ' (p. 62). Such a view is indicative of the very considerable power of quantitative data, possibly because of their association with 'science', to impress by virtue of their apparent rigour.

Qualitative researchers routinely describe the data deriving from ethnographic work as 'rich' and 'deep', often drawing a contrast with quantitative data, which tend to be depicted as superficial. The denotation 'rich' is generally indicative of the attention to often intricate detail which many qualitative researchers provide. Their sustained contact with the people they study permits a penetrating account, which can explore incidents in great detail and can illuminate the full extent of their subjects' accounts of a variety of phenomena. Further, the predilection of ethnographers for conveying social life in the language and style of their subjects adds to this sense of richness. In terms of conventional sampling, Liebow's (1967) street-corner men constitute an unacceptably small, non-random sample of unknown representativeness. But they provide, as in much qualitative research, the route to a vivid, detailed portrayal of a small sector of social life. Further, the potential of the attention to rich detail in qualitative research to policy-making and other 'applied' contexts is gaining increasing recognition (Finch, 1986). An interesting anecdote in this respect has been supplied by Okely (1987, p. 58):

> in the 1983 general election [in the UK], the Conservative party geared its campaign to the daily reactions of the floating voter in marginal seats, mainly in southern England. These potential supporters were the subject of in-depth qualitative interviews several times a week. Feedback from these data was used within days to adjust the emphasis in campaign issues.

To many qualitative researchers, quantitative research produces superficial data. They tend to view survey research, for example, as a source of surface information which relates to the social scientist's abstract categories. By contrast, the quantitative researcher may be suspicious of the limited generality of a study of two dozen men in one area of one city (Liebow, 1967) from which data were collected that may have been heavily influenced by the particular emphases and predispositions of the researcher.

A Question of Epistemology or Technique?

What *are* quantitative and qualitative research, as outlined in the preceding section? In the book thus far, there has been a strong suggestion that epistemological issues underpin the divide between them. By an 'epistemological issue' is meant a matter which has to do with the question of what is to pass as warrantable, and hence acceptable, knowledge. In suggesting that quantitative researchers are committed to a positivist approach to the study of society (Filmer *et al.*, 1972), the view is being taken that they subscribe to a distinctive epistemological position, since the implication is that only research which conforms to the canons of scientific method can be treated as contributing to the stock of knowledge. Similarly, by subscribing to positions, such as phenomenology, *verstehen*, and naturalism, which reject the imitation of the natural scientist's procedures and which advocate that greater attention be paid to actors' interpretations, qualitative research can also be depicted as being underpinned by an epistemological standpoint.[1] The tendency among some writers (e.g. Filstead, 1979) to refer to quantitative and qualitative research as 'paradigms' (following T. S. Kuhn, 1970) underscores the fact that they are frequently conceived of as different epistemological positions. The tendency to view the two research traditions as reflecting different epistemological positions, and hence divergent paradigms, has led to an exaggeration of the differences between them. As a consequence of such thinking, quantitative and qualitative research are frequently depicted as mutually exclusive models of the research process.

The following is a representative version of the view that quantitative and qualitative research reflect different epistemological positions:

Quantitative and qualitative methods are more than just differences between research strategies and data collection procedures. These approaches represent fundamentally different epistemological frameworks for conceptualizing the nature of knowing, social reality, and procedures for comprehending these phenomena. (Filstead, 1979, p. 45)

Similarly, Rist (1977, p. 62) suggests that each of the two research traditions rests on 'an interrelated set of assumptions about the social world'. The view that quantitative and qualitative research constitute different epistemological positions would seem to imply that researchers formulate their views about the proper foundation for the study of social reality and choose their methods of investigation in the light of that decision. This would imply that a researcher's personal commitment to the view that the natural sciences provide the only acceptable basis for generating knowledge would mean that his or her approach to conducting an investigation, as well as the methods of data collection, will be chosen in this light. Likewise, a view that the scientific method provides a poor basis for the study of people, coupled with a commensurate endorsement of a position like phenomenology, will propel an investigator in the direction of a qualitative approach. Alternatively, it might be suggested that a researcher who chooses to carry out a survey, for example, has to recognize that his or her decision to use that method carries with it a train of epistemological implications which need to be recognized at the outset, in case the selection does not fit with the researcher's broader intellectual proclivities.

One might question whether research is conducted in these ways, but the suggestion that the two research traditions are rooted in divergent epistemological implications seems to carry with it connotations of these kinds. However, the view that quantitative and qualitative research represent different epistemological implications is not held by all writers, even though they view the two approaches as distinctive. The alternative standpoint is to suggest that quantitative and qualitative research are each appropriate to different kinds of research problem, implying that the research issue determines (or should determine) which style of research is employed. For example, Walker (1985, p. 16) has proposed: 'Certain questions cannot be answered by quantitative methods, while others cannot be answered by qualitative ones.' This view implies that the decision over whether to use a quantitative or qualitative approach should be based on 'technical' issues regarding the suitability of a particular method in relation to a particular research problem. Accordingly, the different characteristics of quantitative and qualitative research which were summarized in Table 5.1 can be interpreted as pointing to the respective strengths and weaknesses of these two research traditions. Consider the following rationale for the procedures employed in a study of entrepreneurs in Britain:

> As with all social research, the methods adopted in this enquiry were largely dictated by the nature of the research problem. We set out to study the *dynamics* of small-scale capital accumulation and the *social processes* which account for the reproduction of the entrepreneurial middle class. In addition, it was our intention to define more precisely the *nature* and *interrelationships* of the constituent groupings within this class. The complexity of these issues did not favour quantitative investigation; in our view a qualitative approach was more appropriate. [The authors provide three considerations which determined this view] . . . Consequently, we undertook an intensive study of a limited number of proprietors using semi-structured interviews which were, to a considerable extent, shaped by the personal experiences of the respondents. (Scase and Goffee, 1982, p. 198)

In this account, there is a recognition of the strengths and weaknesses of quantitative and qualitative research, coupled with a technical decision that the latter will suit their needs better; epistemological issues are not in evidence. By inference, writers who perceive the distinction between the two styles of research in terms of their relative suitability for a particular research topic are effectively suggesting that the differences between them boil down to little more than 'differences between research strategies and data collection procedures' (see quotation from Filstead, 1979, cited on p. 105). This position is not new; it can be discerned in a celebrated exchange between Becker and Geer (1957) and Trow (1957) in which the former argued that participant observation provides 'the most complete form of sociological datum' (p. 28). In reply, it was suggested that 'the problem under investigation properly dictates the methods of investigation' (Trow, 1957, p. 33).

There seem, then, to be two fairly distinct versions of the nature of the differences between quantitative and qualitative research which might usefully be referred to as the 'epistemological' and 'technical' accounts. However, there is a tendency for many writers to oscillate between these two versions. This is particularly evident in some of the discussions about whether it is possible to integrate quantitative and qualitative research within a single study. The ways in which they might be combined constitute the focus of the next chapter; in the meantime, the broader question of whether in principle they might be combined is addressed here. The technical version of the differences between quantitative and qualitative research seems to provide few impediments to the possibility of a research strategy that integrates them. While a researcher may prefer to use one to the relative exclusion of the other (as with Scase and Goffee, 1982), if the research problem invites a combined approach there is little to prevent such a strategy, other than the usual reasons of time, money, and possibly inclination. The researcher may choose to conduct a predominantly ethnographic study, but decide to add some survey evidence relating to people who are not accessible through the focal method. Woods (1979) buttressed his ethnographic research on a school with a survey of parents for precisely this reason.

The epistemological account would seem to pose more problems in regard to the possibility of combining the two approaches. If quantitative and qualitative research are taken to represent divergent epistemological packages (or paradigms), they are likely to exhibit incompatible views about the way in which social reality ought to be studied, and hence what should be regarded as proper knowledge thereof. This incongruence is particularly evident in the implicit critique of the application of the scientific method to the study of society which phenomenology contains. It is not obvious how a marriage of such divergent epistemological positions as positivism and phenomenology (even in the metaphorical use of the term) can be entertained. Guba (1985) has argued vehemently against the suggestion that the two research traditions might be reconciled. In his view, attempts to combine the two approaches fail to recognize the distinction between a paradigm and a method. He argues that the idea that quantitative and qualitative research can be dovetailed rests on a view that they represent only different methods of investigation; instead, 'we *are* dealing with an either-or proposition, in which one must pledge allegiance to one paradigm or the other' (Guba, 1985, p. 80). Thus in the same way that Kuhn regards paradigms as incommensurable, Guba is suggesting that the collection of assumptions and beliefs about the study of the social order that underpin quantitative and qualitative research should be treated in the same manner.

Not all writers subscribe to this view. Reichardt and Cook (1979) suggest that the tendency to view the two styles of research as paradigms stands in the way of their joint use within a single project, and prefer to see them as 'method-types'. What is somewhat more surprising is that some writers who subscribe to the epistemological view of the differences between quantitative and qualitative research simultaneously suggest that they might be integrated. Filstead (1979), who was quoted above for his view that they represent 'different epistemological frameworks', suggests that 'great advantages can be obtained by creatively combining qualitative and quantitative methods' (p. 42). Bogdan and Biklen (1982), after a discussion of the intellectual foundations of qualitative research (in phenomenology, etc.), ask whether it can be used in tandem with a quantitative approach. They acknowledge that it can, but display a lack of enthusiasm for the idea, not because of any kind of epistemological incompatibility, but for practical reasons. They suggest that research which combines the two approaches 'is likely to produce a big headache' (p. 39), because of the practical problems of producing both a good quantitative and a good qualitative design. Delamont and Hamilton (1984) oscillate in the other direction. In contrasting structured and ethnographic observation in classrooms, they argue against the view that these two styles of observation are 'the equivalent of self-contained epistemological and theoretical paradigms', but then go on to argue that the two methods reflect 'the tension between positivism and interactionism' which 'cannot be done away with by calling for interdisciplinary *rapprochements*' (pp. 5, 6).

There seems, then, to be a tendency for many writers to shuttle uneasily back and forth between epistemological and technical levels of discourse. While much of the exposition of the epistemological debts of qualitative research helped to afford it some credibility, a great many decisions about whether and when to use qualitative methods seems to have little, if any, recourse to these broader intellectual issues.

The Strengths and Weaknesses of Quantitative and Qualitative Research

Underlying much of the preceding discussion is the suggestion that the distinction between quantitative and qualitative research is really a technical matter whereby the choice between them is to do with their suitability in answering particular research questions. Such a view draws attention to the different strengths and weaknesses of the methods of data collection with which the two research traditions are typically associated. It is not uncommon for textbooks on research methods to draw attention to such issues:

> The sample survey is an appropriate and useful means of gathering information under three conditions: when the goals of the research call for quantitative data, when the information sought is reasonably specific and familiar to the respondents, and when the researcher himself has considerable prior knowledge of particular problems and the range of responses likely to emerge . . .
>
> Participant observation is usually more appropriate when the study requires an examination of complex social relationships or intricate patterns of interaction; . . . when the investigator desires first-hand behavioural information on certain social processes . . .; when a major goal of the study is to construct a qualitative contextual picture of a certain situation or flow of events; and when it is necessary to infer latent value patterns or belief systems from such behaviour as ceremonial postures, gestures, dances, facial expressions or subtle inflections of the voice. (Warwick and Lininger, 1975, pp. 9–10)

As they then go on to say, 'Each is useful for some purposes and useless for others' (p. 12).

This passage illustrates well the suggestion that the decision about which method to employ is essentially a technical issue. As such, the decision about whether to employ quantitative or qualitative research stands cheek by jowl with other familiar technical issues on which students of social research methods are reared, such as when it is appropriate to use a postal questionnaire, or to construct a stratified random sample. Warwick and Lininger's list of respective strengths and weaknesses can usefully be expanded. Social surveys are likely to be particularly appropriate where larger scale issues are concerned. The study of social mobility is a case in point (e.g. Goldthorpe, 1980). Of course, it might be argued that much of the recent ethnographic research on schools is concerned with social mobility too (e.g. Lacey, 1970; Woods, 1979; Ball, 1981). However, such research is typically concerned with the processes through which social class is perpetuated by the structure of the school, teachers' practices, and the class based sub-cultures within the school. Studies of social mobility like Goldthorpe's are essentially concerned with the *extent* of social mobility and changes in patterns. Thus, the technical version of the debate would imply that the critical issue about whether a method fits a research problem is not a matter of the area of social life being investigated, but the nature of the issues being raised in relation to it. Similarly, juvenile delinquency may be studied by both survey methods (e.g. Hirschi, 1969) or participant observation (e.g. Patrick, 1973), but the nature of the questions being asked about juvenile delinquency differ. Hirschi was concerned to test the validity of three theories of the causes of delinquency. This preoccupation with the causes of variation in delinquency led him to carry out a survey of over 5,000 school children in California in order to collect sufficient data to separate out the variables which impinged on his dependent variable, delinquency. By contrast, Patrick joined a particularly violent gang in Glasgow as a covert participant observer 'to comprehend and to illuminate their view and to interpret the world as it appears to them' (Matza, 1969, p. 25, cited in Patrick, 1973, p. 9).

Social surveys are also likely to be preferred when, as in the case of Hirschi's study, there is a concern to establish cause-and-effect relationships. Experiments are even stronger in this department, but are likely to be appropriate only to situations in which the independent variable is capable of manipulation and in which random assignment (or at least some form of matching) is feasible. Qualitative researchers are not uninterested in causes, in that they are frequently concerned to establish how flows of events connect and mesh with each other in the social contexts they investigate, or how their subjects perceive the connections between facets of their environment. However, survey and experimental researchers tend to be much more concerned with the precise delineation of a causal factor, relative to other potential causes.

As Warwick and Lininger suggest in the extended quotation above, participant observation has its own strengths. The absence of a highly structured research design means that the investigator can change direction if he or she is lucky enough to hit upon an unexpected but interesting facet of the social setting. The participant observer is better able than the survey researcher to understand social processes.

A further, and neglected, strength of ethnographic studies is their capacity to reveal covert, hidden, even illegal activities. Studies of informal groups in large organizations (Dalton, 1959), output regulation in industrial work groups (Roy, 1960), and pilferage at work (Ditton, 1977) all demonstrate the capacity of ethnographers to look behind the scenes and bring to the centre of the stage aspects of these milieux which would otherwise either be inaccessible or possibly not even uncovered in the first place. The same point can be made about the study of deviant behaviour, a more probing study of which requires sensitivity and a capacity to provide reassurance to the subjects that a survey researcher is unlikely to be able to inculcate. It is difficult to see how Adler's (1985) research on drug dealers could have been conducted with a more formal approach. Indeed, the capacity of ethnographers to gain access to hidden arenas can occasionally cause them difficulties. Serber (1981) sought to conduct an ethnographic study of a government bureaucracy responsible for the state regulation of the insurance industry in California. He rapidly discerned a range of informal practices (e.g. off-the-record meetings) which he chose to make the focus of his investigations, but found his access to people and documents sharply curtailed by senior managers as his awareness of the significance of such undercover processes grew.

The purpose of this discussion was to provide a flavour of the sorts of considerations that are relevant to the technical version of the distinction between quantitative and qualitative research. It is also the case that the choice between the two may derive from reasons other than the epistemological and technical reasons which have been encountered thus far. For example, many women social scientists have drawn attention to the affinity between qualitative research and a feminist perspective (Stanley and Wise, 1983). Oakley (1981) has argued that the typical survey interview, in which the researcher appropriates information from a respondent for the former's use, is incompatible with feminism. A feminist researcher conducting research on women would be setting up an asymmetrical relationship which exploits the already exploited interviewee. In order to mitigate this perpetuation of exploitation she advocates an approach to feminist research whereby the research situation is treated much more as an exchange in which the feminist researcher gives something back − of her own views, experiences, and the like − to those being interviewed. Such an approach implies a much more unstructured interview (and hence one closely associated with the qualitative approach) than that associated with the survey. It is striking that research on women's subordination in the workplace, as well as the interface between the workplace and the home, has tended to be the product of qualitative investigations in which participant observation and unstructured interviews figure strongly (Pollert, 1981; Cavendish, 1982; Griffin, 1985a). The underlying issues to the discussion about the appropriateness of particular methods to feminist research imply that considerations other than those which have figured thus far in this book may impinge on choices of method, e.g. ethical, political, ideological considerations.

Similarities in the Technical Problems Associated with Quantitative and Qualitative Research

One reason for giving greater recognition to the technical aspects of decisions relating to the use of quantitative or qualitative research is that it may result in a appreciation of the common technical problems faced by practitioners working within the two traditions. The emphasis on their epistemological separateness runs the risk of failing to give due attention to these common problems. The recognition of mutual technical problems may also invite a questioning of whether the quantitative and qualitative research traditions are as far apart from each other as the epistemological argument may be taken to imply.[2]

Perhaps the most striking problem which besets both groups of practitioners is that of 'reactivity' – the reaction on the part of those being investigated to the investigator and his or her research instruments. Surveys and experiments create an awareness on the part of subjects that they are being investigated; the problem of reactivity draws attention to the possibility that this awareness creates a variety of undesirable consequences in that people's behaviour or responses may not be indicative of their normal behaviour or views (e.g. Rosenthal, 1966). In experiments subjects may be influenced by what they perceive to be the underlying aims of the investigation, or in interviews respondents may be influenced by characteristics of the interviewer, such as the latter's age, race, gender, or whatever. The recognition of such problems led Webb *et al.* (1966) to propose the greater use of 'non-reactive' methods of gleaning data, such as field experiments in which people do not know that they are under investigation. An example of the latter is Daniel's (1968) study of racial discrimination in England in which actors of different races were hired to seek employment, accommodation, car insurance, and the like in order to determine the extent of such discrimination.

Problems of reactivity confront the ethnographer as well. An obvious solution is to engage in covert observation which simultaneously deals with the problem of access. The study by Festinger, Riecken and Schachter (1956) of a religious cult is an example of this strategy, in that the investigators feigned conversion to a group which was predicting the imminent end of the world. Even here the problem of reactivity was not fully overcome, since the researchers' conversion was treated by the cult's adherents as confirmation of the validity of their beliefs and hardened their resolve to prepare for the fateful day. But the strategy of covert observation is usually frowned upon by social scientists, because it transgresses a number of ethical conventions (Bulmer, 1982), though many of the non-reactive methods suggested by Webb *et al.*

(1966) are suspect in this way as well. By and large, ethnographers prefer to be open about their participation, but frequently display a concern about the effect of their presence on the people they observe. While recognizing the potentially contaminating effects of their presence, ethnographers frequently play down this problem, suggesting that their familiarity to the people they study militates against this reactive effect. Gans's (1967) statement about the impact of this presence in a middle class American suburb is indicative of this position: 'After a while, I became a fixture in the community; people forgot I was there and went on with their business, even at private political gatherings' (p. xxiii). Likewise, Atkinson (1981, p. 129), writing about his experience of a participant observation study of clinical education in a medical school, comments:

> Although my presence on the wards had originally taken a fair amount of negotiation, once access had been granted, I was generally taken very much for granted on the wards, and by the students as they went about the hospital . . . Indeed, for some doctors I became so much a part of the normal scene that they forgot who I was.

The suggestion here is that the participant observer becomes part of the scenery and hence largely invisible. This process of absorption can be enhanced by not taking copious notes in front of subjects.

However, there is some evidence to suggest that reactive effects may occur. For example, Atkinson's assertion that he became unobtrusive jars somewhat with his admission that both clinicians and students often thought that he was engaged in an evaluation exercise (p. 125), which may have had ramifications for the behaviour of these groups in his presence. An interesting insight on the reactive effect in participant observation can be derived from an anecdote relating to research which was not conducted for the purposes of academic social science. During the 1971–2 football season, a journalist, Hunter Davies, was effectively a participant observer with Tottenham Hotspur Football Club, an experience which spawned a book, *The Glory Game* (1972). Writing in his autobiography about one particular game, the then manager of the club, Bill Nicholson (1984, p. 141), remarked:

> Hunter Davies, a Spurs fan, followed us around that season . . . He had been given permission to become virtually one of the players and was allowed in the dressing room which in my view must always be a private place. Permission was not given by me but by someone else at the club. In hindsight I should have overruled the decision.

I know Davies' work was highly acclaimed, but after this particular match I was forced to keep quiet when I wanted to say a lot of things straight away.

It is not apparent whether this was the only incident whereby Davies's presence influenced Nicholson, but the suggestion that he would have overruled the decision indicates that this is at least a possibility. Nor do we know how representative Nicholson's experience is − but then the subjects of participant observation do not normally write books in which they can refer to their experience.

There is, then, at least a possibility that the participant observer's presence may have an effect on what is observed. It is surprising that the widespread acceptance of interviewing in qualitative research has not been given greater critical attention as regards the problem of reactivity. Even unstructured interviewing is an obtrusive method and would seem to share some of the limitations of the familiar survey interview in this regard. Researchers using unstructured interviews, even though such instruments are longer and much more likely to produce repeat visits than those of the survey kind, are unlikely to have the participant observer's capacity for becoming part of the scenery. The potential for reactive effects in the unstructured interview, though arguably less than in survey interviews, would still seem to be more likely than in participant observation.

Indeed, the extensive use of interviews in qualitative research points to another area in which the two research traditions share a common technical problem. The pervasive acceptance of the unstructured interview as a legitimate tool of qualitative research − either in conjunction with participant observation or more especially on its own − is occasionally surprising on at least five further accounts. First, writers like Cicourel (1982, p. 15) have criticized interviews for their lack of 'ecological validity': 'Do our instruments capture the daily life, conditions, opinions, values, attitudes, and knowledge base of those we study as expressed in their natural habitat?' Cicourel points to a lack of ecological validity in interviews in a number of ways; for example, they are very sensitive to slight changes in wording, and the availability of the necessary knowledge to answer a question on the part of the respondent is rarely addressed. Although survey research is certainly more culpable in these respects than unstructured interviews, it is possible that they do not totally escape this criticism. The respondent in an unstructured interview study is questioned in a much more probing manner than in the conventional interview, but the issue of whether this means that ecological validity is obtained tends to be unexplored. This issue again suggests a common thread to the technical problems faced by quantitative and qualitative researchers.

Secondly, it is not always clear how well the unstructured interview fits with the suggestion that qualitative research exhibits a concern for process. Participant observers would seem to be in a much stronger position to impute the interconnections of events over time than researchers who rely exclusively on unstructured interviews. The relative absence of a sense of process in research which relies wholly on unstructured interviews can be mitigated to a certain degree by building in a longitudinal element. In their study of individuals in arrears with their mortgages, Took and Ford (1987) conducted unstructured interviews on three occasions with many of their respondents in order to chart changes in the experience and perception of debt. Thirdly, survey interviews have long been criticized for their tendency to rely on attitudes and people's reports of their behaviour, both of which may bear little relation to actual behaviour (LaPiere, 1934; Deutscher, 1966); participant observation displays a technical advantage in this respect by virtue of the researcher's ability to observe behaviour directly (as recognized in the Warwick and Lininger quotation above). There is little reason to believe that unstructured interviews are substantially superior to survey interviews in this connection which also indicates another similarity in technical problems faced. Fourthly, the qualitative researcher may experience some difficulty in establishing the appropriate climate for an unstructured interview on some occasions. For example, in her qualitative research on grandparenthood, Cunningham-Burley (1985) found that some of her unstructured interviews with grandparents took a more formal, ordered character and departed very little from her schedule. Such interviews seem to have had an adverse effect on the qualitative depth of the data. Finally, the unstructured interview is not obviously consistent with the commitment of much qualitative research to naturalism. The interview is an obtrusive interruption of the natural flow of events, so that it is slightly surprising to find writers like Blumer (1969), who are committed to the naturalistic viewpoint, suggesting that it is a legitimate tool for such research. Cunningham-Burley (1985), for example, found that even her most informal interviews conformed to a question–answer format. Together, these features point to a possible need to question the extent to which unstructured interviewing is entirely consistent with the qualitative approach and to more areas in which the two approaches exhibit similar technical problems.

There has been some re-appraisal of the role of interviews in qualitative research, which may have been motivated slightly by such considerations. Paget's (1983) discussion of interviewing artists in New York is indicative of such a re-orientation. She views the in-depth interview as a scientific means of developing systematic knowledge about subjective experience. She sees the in-depth interview as a medium through which the interviewer and interviewee jointly create this knowledge; the former is fully implicated in the process of gaining knowledge about the interviewee's subjective experience. Paget implicated herself in this process by making clear her own interest in the art world and allowed this personal concern to be reflected in the questions she formulated and her own responses to the interviewees' replies. Her interviews, transcripts from which are quoted at length, include numerous switches of both content and direction which are fully followed up in the course of the sessions. The content of replies is fully explored to discern their meaning and significance. Thus a simple question about the nature of an artist's paintings (e.g. whether they were fun to do) rapidly turns into a statement by the interviewee about her commitments to art and some of the financial problems she encountered during the early years (Paget, 1983, pp. 70–1). These points are then followed up and addressed during the interview. Further, the meaning of replies is embedded in the context of the interview situation itself; thus a particular reply is examined by the interviewer in the context of the interviewee's other replies and is possibly returned to when, for example, later exchanges produce information which is puzzling, when viewed in relation to the earlier reply. It is the contextual understanding of respondents' replies that sharply distinguishes this emerging conception of the role of the unstructured interview from the survey interview (Mishler, 1986). The unstructured interview is viewed by writers like Paget as a dynamic process whereby the researcher seeks to gain knowledge – by which she means 'illuminating human experience' (p. 88) – about what art work or whatever entails. This perspective on interviewing seems to harmonize somewhat better with the qualitative research tradition than much unstructured interviewing, by virtue of its explicit concern with respondents' subjective experiences. Further, the tendency to invite interviewees to speak at length possibly renders such interviewing less obtrusive than much unstructured interviewing. The problem of ecological validity may also be reduced since the focus is very explicitly upon what is important to the interviewee rather than to the researcher.

A further technical problem shared by both research traditions relates to the selection of people who are the focus of the research. Quantitative research is concerned to establish that respondents are representative of a wider population, so that the generalizability of findings can be enhanced. In fact, much research departs significantly from this ideal in a number of ways. However, there is a case for suggesting that the issue of representativeness confronts the qualitative researcher too. The avowal to see through the eyes of one's subjects can be interpreted to imply that the ethnographer needs to attend to the question of the typicality of the eyes through which he or she is seeing. This kind of concern may be regarded as indicative of the application of an inappropriate criterion (that is, one deriving from the framework of quantitative research) to the ethnographer's mode of research. For example, in their exposition of grounded theory, Glaser and Strauss (1967) advocate that the qualitative researcher should give less attention to the need to meet statistical sampling criteria in assessing the adequacy of a 'sample'; rather, the researcher should be much more concerned with the issue of whether the sample conforms to the investigator's emerging theoretical framework. For example, in an ethnographic study of power in a medical school in the USA, Bucher (1970, p. 5) proposed that, following a preliminary analysis of her initial observations, 'data are being sought from areas of the organization which should provide test cases, so to speak, for emerging propositions'. According to the principles of 'theoretical sampling' (the term coined by Glaser and Strauss), the researcher observes only as many activities, or interviews as many people, as are needed in order to 'saturate' the categories being developed, and then turns to the next theoretical issue and carries out the same process over again. Thus the question of the adequacy of a sample is determined by the degree to which it permits the qualitative reseacher to develop and confirm one or more categories; as soon as the researcher feels satisfied that the theoretical point has been established, he or she can move on to the next issue. This procedure allows the constant interplay between theory and research that Glaser and Strauss are keen to develop.

While Glaser and Strauss's view of sampling serves well to exemplify the disinclination of qualitative researchers to accept the quantitative researcher's preoccupation with representativeness, like other aspects of grounded theory, their particular view of the sampling process is probably cited far more frequently than it is used. Of course, qualitative researchers (especially ethnographers) may not simply sample people, but also activities, time periods, and locations (Burgess, 1984). None the less, if the aim of the exercise is to see as one's subjects see, there is still a problem of the representativeness of the eyes. For example, qualitative researchers sometimes display a concern that the people with whom they come into contact may be marginal to the social setting. Blau (1964) found that during the early period of his field-work in a federal agency, his early contacts and suppliers of information were marginal officials who were keen to voice their criticisms of the agency and their colleagues. As Blau acknowledged, had he not recognized this problem, a distorted picture of the agency would have been generated. Interestingly, Blau (1964, p. 30) argues that the field researcher's own marginality may render him attractive to those who are marginal to the settings in which research is carried out. Similarly, Ball (1984, p. 81), drawing on his ethnographic study of a comprehensive school, has remarked on the untypicality and, in the case of two teachers, marginality of his main informants. Other writers (e.g. Hammersley, 1984, pp. 51–3) have drawn attention to biases which stem from the problem of establishing a picture drawn from a representative spread of contacts and informants.

The purpose of drawing attention to some common technical problems faced by quantitative and qualitative researchers has been to highlight the possibility that discussions of the differences between the two traditions purely in terms of epistemological issues run the risk of exaggerating their distinctiveness. This is not to imply that the differences between quantitative and qualitative research are insignificant, but that they may not be as far apart as is sometimes implied by the epistemological version of the debate about the two research traditions.

The Link between Epistemology and Technique

Quantitative and qualitative research are each associated with distinctive methods of data collection and research strategy, although their differences are not as clear cut as some of the more programmatic statements imply. In particular, it has been suggested in this chapter that the differences between the two research traditions are less precise than writers who emphasize epistemological issues suggest. According to the epistemological version of the debate about the two research traditions, the choice of research method flows from an allegiance to a distinctive position in relation to how social reality ought to be studied. This view suggests that, for example, it would be wholly inappropriate to use a survey in order to conduct research which is grounded in the cluster of intellectual predilections associated with qualitative research. It is not simply that the survey is likely to generate quantitative data; rather, it is seen as better suited to a natural science conception of how social reality ought to be studied, while a technique like participant observation is better attuned to the epistemological commitments of qualitative research.

In other words, the epistemological version of the debate assumes a correspondence between epistemological position and research method. Is this an acceptable view of the way social research is conducted? This question can be tackled in a number of ways, but in the rest of this section some problems with assuming a clear correspondence between epistemology and research technique will be examined.

Ethnography and Positivism

Not all commentators on the nature of social research have accepted the bond between ethnographic research and a non-positivist approach to the study of social research. In particular, the view has been expressed that ethnographic investigations may also engender a form of empiricism. Willer and Willer (1973) argue that, although participant observation differs from what they call 'systematic empiricism' (as exemplified by the experiment and the social survey), it is none the less empiricist in that it establishes the connections between observed categories. According to this view, the empiricism of participant observation resides in the researcher's distrust of categories which are not directly amenable to the senses. This point is highly congruent with Rock's (1973) view that much research in the sociology of deviance (a great deal of which stems from ethnographic investigations) is phenomenalist by virtue of a disinclination among many researchers to dig themselves out of the data on the social world in which they bury themselves. This phenomenalism can be discerned in the following passage from a text on field research by a proponent of qualitative research in the sociology of deviance:

> We begin with direct experience and all else builds on that . . . [W]e begin with and continually return to direct experience as the most reliable form of knowledge about the social world. (Douglas, 1976, p. 7)

In like fashion, Willis (1980), the author of a celebrated ethnographic study of working class youth (1977), has referred to a 'covert positivism' in participant observation. By this phrase, Willis means that the researcher sees the subject of his or her research as an object who can provide data; further, he argues, the preference of participant observers to postpone the generation of theory in relation to their data enhances a positivist hue by virtue of deferring to what is directly observable. Finally, Delamont and Atkinson (1980) have argued that the tendency towards atheoretical investigations in much school ethnography is conspiring to produce a form of empiricism.

In each of these comments is a view that participant observation does not depart radically from a positivist epistemology. In the view of these authors, the empiricism in much ethnographic research is exaggerated by the widespread tendency to postpone theoretical reflection, if indeed theory comes into the reckoning at all. In Glaser and Strauss's (1967) grounded theory, the view of theory as an emergent product of an investigation is systematized. However, the positioning of theory at the outset of an investigation can also be regarded as retaining positivist elements, by virtue of 'theory' being envisioned as something which needs to be tested by recourse to an examination of the real world. The problem here is that, irrespective of whether theory is seen as something which precedes or succeeds the collection of ethnographic data, a basically positivist precept is being adhered to, since the world of the senses is the ultimate arbiter of whether a theory is acceptable or not. Thus the quest for a more explicit grounding of qualitative research in theory (which some writers have expressed − see Chapter 4) supplants the more obvious empiricism of waiting for the theory to emerge, with the positivist preference for being 'entitled to record only that which is actually manifested in experience' (Kolakowski, 1972, p. 11). It is the manner in which theory is conceptualized in relation to the collection of data that points to an affinity with positivism, and not simply whether theory comes before, during, or after the data collection phase.

Qualitative research may also allow the investigator to impute causal processes which bear a strong resemblance to the kinds of causal statements that are the hallmark of quantitative research (although without the precise delineation of cause and effect which quantitative researchers seek to generate). McCleary (1977) conducted participant observation and interviews with parole officers in a division of a state parole agency in Chicago. He notes that officers should report parole violations known to have been committed by their parolees, but frequently they do not. Through his research, he was able to identify five factors which result in officers' disinclination to report their parolees: full reporting cuts into the officer's time; it may reflect badly on the officer and result in a negative evaluation by his or her superior; the officer's options may be restricted as a result of reporting a violation; and so on. Thus, McCleary was able to identify causes of failure to report parolees, whilst retaining fidelity to the perspectives of parole officers themselves.

Quantitative Research and Meaning

The recurring theme within qualitative research of viewing attributes of the social world through the eyes of the people being studied has led to a convention that only methods like participant observation and intensive interviewing are acceptable in this light.

But quantitative researchers also make frequent claims to addressing issues relating to the meaning of aspects of the social world to the people being studied. Social science research on work provides a number of examples of such investigations. The classic study of a sample of adults in the USA by Morse and Weiss (1955) used a survey to discern the range of reasons why people work and what meaning work has for them. The authors found that work does not simply mean the ability to earn money, but has a number of other meanings for people. Goldthorpe *et al.* (1968) conducted a survey in Luton to examine industrial attitudes and behaviour. One of the study's central notions − the idea of 'orientation to work' − draws attention to the variety of meanings which work may have for industrial workers. Finally, in their monograph on social stratification which reports a large scale survey of white-collar employees, Stewart, Prandy and Blackburn (1980) draw attention to the tendency to treat clerks as an undifferentiated category in many discussions of their position in the class structure. By contrast, the purpose of their research was to show that 'the *meaning* of clerical work will not be the same for all engaged in it' (Stewart, Prandy and Blackburn, 1980, p. 112 − emphasis added).

Marsh (1982) has also drawn attention to the capacity of social surveys to provide insights into questions of meaning. For example, the widespread tendency among social researchers to solicit their respondents' reasons for their actions, views, and the like, provides the researcher with people's interpretations of a variety of phenomena. She also points to the research by Brown and Harris (1978), which examined the connection between critical life events (e.g loss of job, death of husband, childbirth) and depression. Marsh observes that the researchers went to great pains to establish the meaning of each life event to each respondent. For example: 'Childbirth was not normally rated severe unless it happened in the context of bad housing and shortage of money' (Marsh, 1982, p. 117).

The field of cognitive social psychology provides a contrasting example of a subject which is explicitly concerned with meaning but which relies heavily upon quantitative experimental research as a prominent data gathering procedure. Cognitive social psychologists are concerned with 'how people make sense of other people and themselves' and 'people's everyday understanding both as the phenomenon of interest and as a basis for theory about people's everyday understanding' (Fiske and Taylor, 1984, p. 17). For example, in the field of leadership research, a prominent interest has been leaders' perceptions of the causes of their subordinates' success or failure (Bryman, 1986). This level of analysis is concerned with everyday understandings of the meanings of success and failure. Such research has proceeded by experimentally manipulating subordinate behaviour and then gauging leaders' perceptions of the causes of particular levels of that behaviour. Investigators have been particularly concerned to establish the circumstances in which good or poor subordinate performance is deemed by leaders to be a consequence of internal factors (e.g. subordinates' levels of ability or effort), or of external factors (e.g. task difficulty or luck). Thus such research is concerned with the meanings people ascribe to events and to others' behaviour.

It seems, then, that quantitative researchers also make the claim that their methods can gain access to people's interpretations and to the ways in which they view the world.

Participant Observation and Theory Testing

Quantitative research tends to be depicted as well suited to the task of testing explicitly formulated theories, whereas qualitative research is typically associated with the generation of theories. However, there is nothing intrinsic to participant observation, for example, that renders it inappropriate for the testing of preformulated theories. Becker (1958) provided a framework which would facilitate the examination of previously formulated theories by participant observation. He anticipated that his proposed approach would allow qualitative research to assume a more scientific character than that with which it is most closely associated. Other writers, like McCall (1969) and Campbell (1979), have argued along similar lines that the association of qualitative research solely with theory-creation does less than justice to its potential.

Indeed, one of the most celebrated studies using participant observation – Festinger, Riecken and Schachter's (1956) investigation of a religious cult – was designed to test a theory about how people are likely to respond to the disconfirmation of a belief to which they are fervently wedded. The authors suggested that a number of conditions can be envisaged which would allow the belief to be held with greater zeal even when it has been proved to be wrong. Festinger *et al.* learned of a millenarian group that was prophesying the imminent end of the world and felt that it would provide an ideal case for the examination of their theoretical concerns. As mentioned on p. 112, along with some hired observers, they joined the group as participants and 'gathered data about the conviction, commitment and proselytizing activity' (p. 31) of its adherents. More recently, as observed above, some writers have argued for a more explicit approach to the testing of theory by qualitative researchers (e.g. Hammersley, 1985; Hammersley, Scarth and Webb, 1985). Further, the view that qualitative research is compatible with a theory testing approach is implicit in the more recent treatments of the issue of case study generalization which were mentioned in Chapter 4. It will be recalled that Mitchell (1983) and Yin (1984) have both suggested that the question of the generalizability of case studies (and thereby much qualitative research) misses the central point of such investigations, in that the critical issue is 'the cogency of the theoretical reasoning' (Mitchell, 1983, p. 207). The Festinger, Riecken and Schachter study is a case in point: the representativeness of the cult is not particularly important; it is its relevance to the theoretical framework which constitutes the most important criterion for assessing the study. Accordingly, the view of qualitative research which plays down its role in relation to the testing of theory may be missing an important strength that qualitative investigations possess. In other words, there is nothing intrinsic to the techniques of data collection with which qualitative research is connected that renders them unacceptable as a means of testing theory.

Conclusion

It has been suggested that there are a number of ways in which the posited connection between epistemology and data collection can be questioned: participant observation (and indeed unstructured interviewing) is not without positivist leanings; survey researchers frequently claim to be looking at the social world from their respondents' perspectives; and participant observation can be deployed within a theory testing framework with which the epistemological basis of quantitative research is conventionally associated. None the less, a recurring theme of this book thus far is that a prominent view of the debate about quantitative and qualitative research is that they are competing epistemological positions, each of which is associated with particular approaches to data collection and research strategy. How should we understand the apparent clash between the suggestion presented here that the link between epistemology and method is not clear-cut and the epistemological account of the debate about quantitative and qualitative research?

One of the most unsatisfactory aspects of the epistemological version of the debate is that it is unclear whether its proponents are arguing that there *is* a link between epistemology and method of data collection or whether there *ought* to be such a bond. If the argument is that there *is* such a link, the epistemological argument runs into difficulties. In addition to the points made in the previous section, which suggest that the bond between epistemology and method may be exaggerated, it is also clear that methods like participant observation and unstructured interviewing have been used by various practitioners who have not had an epistemological axe to grind. Writers like Lupton (1963), Gans (1962), and Skolnick (1966), all of whom have written much admired monographs deriving from the use of such methods, seem to have exhibited few, if any, philosophical pretensions in their justifications for the use of qualitative research. These researchers were able to produce highly regarded ethnographic studies without recourse to the programmatic statements surrounding qualitative research. This very fact invites a questioning of the role of programmatic statements in relation to the pursuit of good social research. Rather, these researchers were concerned to get close to the people they were studying, to allow for the possibility of novel findings, and to elucidate their findings from the perspective of the people they studied. While the last of these three concerns is invariably taken as a keynote of the epistemological substructure of qualitative research, a preoccupation with meaning and subjects' perspectives is not exclusive to the qualitative tradition. Further, the methods with which qualitative research is associated have often been chosen on technical grounds rather than epistemological grounds.

The lack of a definitive link between broad epistemological positions and methods has also been suggested by Snizek (1976), who analysed 1,434 articles in sociological journals covering the period 1950 to 1970. Snizek was concerned to find out whether there was a connection between the three paradigms which Ritzer (1975) had suggested underpin sociology and the methods with which they are associated. If these three basic approaches to sociology really are paradigms (T. S. Kuhn, 1970), one would anticipate a link between the endorsement of the epistemology with which each is associated and the methods of research used. Two of the paradigms – the 'social factist' and 'social definitionist' orientations – correspond to quantitative and qualitative research respectively to a fair degree. However, Snizek was unable to discern a clear pattern which linked the general orientation of each paradigm with the methods of investigation employed.

The alternative position is to suggest that there *ought* to be a connection between epistemological positions and methods of data collection. This view would imply that researchers should be much more sensitive to the wider epistemological context of methods of data collection and that they are not neutral technical devices to be deployed under a variety of auspices. Choosing to conduct a survey or an ethnographic study would mean accepting a package of views about social reality and how it ought to be studied. Accordingly, it might be argued that researchers who claim to study subjects' views of the world with a survey (e.g. Goldthorpe *et al.*, 1968) are misguided, since they should have chosen a method more suited to this perspective, like unstructured interviewing. It is not at all clear from the various writings on the debate about quantitative and qualitative research that the view exists that there ought to be a recognition of a mutual interdependence of epistemology and method (as against a view that there *is* such a connection). The problem with the 'ought' view is that it fails to recognize that a whole cluster of considerations are likely to impinge on decisions about methods of data collection. In particular, the investigator's judgements regarding the technical viability of a method in relation to a particular problem will be important, as the technical version of the debate about the two research traditions implies.

Methods are probably much more autonomous than many commentators (particularly those who espouse the epistemological versions of the debate) acknowledge. They can be used in a variety of contexts and with an assortment of purposes in mind. Indeed, the very fact that many qualitative researchers instil an element of quantitative data collection into their investigations underlines this point to a certain degree. Similar points can be made in relation to the connection between broad theories and methods. As pointed out in Chapter 2, Platt (1986) has strongly questioned the supposed link between functionalism and the survey. Similarly, while some writers have found an affinity between a Marxist perspective and qualitative research (e.g. Sharp and Green, 1975; Willis, 1977), others have preferred the methods of quantitative research for the empirical elucidation of concepts associated with this theoretical perspective (e.g. Wright and Perrone, 1977). Symbolic interactionism, while typically associated with participant observation (Rock, 1979), is not universally identified with qualitative research and an anti-positivist epistemology: M. H. Kuhn (1964) used the techniques and research strategies of quantitative research in his attempt to use symbolic interactionist notions; many studies conducted within this theoretical tradition make substantial use of standard survey techniques alongside participant observation; and there is even a questioning of whether G. H. Mead's (1934) writings lead in a direction which is antithetical to the application of the methods of the natural sciences (McPhail and Rexroat, 1979). The tendency to associate particular methods with particular epistemological positions is little more than a convention (which took root in the 1960s), but which has little to recommend it, either as a description of the research process or as a prescriptive view of how research ought to be done.

In comparison with the rather stark contrasts between quantitative and qualitative research which have permeated the pages thus far, the next chapter examines some of the ways in which the two traditions may be used in tandem. The epistemological version of the debate does not readily admit a blending of quantitative and qualitative research since the two traditions are deemed to represent highly contrasting views about how social reality should be studied. The technical version of the debate much more readily accommodates a marriage of the two since it acknowledges the respective strengths and weaknesses of the two approaches as methods of data collection. Many writers shuttle uneasily back and forth between the two ways of thinking about the two traditions. It is little wonder that confusion ensues when there is a lack of clarity about what quantitative and qualitative research are. In this context, the view of a leading writer on the ethnography of schooling is instructive:

> It is not surprising that some work called 'ethnography' is marked by obscurity of purpose, lax relationships between concepts and observation, indifferent or absent conceptual structure and theory, weak implementation of research method, confusion about whether there should be hypotheses and, if so, how they should be tested, confusion over whether quantitative methods can be relevant . . . and so forth. (Spindler, 1982, p. 2)

Precisely because many qualitative researchers have failed to sort out whether the style of research to which they adhere is an epistemological or a technical position, it is possible for such confusion to reign. However, when quantitative and qualitative research are jointly pursued, much more complete accounts of social reality can ensue, as many of the examples cited in the next chapter imply.

Notes

1 Symbolic interactionism, by contrast, is a theoretical position developed largely within the social sciences, but which has its roots in an epistemological position, namely, pragmatism.
2 Frequently, discussion in the literature of such issues takes the form of evaluating qualitative research in terms of its validity and reliability (e.g. LeCompte and Goetz, 1982). I have resisted such an approach in this book, because I feel that it imposes a cluster of standards upon qualitative research which to a large extent are more relevant to the quantitative tradition, within which such terms were originally developed.

6

Combining Quantitative and Qualitative Research

The rather partisan, either/or tenor of the debate about quantitative and qualitative research may appear somewhat bizarre to an outsider, for whom the obvious way forward is likely to be a fusion of the two approaches so that their respective strengths might be reaped. The technical version of the debate more readily allows this solution to be accommodated because it is much less wedded than the epistemological version to a view that the two traditions reflect antagonistic views about how the social sciences ought to be conducted. In this chapter, the focal concern will be the ways in which the methods associated with quantitative and qualitative research can be, and have been, combined. As noted in Chapter 3, there are examples of investigations carried out by investigators who locate their work largely within the tradition of qualitative research, but who have used survey procedures in tandem with participant observation (e.g. Woods, 1979; Ball, 1981). Such research will be employed as an example of the combination of quantitative and qualitative research, because the chief concern of the present chapter is with the *methods* with which each is associated.

The focus on methods of investigation should not lose sight of the significance of a distinction between quantitative and qualitative *data*. For example, some of the findings associated with an ethnographic study may be presented in a quantified form. In their research on the de-skilling of clerical work, Crompton and Jones (1988) collected much detailed qualitative information, in the form of verbatim reports, on the work of their respondents. In spite of considerable reservations about coding these data, they aggregated people's accounts of their work in terms of the amounts of control they were able to exercise in their work. Even among qualitative researchers who prefer to resist such temptations, the use of quasi-quantitative terms like 'many', 'frequently', 'some', and the like, is common (e.g. Gans, 1982, p. 408). Further, survey researchers provide the occasional verbatim quotation from an interview, or one or two case examples of respondents who exemplify a particular pattern. Sometimes, the reporting of qualitative data deriving from a survey can be quite considerable. In addition, researchers sometimes use a structured interview for the simultaneous collection of both quantitative and qualitative data. For example, Ford *et al.* (1982) employed such a structured interview schedule to investigate employers' recruitment practices. Quantitative data were collected on such topics as the frequency of use of particular methods of recruitment. The schedule also permitted qualitative data to be collected on employers' reasons for the use and non-use of particular recruitment channels. Such cases may be viewed as indicative of a slight limitation in discussing quantitative and qualitative research largely in terms of methods of data collection. However, there is little doubt that methods like surveys and participant observation are typically seen as sources of quantitative and qualitative data respectively, so that it is not proposed to challenge this convention but merely to alert the reader to the lack of a hard and fast distinction.

Even though the studies which will be cited in this chapter as examples of the fusion of quantitative and qualitative styles of research give considerable weight to both approaches, they rarely accord them equal or even nearly equal weight. Most researchers rely primarily on a method associated with one of the two research traditions, but buttress their findings with a method associated with the other tradition. However, the relative weight accorded to quantitative or qualitative research within a single study may shift over time. For example, Fuller (1984) sought to examine the variables which affect school children's perceptions of gender using a measurement device – the Bem Sex Role Inventory (BSRI) – as the core method, along with interviews. Although she perceived this strategy as the central strand in her research, she also chose to undertake some participant observation (although not as a teacher) in the school in which she was administering her instruments. In the end, the qualitative materials assumed far greater prominence in her PhD thesis. In particular, the inventory seemed to give a misleading picture of children's 'real' perceptions:

> Instead of being treated as an accurate reflection of how pupils saw themselves, the BSRI results are discussed in the thesis as an indicator of the extent to which pupils were aware of and subscribed to essentially American norms of masculinity and femininity. There was often a big discrepancy between pupils' awareness of what they were 'supposed' to think, feel and do as females or males and their self-descriptions as gendered people, a discrepancy which I was able to observe in their school life. (Fuller, 1984, p. 109)

This example also suggests that it is important to realize that the ways in which quantitative and qualitative research are fused may on occasions be unplanned outcomes. In most instances, investigators are likely to be aware of the uses of integrating methods of data collection and they organize their overall research strategy in this light, but, as Fuller's experience suggests, the precise uses and advantages of the strategy may well not be envisaged at the outset.

One Case or Many?

One of the contexts in which the marriage of methods frequently occurs is where the investigator is pursuing an examination of one fairly discrete social collectivity (or possibly two or three collectivities). Many of the example studies below will be drawn from the study of one school, one community, one religious sect, one police force, and so on. This style of research will be familiar, at least in part, from frequent recourse to such research in Chapters 3 and 4. Another context for an integrated research approach is possibly less familiar − the 'multisite/multimethod' study (Louis, 1982a). Such research entails the investigation of a large number of sites by a battery of quantitative and qualitative research techniques, and has gained some support, especially in the USA, as a strategy for examining policy innovations.

The study of parental involvement in Federal Educational Programs by Smith and Robbins (1982) is a case in point. The investigators carried out a questionnaire survey of a national sample of representatives of 1,155 schools and school districts to gather data on the amount, nature, causes, and effects of parental participation. In addition, fifty-seven local projects were selected from the survey sample for more intensive research. The fifty-seven cases were chosen to reflect a variety of characteristics, so that a good 'spread' of intensively studied sites was possible. Each site had its own separately recruited field researcher, each of whom was assigned a clutch of 'analysis packets' which were to act as guides for the topics and issues to be addressed. Three types of packet were designed: highly specific ones giving precise details including interview questions, general ones providing indications of the sorts of topics that should be covered in interviews, and exploratory packets which 'alerted the [field] researcher to explore the area further so that important issues could be identified' (Smith and Robbins, p. 49). Site co-ordinators each kept contact with four to eight researchers.

The end-product was an amalgam of interview transcripts, observational data, documentary evidence, and quantitative data. The investigators then sought to conduct cross-site analyses of the data and to integrate the fruits of their analysis with the survey findings.

This 'structured ethnography' (as Smith and Robbins call it) departs from conventional qualitative research in a number of ways. The need to investigate specific policy initiatives makes it much more problem-focused than conventional ethnography. The decision to study a large number of sites by an equally large force of field-workers means that a substantial degree of standardization had to be imposed in order to ensure that roughly the same issues could be addressed in a roughly comparable way. This approach contrasts sharply with the qualitative researcher's dislike of structured investigations. Also, the need to engender inferences across sites means that the data have to be 'reduced' to comparable categories and units, thereby losing some of the richness of texture with which qualitative investigations are associated. None the less, it exhibits some of ethnography's familiar virtues, such as the ability to observe behaviour and to examine a particular unit holistically and hence become aware of contextual nuances. In addition, some flexibility was instilled to allow local issues to surface.

Other examples of such research may be cited. Huberman and Crandall (1982), for example, discuss their study of the factors associated with the successful implementation of innovations in schools in the USA. This research combined a quantitative approach, in which 4,000 individuals responded to questionnaires in relation to 145 school districts, with a more intensive ethnographic study of a purposively selected sub-sample of twelve sites. The latter investigations entailed prolonged periods of participant observation and some interviewing by field investigators. What is striking about the multisite, multimethod approach is that it does not readily allow classification as either quantitative or qualitative research; also, these studies provide examples of methodological integration in a slightly unfamiliar framework, since there is a strong preoccupation with policy issues. Not all contributors to the qualitative research tradition are enthusiastic about such developments. Rist (1980) has observed that such research has arisen because of the greater preparedness of federal agencies in the USA to fund qualitative research. He suggests that the greater funding opportunities have enticed some applicants for research funds to flirt with methods which they dub 'ethnographic' but which are not genuine ethnographies. In particular, Rist contrasts the often brief forays into the field which multisite, multimethod studies entail with the lengthy involvement of 'genuine' ethnographers seeking to elucidate the systems they investigate in rich detail. He also objects to the ways in which research foci are decided in advance rather than allowed to emerge after prolonged immersion in the field. He refers to multisite research disparagingly as 'blitzkrieg ethnography' and finds it 'superficial and trite' in comparison with conventional ethnography.

Approaches to Blending Quantitative and Qualitative Research

The purpose of this section is to describe the ways in which quantitative and qualitative research have been combined in a number of studies. While reasonably comprehensive, this overview details only those instances with which the author is familiar. It should also be noted that some studies appear under more than one heading, reflecting the fact that the merger of the two styles of research may produce a number of pay-offs within a single investigation.

The Logic of 'Triangulation'

Webb *et al.* (1966) have suggested that social scientists are likely to exhibit greater confidence in their findings when these are derived from more than one method of investigation. Their focus was largely on the need, as they perceived it, for more than one research instrument to be used in the measurement of the main variables in a study, a strategy which was referred to as 'triangulation of measurement'. While this emphasis would seem to relate to the quantitative research tradition, many writers have stretched its potential meaning to embrace a wider range of concerns. Denzin (1970, p. 310), for example, treats triangulation as an approach in which 'multiple observers, theoretical perspectives, sources of data, and methodologies' are combined. By and large, researchers have viewed the main message of the idea of triangulation as entailing a need to employ more than one method of investigation and hence more than one type of data. Within this context, quantitative and qualitative research may be perceived as different ways of examining the same research problem. By combining the two, the researcher's claims for the validity of his or her conclusions are enhanced if they can be shown to provide mutual confirmation.

In his study of a grammar school, Lacey (1970) was primarily a participant observer, but supplemented this method with others for a variety of reasons, one of which was to confirm his observations. In a commentary on his research, Lacey (1976) describes how he gradually evolved a picture of the patterns of interaction. This image was derived from his observations and from discussions with one of the teachers. In order to check the patterns he was developing, he employed sociometric indicators:

> The analysis of the sociometric data was a completely new experience. I can still remember the excitement as one after another of my ideas about the patterns of relationships held up during the analysis. The conceptualization of the processes of differentiation and polarization grew out of the interplay between observation and analysis of the sociometric data. (Lacey, 1976, p. 60).

Another example of the use of quantitative and qualitative approaches within a strategy of mutual corroboration is Cook's (1984) study of the influence of parents' gender on the way they experience having a child who is dying of cancer. For the qualitative side of her investigation, Cook used a lengthy interview schedule which comprised a large number of open-ended questions. The data from these interviews were analysed, following Glaser and Strauss (1967), to detect underlying themes, and then submitted to the procedures associated with analytic induction to discern patterns which suggested that the adjustment responses of parents differed by gender. She also developed a scale of items to measure the problems encountered by parents during the child's illness. The scale was then correlated with the parent's gender. Together, the two sets of data revealed that 'women seem more pervasively steeped in the culture of the child's illness – a culture in which many men feel out of place and uncomfortable' (Cook, 1984, p. 89). As the author observes, this study is an example of the triangulation of methods whereby the two approaches corroborate each other (Cook and Fonow, 1986, p. 16).

In the ORACLE research referred to in Chapter 3, structured observation, in the form of coding schedules dealing with patterns of interaction in schools, was combined with ethnographic research in classrooms by hired observers during one phase of the investigation, namely the examination of the transfer of pupils between schools or classes (Galton and Delamont, 1985; Galton and Willcocks, 1983). However, as if often the case with studies in which quantitative and qualitative research are combined, one method of data collection tended to be accorded greater prominence than the other. In the ORACLE case, the quantitative data collection through systematic observation was the hub, while the ethnographic research put 'flesh on the bones' (Galton and Delamont, 1985, p. 174) of the statistical findings. The qualitative research largely supported the main findings deriving from the systematic observation, e.g. the impact of different subjects on the ease with which transfer was dealt with by pupils. However, the ethnographic work was able to add to the findings because observers using this approach picked up certain features which were not included in the systematic observation schedules. For example, all ethnographic observers noted incidents of sex stereotyping in classrooms which the coding schedules had not been designed to highlight.

In these examples, the combination of quantitative and qualitative research techniques provide broadly consistent data. It is not surprising that this is not always the case. One notable example of incongruent findings is Shapiro's (1973) evaluation of a

Follow Through (FT) programme in the USA. Such programmes entail

> a comprehensive approach to the education of young children which has multiple goals for both children and teachers. It is expected that teachers will embrace new ways of teaching . . . [FT programmes] also share a stake in maintaining flexibility in the teaching–learning process, a dislike of 'packaging', a commitment to a basic philosophy of education rather than to a set of educational prescriptions. (Shapiro, 1973, p. 527)

Shapiro compared children in three schools which were experiencing FT programme with three which were not. She employed quantitative indicators of performance and classroom observations. Her observational data suggested that in FT classrooms 'the quality of the relationships between teacher and children and among the children, the variety and interest of the curriculum, and the general atmosphere of the classroom were notably different' (pp. 528–9). Her quantitative test measures were designed to tap feelings about the self, school and learning and aspects of cognitive functioning. However, she failed to discern any differences between the two groups of schools in terms of the quantitative indicators.

What is particularly interesting about this example is that the question of which account is correct is not addressed. Shapiro points to a number of research design problems which may have contributed to the failure of the quantitative study (e.g. failure to control all variables which distinguished the FT and non-FT schools), but it is apparent that the observational study is deemed to provide the accurate portrayal. Similarly, Patton, a prominent advocate of a qualitative approach to evaluation research, has commented that Shapiro's 'quantitative methodological procedures determined the research results' (Patton, 1975, p. 15). How do we know? What are the rules of inference which permit a clear statement which allows one to plump for one version rather than another? The answers to such critical questions are not addressed; instead, the qualitative research is assumed to be correct. A better solution would be to use the incongruent findings as a springboard for the investigation of the reasons for such contrasting findings. After all, since quantitative and qualitative research undertaken in the same investigation may provide mutually reinforcing results (as in the three examples cited above), the possibility of discrepant findings also exists. When there is evidence of a clash, further exploration of the issue would seem warranted. For example, in their multisite, multimethod study of educational innovations, Huberman and Crandall (1982) found that two-thirds of the way through the collection of their ethnographic data, their survey data became available. The two sets of data were cross-checked and discrepancies were noted and followed up. Trend (1978) reports a study of the management issues associated with a scheme to provide direct cash allowance payments to assist low-income families to obtain housing on the open market. Both quantitative and qualitative data were collected. In one of the regions in which the evaluations were taking place a substantial clash was found between the two sets of findings. Whereas the qualitative findings tended to suggest managerial incompetence and a failure to attract the appropriate clientele (and hence to meet programme objectives), the survey data strongly implied that the site was performing well relative to others in terms of the scheme's aims. On further probing, Trend found that the clash between the two sets of data could be attributed to the failure of the quantitative findings to reflect the different ethnic characteristics of the three areas which made up the site in question, this being an interesting discovery in its own right. Thus, discrepancies between the findings deriving from research in which quantitative and qualitative research are combined are not in the least unusual. Further, it is in the spirit of the idea of triangulation that inconsistent results may emerge; it is not in its spirit that one should simply opt for one set of findings rather than another. Discrepancies may also prompt the researcher to probe certain issues in greater depth, which may lead to fruitful areas of inquiry in their own right.

Qualitative Research Facilitates Quantitative Research

There are a number of ways in which qualitative research can act as a precursor to the formulation of problems and the development of instruments for quantitative research. One of the most obvious senses in which this may occur has been encountered previously in this book: qualitative research may act as a source of hunches or hypotheses to be tested by quantitative research. Sieber (1973) observes that many survey researchers have an intensive knowledge of a locale, organization, or whatever, which informs the formulation of problems to be investigated. For example, Lipset's personal knowledge of the International Typographical Union, through his father's membership, influenced some aspects of the social survey component of his case study of this organization (Lipset, 1964). In other instances, the use of a field-work phase which precedes the collection of survey data may be more systematic. Sieber cites the case of Stinchcombe's (1964) study of high school rebellion in which a period of six months was spent conducting 'anthropological observation'. This phase generated a number of hypotheses, which could be tested by a conventional survey approach. Sieber argues that periods of intensive qualitative research prior to conducting a survey rarely occurs. What probably occurs more frequently is that an ethnographic study produces hypotheses which are tested by a survey researcher on another occasion.

Qualitative research may also facilitate the construction of scales and indices for quantitative research. Sieber (1973) notes the case of Carlin's (1966) investigation of the ethical behaviour of lawyers which was preceded by intensive interviews with twelve lawyers. Respondents were asked questions relating to professional ethics and requested to stipulate unethical practices. From the answers to these questions, Carlin was able to develop hypothetical situations which offered the potential for unethical conduct. These formed an index which facilitated the scoring of respondents in question-naires. Similarly, in her study of a programme for the development and implementation of innovations in schools, Louis (1982b) used a multimethod, multisite approach. This strategy served her well in a number of ways, but in the development of an indicator of suc-cess for each site it proved particularly helpful. The researchers discussed a potential definition of success with staff and then developed an indicator (based on these discussions) from data deriving from surveys of principals and teachers. Ninety sites were then classified in terms of this indicator. Previously collected qualitative data were then re-examined in order to discern whether the classification of each site was consistent with these data.

The presence of qualitative data may greatly assist the analysis of quantitative data. In their multisite, multimethod study of parental involvement in Federal Educational Programs, Smith and Robbins (1982) found that their ethnographic data enhanced their ability to construct path analyses of their survey data. In view of the problem (noted in Chapter 2) that path analysis is capable of sustaining a number of logical models of the relationships between variables, the ability to construct models deriving from intensive knowledge of the domain in which the investigation has taken place is a considerable benefit.

A different view of the ways in which qualitative and quan-titative findings may interrelate is provided by Whyte (1976) in the context of team research he had been directing on Peruvian villages. One of the chief areas of interest was the characterization of the villages in terms of the contrast between consensus or con-flict − the focus of the clash between Lewis and Redfield which was referred to in Chapter 4. Whyte was reading a report by one of his researchers of the village of Mito and noted with surprise that the village was described as exhibiting a low level of both conflict *and* co-operation. This finding was based on ethnographic field observations. Whyte realized that he was surprised because writers like Lewis and Redfield had tended to view conflict and co-operation as opposite ends of a continuum. He reformulated his thinking on this issue in such a way that conflict and co-operation were visualized as orthogonal variables, i.e. separate, uncorrelated continua. He was then able to validate his emerging framework with reference to survey data he had collected on a number of villages, which confirmed that conflict and co-operation were separate but cross-cutting dimensions.

As Whyte points out, this finding may go some of the way towards explaining the clash between Redfield's (1930) and Lewis's (1951) accounts of Tepoztlán. However, he is also at great pains to point out that his example should not be used simply as an instance of qualitative research providing hypotheses for empirical confirmation by quantitative research. For example, having noted the potential validity of his reconceptualization of conflict and co-operation, Whyte examined each village in the context of each of two waves of survey data collection (in 1964 and 1969) which had addressed these variables. He found that one village had moved markedly from high co-operation/low conflict to a considerably lower level of co-operation coupled with a high level of conflict. In order to understand this shift better, he carried out further anthropological investigations. Whyte's (1976, p. 216) strategy of 'weaving back and forth among methods' is not only much less rigid than the view that the soft findings of qualitative research have to be confirmed by the hard data of a quantitative approach, but is also a view which entails a much more positive role for the former.

Quantitative Research Facilitates Qualitative Research

Examples of investigations in which quantitative research precedes and provides an aid to the collection of qualitative data are less numerous than the preceding category. In a sense, Whyte's experience could be viewed as relevant to the present section, since his examination of the survey data led him to conduct further ethnographic investigation of the village whose conflict–co-operation profile had shifted. Indeed, one of the ways in which quantitative research may facilitate qualitative research is in the judicious selection of cases for further study. Kahl (1953) was interested in the reasons why some working class school boys in the USA aspire to 'better' occupations, while others do not. Having noted the differential college and occupational aspirations of working class boys from a questionnaire survey of nearly 4,000 boys, he selected a sub-sample of twenty-four of comparable IQ – twelve of whom planned to go to college and twelve of whom did not.

These two groups of boys (as well as their parents) were then subjected to intensive interviewing in order to tease out the differences in orientation between them.

In their research on juvenile delinquency in the UK, Reicher and Emler (1986) asked six hundred 12 to 15-year-olds to complete questionnaire measures of self-reported delinquency and social attitudes. This exercise allowed the researchers to relate delinquency to the respondent's perceptions of his or her relationship to a number of different forms of institutional authority. It also enabled them to select groups of young people who differed sharply in their degree of involvement in delinquency. One hundred and fifty of the original sample were then interviewed in order to provide data on young people's views of delinquency. These interviews formed the basis for an intensive interview study of sixty young people (with contrasting levels of involvement in delinquent activities). As with Kahl's research, the initial quantitative research allows a 'mapping' of the issue to be addressed and also provides the basis for the selection of comparison groups for in-depth qualitative interviewing.

Quantitative and Qualitative Research are Combined in Order to Produce a General Picture

One of the contexts in which quantitative and qualitative research are most frequently united is where an ethnographer carries out a survey in order to fill some gaps in his or her knowledge of a community, group, organization, or whatever, because the gaps cannot be readily filled by a reliance on participant observation or unstructured interviewing alone. Such gaps may occur for a variety of reasons, such as the inaccessibility either of particular people or of particular situations.

In his study of a new suburban community in the USA (known as a Levittown, after the name of the builders), Gans (1967) made much greater use of questionnaires and formal interviewing (although participant observation was the dominant method) than in his earlier ethnographic research on a working class area in Boston (Gans, 1962). Gans was interested in the ways in which a new community comes about and in the nature and effects of suburban life. Consequently, a major component of his proposed investigation entailed attention to people's aspirations, expectations and reasons for moving prior to their departure from the city to suburbia. In addition, a follow-up was required to examine changes in orientations after moving into suburbia and the consequences of suburban living for the individual. These are highly specific questions which required access to people prior to their arrival and systematic information on changes in their views over time. Gans used a postal questionnaire which was sent to 3,100 individuals who were on the point of moving to the Levittown. The data deriving from this exercise provided Gans with information about respondents' reasons for moving. In addition, structured interviews were carried out with a small sample of Levittowners to find out about their hopes and expectations before moving in, and again two years later to determine the changes that had occurred for them. This information provided data on feelings of loneliness and boredom and also allowed Gans to establish changes in attitudes and behaviour over the two-year period. Interestingly, Gans did not himself conduct these interviews (which were carried out by graduate students) because he felt that his participant observation cast him in the role of resident, so that he could less readily ask personal questions. These quantitative data were combined with Gans's participant observation in the community to provide a rounded portrayal of people's experiences of suburban living.

A contrasting context is provided by Barker's (1984) investigation of the processes by which one becomes a member of the Unification Church, i.e. a Moonie. Her views about how this issue ought to be tackled led her to view her research as requiring attention to a number of different levels of analysis:

> It was obvious that no one method would be sufficient to obtain all the information that I would need . . . In order to deal with [the varied perspectives within and outside the movement of the church and its leaders] I needed to speak to outsiders as well as insiders. [In addition,] I needed information about individual Moonies, their backgrounds, their hopes, values and general perspectives on life both inside and outside the movement. I also needed to observe them 'at work' as they interacted with other people in order to see how they were influenced by, and would themselves influence, others on a day-to-day basis. Finally, I needed to see how the movement as a whole was organized and how it influenced the day-to-day actions and interactions of its members. (Barker, 1984, p. 17)

In line with her commitment to an empathetic investigation of becoming a Moonie (p. 20), Barker relied a great deal on in-depth interviewing and participant observation. She conducted thirty intensive interviews in which a prepared schedule was used, although a good deal of flexibility was possible. Her participant observation entailed living in various centres and attending seminars or workshops. She visited many centres in the USA and Scandinavia, although the bulk of her research was centred in the UK. Through her participant observation she came into contact with a great many Moonies and their parents. In addition, she conducted a number of questionnaire surveys, which were administered to various groups at different times in diverse places. Her rationale for their use was that she had formulated a number of 'hypotheses' about connections between various 'variables' which she felt warranted testing (p. 26). In addition, informants and documents were used prodigiously in order to capture an overall view. Thus the use of quantitative methods allowed Barker access to connections which a sole reliance on qualitative techniques would not readily permit, such as social class backgrounds and religious commitments and experiences before joining the movement. Further, some of the issues which she wanted to examine (which are referred to in the extended quotation above) were more obviously suited to survey instruments. For example, much of her data on Moonies' general perspectives and their feelings before joining the movement stem from her survey investigations. Her qualitative investigations provided her with information about how Moonies view the world and what being a Moonie means to them.

Jenkins (1983) used structured interview schedules in his ethnographic study of a working class estate in Belfast. He took samples of the three groupings he had identified – 'lads', 'citizens' and 'ordinary kids' – and showed how the three life-styles were related to attitudes to school, truancy, and social class background. He used his understanding of the area and the people to facilitate an interpretation of the relationships and patterns revealed by his survey data (p. 54). Jenkins's participant observation allowed him to establish the three broad categorical groupings of the young men, but the interviews allowed much finer distinctions to be made between them (e.g. their attitudes to the area in which they lived).[1] The interviews also allowed him access to matters which were rarely publicly discussed, or which were not discussed very honestly in a public context. Jenkins's *rapport* with the 'citizens' was not as strong as with the other two groups (because of his local identification with the latter), so that the interviews constituted a vital source of comparative data. Further, not all situations were open to him, so that the interviews allowed him to fill some of the gaps in his knowledge regarding aspects of these situations. The problem of inaccessibility was exacerbated by the scale of the area in which the research was being conducted, since he could not be available in all quarters at all times. Again, the interviews were able to provide information on missed events. Finally, past events, such as job histories and criminal records, could only be established by structured interviews. Thus the interviews allowed leverage on matters which were not amenable to participant observation.

In each of these instances the researcher is concerned to come to as full an account of his or her focus of interest as possible. The resort to quantitative methods of data collection in predominantly qualitative studies occurs in large part because of the researcher's calculation that a reliance on qualitative methods will not allow all the relevant issues to be fully addressed. The survey data sit side-by-side with the ethnographic data as indications of the ways in which subjects think and feel. The qualitative research in each case provides rich data about the world-views and interpretations of Levittowners, Moonies and Belfast youth, but additional information is deemed to be necessary to provide a complete picture. In much the same way that Gans (1967, table 7) documents the changes in Levittowners' attitudes, Barker (1984, tables 12–15) portrays various shifts in Moonies' perceptions of how they, their lives, and their ideals have changed, while Jenkins (1983, tables 6.6 and 6.7) details such 'unobservables' as the methods of obtaining jobs used by each of the three groups of boys and their reasons for leaving jobs. In each case, the researcher has judged the establishment of various patterns to be inaccessible through qualitative research and has made a technical decision to augment the investigation with quantitative methods in order to gain access to the areas and issues that cannot otherwise be reached so that a complete account could be provided.

Structure and Process
As suggested in Table 5.1, qualitative research presents a processual view of social life, whereas quantitative research provides a static account. The attribution 'static' may be taken to have a negative connotation, but this need not be so. By adopting a static view, much quantitative research can provide an account of the regularities, and hence patterns of structure, which are a feature of social life. A division of labour is suggested here in that quantitative research may be conceived of as a means of establishing the structural element in social life, qualitative research the processual. This view can be seen as an elaboration of the previous theme in which the two traditions were depicted as being integrated to present a general picture.

The use made of sociometric instruments in school ethnographies (as in the case of Lacey's study of a grammar school which was cited above) exemplifies this division of labour. Ball used such techniques in his ethnographic study of a comprehensive school because of their appropriateness to the examination of

> the stability of the social structures over time. This seems to suggest that, rather than being the product of momentary whim or the variations in data-collection procedures, the choices made by

the pupils in the sociometric questionnaires accurately reflect the structure of friendship patterns in the form. (Ball, 1981, pp. 53–4)

Ball was able to show how friendship patterns and cliques related to social class background, attitudes to school, and academic performance. His ethnographic research served to provide a portrayal of the processes which link these variables, and in particular how they conspire to precipitate the underachievement of working class pupils.

Another example of the integration of the two research traditions in this section is a study of 'omega children', that is, 'child participants in kindergarten classroom interactions who have very low social standing in the dominance hierarchy of the group' (Garnica, 1981, p. 230). In one part of her study, Garnica obtained measurements of the verbal behaviour of six omega children and a comparison group of six randomly chosen children (but matched for sex) from the same class. The data were three 20-minute speech sequences for each child. Garnica established some sharp quantitative differences between the two groups; for example, omega children had a much smaller number of conversations initiated by another child towards them and fewer conversational partners. As Garnica (1981, p. 242) notes, although her quantitative indicators provide useful information about patterns of interaction, they say 'little about how these patterns are actually carried out'. Garnica then presents transcripts of verbal interaction which demonstrate how the omega child's inferiority is expressed and reinforced in verbal interaction.

A final example to be cited is a study of teachers' expectations of their pupils' performance by Blease and Bryman (1986). Using a quantitative procedure – based on the personal construct approach developed by Kelly (1955) – the teachers' ways of thinking about each of their pupils, and how these perspectives related to the rank ordering of the pupils in each class, were gleaned. Thus the investigators were able to establish the connection between the ability ranking of the pupils and teachers' expectations about the pupils. In addition, a high degree of concordance was found in the rankings and rating criteria used by the six teachers who taught the class which was the focus of the research. Transcripts drawn from the observation of lessons were then used to show how these expectations are communicated. One way in which this occurs is through public comparisons between children. For example, in one Physical Education lesson, John Perry (rank order 24) is compared with Dean Berwick (rank order 2). The teacher, Miss Shiels, asks John Perry to help her to demonstrate how to dribble a basketball.

He has to count with his fingers the number of times she bounces the ball but experiences some difficulty:

> *Miss Shiels*: . . . Now there's no fingers there (bounce). (Giggles from class who are sitting around watching)
> There's still five fingers there, (bounce) still five (bounce). There's four (bounce), still four (bounce), three, yes good (bounce) two, yes good, (bounce) one. (She laughs). Is he always like this?
> *The class in chorus*: Yes. (laughter)
> *Miss Shiels*: Remind me to pick Dean Berwick next time, he usually manages to do what I ask! (Blease and Bryman, 1986, p. 165)

Thus the researchers are able to establish the ability structure of the class and its connection with teachers' ways of thinking about each pupil, and to demonstrate the processes by which these aspects of the classroom are communicated.

Quantitative research can establish regularities in social life while qualitative evidence can allow the processes which link the variables identified to be revealed. Qualitative research *may* be able to establish the structural features of social life in many instances, but the use of questionnaires or structured observation can be a more efficient way of forging connections and gleaning underlying patterns, which might take an age to produce when relying solely on ethnographic methods.

Researchers' and Subjects' Perspectives

One facet of the distinction between quantitative and qualitative research is that the former is orientated to the specific concerns of the investigator and the latter to subjects' perspectives. In Table 5.1, the distinction between outsider and insider perspectives is an expression of this point. One possible role for the integration of quantitative research would be the combination of insider and outsider perspectives within a single project.

Studies of debtors and debt actions in Scotland carried out for the Scottish Law Commission illustrate this possibility. One of the studies (Gregory and Monk, 1981) used a structured interview survey of over 1,200 people in 1978 who had been identified as having had court action taken against them for the recovery of debt. The interviews covered a variety of topics such as: details of the debt and the court action, reasons for the debt, respondents' understandings of the procedures, and so on. Much of the quantitative data were cross-tabulated, so that, for example, various aspects of debt could be linked to household circumstances.

This study contains the main attributes of quantitative research in that the focus derived exclusively from the researchers' (or more accurately the Scottish Law Commission's) concerns. A linked study by Adler and Wozniak (1981) adopted a different tack by conducting lengthy in-depth interviews with a hundred default debtors. Some of the resulting data were quantified, but a large proportion of the information deriving from the interviews was presented in the form of verbatim transcripts, from which numerous generalizations about the experience of debt were forged. The utility of nesting a qualitative study which seeks to elicit subjects' perspectives within a quantitative investigation is particularly striking in connection with this topic of inquiry. Debtors are often regarded as feckless or inadequate people, even as 'scroungers', so that such deprecating views could be contrasted with the considerable variety in the causes and experiences of debt from debtors' perspectives. An approach such as that associated with the Scottish Law Commission's research allows a fruitful combination of the Commission's own focal areas of interest with subjects' interpretations of their circumstances.

The Problem of Generality
A problem that is sometimes identified in qualitative research is that it fails to provide a sense of the typicality or generality of the events described. The tendency to rely on illustrative or anecdotal methods of presenting qualitative data adds to this unease. As Silverman (1985, p. 140) has put it, 'The critical reader is forced to ponder whether the researcher has selected only those fragments of data which support his argument.' Silverman argues that the use of 'simple counting techniques' allows the qualitative researcher to survey the bulk of his or her data and to provide the reader with an overall impression of those data. Further, Silverman argues that the exercise may greatly benefit qualitative researchers themselves in that they may come to revise their understandings of their data when 'simple counting' reveals that their impressions were mistaken.

On the face of it, the advocacy of counting by a writer like Silverman who once inveighed against the corrupting influence of positivism and the quantitative approach in sociology (Silverman, 1972) is surprising. However, what he is encouraging 'is to count the countable preferably in terms of the categories actually used by the participants' (Silverman, 1985, p. 140). In other words, Silverman is maintaining his distate for the procedures associated with operationalism, but suggests that counting in terms of natural categories which are consistent with people's own understandings is not only acceptable but also desirable in order to provide complete versions of social reality. By relying exclusively on illustrations of their data, qualitative researchers, in Silverman's view, lose large amounts of data.

In Silverman's (1984) study of oncology clinics, counting procedures were adopted 'to demonstrate that the qualitative analysis was reasonably representative of the whole' (Silverman, 1985, p. 143). The main focus of interest derived from the suggestion by Strong (1977) that consultations within the National Health Service are somewhat standardized and impersonal, whereas private consultations are more particularistic and personalized affairs. Silverman treated this suggestion as a hypothesis. He compared consultations in a private oncology clinic with consultations in two NHS oncology clinics in order to flesh out the differences between the two types of clinic in terms of the nature of the services each provides. Brief transcripts of doctor–patient transactions (at which Silverman was an observer) and also quantitative comparisons of various indicators of interaction are used as evidence. Silverman's approach is to use the quantitative contrasts between private and NHS clinics as the starting point for various themes and to expand on them with the transcripts. For example, he shows the greater participation of patients in private consultations based on 'crude counts of the numbers of questions and unelicited statements made by patients or those accompanying them' (Silverman, 1984, p. 199), but goes on to say 'although these figures do tell part of the story, we must rely on qualitative data to obtain a broader picture of patient behaviour' (p. 200). The latter data demonstrate, for example, that in private clinics there is a greater initiation of the patient's own care and greater control of both physical space and the agenda by the patient. As an example of Silverman's qualitative analysis of the data − relating to the patient's control of the agenda − the following passage serves well:

1   *Mrs. B*: Now where do we go from here?
2   *Dr.*:   May I ask you something?
3   (after a further 10 minutes)
    Mrs. B: (standing up) Thank you for your kind attention . . .
Viewed in comparison with the NHS consultations, this extract is remarkable in three ways: (1) The patient herself raised the question of the agenda; (2) The doctor has to ask permission to ask a question . . .; (3) the patient signals the end of the consultation by standing up.

Nonetheless, the consultation only depicts, in a slightly more exaggerated form, the *rule* at the private clinic. (Silverman, 1984, p. 201)

Thus Silverman emphasized mainly the qualitative data in his research, employing his quantitative information as a means of establishing the generality of his observations. His suggestion that the quantitative data should reflect subjects' own ways of understanding the world is especially interesting in that this view is one way in which the plea to integrate quantitative and qualitative research is consistent with the epistemological version of the debate about the two research traditions. This position allows the researcher to collect quantitative data in terms of categories which are not alien to those to whom the data are supposed to refer. This standpoint means that the researcher must have acquired some familiarity with the setting before the collection of quantitative data can get under way, since some understanding of subjects' concepts and categories would be a prerequisite.

Qualitative Research May Facilitate the Interpretation of Relationships between Variables

The researcher who establishes a correlation between two variables, or who believes that a causal connection has been discerned, is faced with the problem of interpreting the relationship – how does it come about? Within the framework of quantitative research, the method of elaboration through the search for intervening variables is one way forward (Rosenberg, 1968). Thus, if it is found that there is a connection between race and occupational status, the question 'why?' may lead to the suggestion that education is an intervening variable. Because blacks are more likely to receive a poorer education than whites, they are less likely to be able to attain higher status jobs. However, the 'why?' question can then be levelled at the connection between race and education, and between education and occupational status. Of course, further intervening variables may then be introduced (if the data have been collected).

An alternative procedure may be to combine qualitative research to provide an understanding of the processes and mechanisms which 'produce' statistical relationships. In his study of working class boys in the USA, Kahl (1953) employed intensive interviews to establish the reasons for the different patterns of aspiration which had been established in a survey. For example, Kahl documents the influence of a boy's family on his attitudes to school and careers. In particular, Kahl shows how a positive regard for school and its relevance for a good career could largely be attributed to their positive evaluation by parents.

In her research on a girls' public school, Delamont (1976) used the Flanders Interaction Analysis Categories (FIAC) scheme to provide quantitative indicators of patterns of interaction in school classrooms. The FIAC approach is one of a number of methods of systematic observation which have been developed for research in classrooms and which counts incidents in terms of pre-specified categories. Not surprisingly, the teachers differed quite substantially in terms of these quantitative indicators, but, as Delamont found, the reasons for the observed differences could not readily be discerned from FIAC data. However, she was able to deploy data collected by 'anthropological' observation and interviews as a means of interpreting the quantitative information. In Delamont (1976) she concentrates on two pairs of teachers: two Latin teachers who were similar to each other 'in the proportions of acceptance in their reactions to pupil-talk and in the low proportions of pupil initiated speech they receive, but very different in the proportion of questioning to lecturing in their speech' (p. 108); and two science teachers who were similar to each other in terms of the FIAC categories, but considerably different from all the other science teachers. In the case of the two Latin teachers, the transcripts of lessons and of interviews with pupils reveal that the difference between the two teachers is a product of their dissimilar philosophies of teaching their subject and differences in personal demeanour:

> The high ratio of questioning to lecturing which characterizes Miss Odyssey is closely related to her discursive, idiomatic 'angle' on her subject . . . and to her marginality and undefined self-presentation. The low proportion of questioning which characterizes Miss Iliad's teaching is . . . due to her emphasis on factual accuracy and 'drill and practice' and her stable, well-defined self-presentation. (Delamont, 1976, pp. 117–18)

Similarly, the differences between the two science teachers and their colleagues in this subject were also largely attributed to different schools of thought about how science ought to be put across. Whereas their colleagues preferred a pre-structured approach, the two focal science teachers 'believe in less interference in the discovery process, hide their structuring and rely on informal, pupil initiated interaction to emphasize points' (p. 127).

A further context in which qualitative research may facilitate an interpretation of quantitative findings is suggested by an investigation by Fielding and Fielding (1986) of the training and occupational socialization of the police. This study comprised both quantitative research (in the form of a number of different questionnaires and structured interviews administered at different points during the duration of the project) and qualitative research (observation of training sessions and unstructured interviews). Fielding and Fielding came across an apparently paradoxical finding, deriving from one of their questionnaire studies, in that recruits were considerably more likely to give a racist response to a question on whether coloured immigration to Britain ought to be curtailed than when they were asked about whether the police should seek to recruit coloured people. This apparent anomaly was resolved when some of the data deriving from intensive interviews were examined. The answers revealed intensely racist remarks and views about coloured immigration co-existing with views about the strategy of policing in a multi-racial society.

In these examples, the recourse to qualitative research allows the investigator to flesh out the meaning of findings established through quantitative methods. This approach can be viewed as a route by which findings which are adequate at the levels of both cause and meaning – to use Weber's (1947) terminology – may be established, and as such contrasts with Marsh's (1982) reliance on the social survey alone as a means of generating data which meet both of these criteria. Thus, while Marsh seeks to develop a framework within which findings which are adequate at the levels of both cause and meaning can be generated by the survey alone, the research reported in this section points to the advantages of conjoining quantitative and qualitative research in order to achieve much the same end.

The Relationship between 'Macro' and 'Micro' Levels

It is very tempting to view qualitative research as concerned with, and best suited to, the investigation of the micro level of social life. Many of the classic ethnographic studies which have been referred to in this volume concentrated on the elucidation of social behaviour and culture in relatively small groups. Quantitative research, by contrast, may be depicted as relevant to the establishment of findings at the larger scale, macro level. A number of writers have drawn attention to the tendency for the investigation of different levels of analysis to be associated with particular methods and research strategies (e.g. Cicourel, 1981). The relationship is by no means perfect. Quantitative research is often used for the study of micro level phenomena, as in the employment of the FIAC approach for the examination of patterns of interaction in schools. Further, the findings generated by much experimental research in social psychology rarely rise above the micro level.

Qualitative researchers on occasions seek to move from the study of apparently small scale phenomena to the macro level. In the field of the sociology of education, the intrusion of Marxist ideas into school ethnographies has been especially responsible for the injection of a sense of the macro level, as Hammersley (1984) and A. Hargreaves (1985) have recognized. One example of such an approach is an ethnographic study of a school by Sharp and Green

(1975), which exhibits a clear concern to elaborate the inter-relationships between the classroom and the wider social structure via Marxist concepts. For example, one of the authors' main concerns was 'to locate . . . the teachers' classroom practice in the context of the wider context of extra classroom relationships' (p. 176), which entailed, *inter alia*, attention being paid to the constraints on teachers. Their concern with macro level phenomena is even more apparent when they write:

> Thus, whilst the teachers display a moral concern that every child matters, in practice there is a subtle process of sponsorship developing where opportunity is being offered to some and closed off to others. Social stratification is emerging.
>
> We have tried to show how these practices are a function of the constraints both ideological and material which influence the practice of the individual teacher. Far from the stratification system being a mere product of interaction patterns at the micro level, we have suggested that such interactions are socially structured by the wide context of which they are a part and whose major features they reflect and in turn reproduce. (Sharp and Green, 1975, pp. 218–19)

Such research has not found favour with many qualitative researchers, who display the familiar concern that too many of the conclusions are insufficiently grounded in the data which are collected (e.g. D. H. Hargreaves, 1978; West, 1984). Thus it is suggested that the proffered linkages between the observation of classroom life and the macro, social structural level are not adequately demonstrated. This distaste for Marxist ethnography is indicative of the unease among many qualitative researchers with theoretically inspired investigations which may depart excessively from participants' own perspectives. Further, it is also indicative of the empiricist streak in much ethnography in that part of the unease is produced by the apparent lack of a definitive demonstration of the posited linkages between macro and micro levels.[2]

One approach to the bridging of the two levels of analysis is through a combination of quantitative and qualitative research. Such an approach has been suggested by Duster (1981), who uses the metaphor of a ladder to show how the distance between macro and micro levels of analysis might be bridged. The metaphor draws attention to the need for 'rungs' which allow better movement between the two levels, and hence facilitate their integration. Duster outlines a model for the investigation of screening for inherited disorders, such as Sickle Cell and Tay-Sachs diseases, which are known to be associated with certain ethnic groups. Four chief levels are addressed: the *step to macro analysis* which entails attention to the formulation of laws relating to screening and the associated lobbying by interested parties; an *intermediate* rung which relates to the operation of relevant institutions, such as federal and state agencies and local hospitals; two *micro observational levels*, one of which entails the doctor (as representative of state and medical interests) and patients (as representatives of the community), and the other embracing family and community (as routes to an appreciation of the acceptability of screening); and finally the grounding of the other levels in *history and context*, whereby the researcher attends to the history and technology of screening and the examination of quantitative data showing which sections of the population are at greatest risk.

Duster is not entirely clear in his explication regarding the connection between levels and methods of data collection. However, he indicates that the micro observational level implies the collection of ethnographic data in clinics and communities in order to gauge patterns of response to screening, as well as case studies of families with members who have a relevant disease. By contrast, he suggests that the history and context level requires an examination of historical records and oral history materials, as well as demographic analyses of migration, employment, and the like. One might imagine that the intermediate rung would entail the collection of quantitative data which may allow different agency responses to various ethnic groups and diseases to be investigated, while also collecting ethnographic case study data on the operation of specific agencies.

Although he is highly programmatic and somewhat unclear about the nature of the fit between levels and methods, Duster provides an interesting model of how the macro–micro gap may be bridged and how the integration of quantitative and qualitative research may be a necessary component of such an exercise.[3] The idea of the ladder does not rely on the leaps between levels which seem to have disconcerted some commentators on the Marxist approach to educational ethnography.

Stages in the Research Process
Quantitative and qualitative research may be relevant at different stages in the research process. A case study by Gross, Giacquinta and Bernstein (1971) of an organizational innovation in a school in the USA illustrates this possibility well. The investigators had formulated a number of hunches about the factors which influence the degree to which a major innovation is implemented by an organization, even when there appears to be little resistance to change among its members. They were then presented with the opportunity

of carrying out an apposite case study in an inner city elementary school (referred to as Cambire in the study). The educational innovation was a new understanding of the teacher's role, called 'the catalytic role model', and was conceived as a means of mitigating the poor motivation and achievement of working class children.

Gross *et al.* broke down the research process into three phases. In the first phase, they were concerned to come to an understanding of the culture and ethos of the school. While some structured interviewing took place with teachers, the bulk of the data collection during this phase was more in keeping with the unstructured approach associated with qualitative research. Unstructured interviews were carried out with teachers and 'subject-matter specialists' to glean an understanding of perceptions of Cambire and its climate and social structure. Informal conversations and informal observation of classrooms were also used as sources of data during this phase. The second phase was to embrace the period in which the innovation was implemented. Informal observations and interviews were focused increasingly on the innovation, revealing somewhat greater variation in enthusiasm for, and knowledge about, the innovation than had originally been anticipated. However, during this phase the emphasis in the data collection methods shifted towards the more structured approach of quantitative research. Formal interview schedules were prepared 'to secure from the teachers their perceptions about the events that transpired over a five-month period in connection with the innovation, whether their feelings and perceptions about it had changed during this period, and, if they had, why they had changed' (Gross, Giacquinta and Bernstein, p. 57). In the final phase, the use of a structured observation schedule was the chief method of data collection. This schedule covered such topics as whether the teacher encouraged pupils to choose their own activities, whether pupils were allowed to decide for themselves to work alone or with other pupils, whether they were allowed to move freely about the room, and the like. In addition, teachers filled in questionnaires on background, career aspirations, and job satisfaction, as well as a personality inventory.

Thus the initial phase, in which qualitative research predominated, allowed the investigators to discern a positive and receptive climate for the innovation, although they also noted that the curriculum was largely traditional in nature. The second and third phases revealed that some six months after the innovation should have been implemented, teachers were still using traditional methods of instruction and indeed were doing little to introduce the innovation's apparent directives into their teaching. The structured observation played a major role in drawing this conclusion. Gross *et al.* point to a number of factors which contributed to the failure of the innovation to be introduced. For example, the early qualitative research revealed that the teachers were unclear about the nature and implications of the innovation. Further, the more focused informal interviews and observations associated with the second phase strongly suggested that resistance to change built up *during* the period that the innovation was to be introduced, i.e. resistance to change was not a pre-existing state of affairs.

The interesting feature of this study for the present discussion is that it shows how quantitative and qualitative research may achieve different types of fit with the various stages of a longitudinal case study of this kind. The qualitative investigations seem to have been very adept at establishing general orientations within the school, while the quantitative research brought out the degree to which change had failed to materialize and some of the reasons for the lack of progress with the innovation.

Hybrids

Not all examples of research in which the quantitative and qualitative traditions appear to be represented can readily be subsumed under the different headings encountered in this chapter. One reason for this state of affairs is that some investigations may be better conceptualized as hybrids which have elements of both research traditions.

Hall and Guthrie (1981) were concerned to examine the suggestion that children from poor and minority group backgrounds use language in ways which put them at a disadvantage at school. They decided that the most appropriate approach would be an ethnographic study in which talk and the context in which it occurs were the main areas of interest. They audiotaped samples of language from pre-school children in a variety of locales, such as homes and shops, and in ten temporal situations, for example, before school, on the way to school, in kindergarten classrooms, and the like. The subjects were forty pre-school age children who had been selected in order to be included in one of four groupings of ten children each: lower class black, lower class white, middle class black, and middle class white. The field-workers took copious notes about the contexts in which conversations took place, such as place, subjects, and what interactants were doing. In addition, formal interviews were recorded with parents in order to collect data about the children and their home and school environments. The data were analysed in order to determine the answers to nine questions about the differences in language use between the groups and how far language use was sensitive to diverse contexts. What makes this study a hybrid is its combination of ethnographic methods of data collection with a quasi-experimental research design which was fashioned to answer a number of highly specific questions. The different 'mixes' of ethnicity and social class, along with the different contexts in which each child's use of language was recorded, are like experimental treatments, albeit naturally occurring ones. The researchers do not use a combination of quantitative and qualitative methods of data collection, which is the context in which the two research traditions are usually deemed to achieve a *rapprochement* (as in the bulk of the examples cited in this chapter thus far); rather, they use qualitative methods of data collection within a research design typically associated with quantitative research.

Another instance of a hybrid can be discerned in a study of the effect of teachers' expectations of students' communicative competence on teachers' language by Wilkinson (1981). The research is based on data collected on seventy-six pupils in nursery, kindergarten, and first, second and third grade classes. Wilkinson established the teachers' rankings of the ability of the seventy-six children upon whom she focused in terms of their use of language to communicate effectively. She both audio- and video-taped fifteen lessons in which the focal children were participants. The tapes were transcribed and contextual information (such as nonverbal responses by children and whether pupils did or did not comply with teachers' requests for information) was included. The transcripts were then coded in terms of a number of discourse characteristics, such as the nature of the teacher's request for information and the nature of the feedback provided for the children. Wilkinson then statistically analysed the relationship between teachers' estimations of their pupils' communicative competence and characteristics of the teachers' language in relation to the pupils. Ostensibly, the research entails the quantitative analysis of behaviour and speech, and therefore might be considered an example of structured observation, like the aforementioned FIAC approach. However, Wilkinson's study involves the collection of qualitative data and a subsequent coding into categories. Moreover, the coding is highly sensitive to the context in which teacher–pupil verbal exchanges are grounded and so has a strong ethnographic emphasis. As in the previous example, this study does not qualify as an instance of the combination of quantitative and qualitative research by virtue of two types of data being dovetailed; rather, ethnographic data are collected, then coded with a 'filling in' of the contexts of exchanges, and are then submitted to a quantitative analysis. Like the Hall and Guthrie (1981) study, Wilkinson's investigation uses qualitative data within a research design conventionally associated with quantitative research.

Conclusion

The chief focus of this chapter has been the ways in which quantitative and qualitative research can be combined. Such integration is clearly possible, though researchers' implicit or explicit reasons for employing such a strategy are highly varied. No claim has been made that the full range of possible ways of combining quantitative and qualitative research have been covered. Indeed, a useful exercise for the reader would be to find (a) other approaches to the integration of the two research traditions and (b) other examples of studies which can be subsumed under the eleven headings. It will be noted that certain kinds of apparent integration are not covered in the discussion above. For example, the reporting of survey research in which there is the occasional verbatim quotation from a respondent to a structured interview schedule seems to be stretching the notion of a combination of the two research traditions somewhat.

There are a number of barriers to the integration of quantitative and qualitative research. One barrier has been a major theme of this book thus far – the view that quantitative and qualitative research are based upon fundamentally incompatible epistemological positions. The suggestion that they derive from different views about how social reality ought to be studied has led some qualitative researchers to eschew survey procedures because of their positivist taint. Consequently, the possible role of the methods associated with quantitative research within a qualitative investigation is a source of some controversy and confusion. Another obstacle is cost. The impact of resources on the conduct of social research is an underdeveloped topic (Bryman, 1988), but the substantial costs involved in carrying out investigations in which the two traditions are brought together are considerable. It is striking that a large proportion of the studies cited in this chapter derive either from fairly lavishly funded federal projects in the USA or from limited survey exercises conducted by ethnographers. Large scale survey research comparatively rarely has an ethnographic component welded on to it. Such survey research frequently involves a team of researchers and tends therefore to be costly even without the addition of an ethnographic component. The ORACLE research is a comparatively unusual example of a study which relies predominantly on methods associated with quantitative research, but which has a fairly strong ethnographic component (Galton and Delamont, 1985).

Indeed, it is quite unusual to find examples of investigations in which quantitative and qualitative research have a roughly equal role. The multisite, multimethod projects which have been mentioned sometimes provide exceptions to this rule, although some commentators (adopting a somewhat purist stance) have questioned whether the ethnographic component in such studies is 'true' ethnography (e.g. Rist, 1980). However, in most instances one approach tends to prevail as the major source of data collection. Behind this tendency can be discerned a further obstacle to integration – the training of researchers and its effect on their methodological competence and inclination. Because researchers are often trained in the ways of particular styles of research, their ability and inclination to flirt with other approaches is often limited. Reiss (1968, p. 351), for example, cites the 'trained incapacities' of researchers as a cause of the disinclination to combine social survey research and participant observation. If this point has any veracity, it has implications for the technical version of the debate about the two research traditions. The technical version implies that the decision about which method should be used is predicated upon a judgement about the appropriateness of methods in relation to problems. However, if a researcher's personal inclination and competence play a determinative role, it is likely to do so in the formulation of the research problem from which the appropriate method is supposed to flow. Thus a researcher who is inclined towards survey methods is likely routinely to formulate his or her research problem in such a way that it will be amenable to a survey approach; he or she does not decide the problem and then select the appropriate method.

In many respects, it is not easy to detect the ways in which quantitative and qualitative research can be fruitfully amalgamated, since, when they are used in tandem, the products of such blending are not directly recognizable. In his study of Suffolk farm workers, Newby (1977a, 1977b) chose to carry out a structured interview survey as his main source of data, but decided to conduct some participant observation in order 'to make valid inferences from the survey data, while insights gained from the participant observation could be checked for representativeness against knowledge gained through the survey' (Newby, 1977b, p. 116). Newby notes that the survey data largely dominated the presentation of data in his monograph, which

> contains little of the material gathered through participant observation, despite my voluminous fieldnotes which I faithfully wrote up every evening. The participant observation was not, of course, lost altogether. It remains *between the lines* in my interpretation of the survey data, but I suspect that most readers will not recognise this. This seems unfortunate, for not only did the participant observation crucially affect my understanding of deference [the key conceptual focus in the monograph], but

also, given my reformulation of the concept, it was this method which was providing me with valid data, and where survey and participant observation data conflicted I instinctively trusted the latter. (Newby, 1977b, p.127, emphasis added)

Two closely related points stand out in this passage. First, the survey data tend to be emphasized in the monograph; the participant observation data facilitated the interpretation of the survey data and hence are 'between the lines'. This remark suggests that the precise manner in which quantitative and qualitative research and data are dovetailed may be somewhat hidden from view, and that possibly even researchers themselves may not be fully aware of the impact of one set of findings on the other. Secondly, Newby's observation that his participant observation data were more valid and hence more trustworthy reflects a tendency, noted previously in this chapter, to accord such data preferential treatment when they clash with findings gleaned from a social survey. The reasons for this privileged treatment are rarely given, but one might hazard a guess that the researcher's greater proximity to, and involvement with, his or her subjects in qualitative research induces a feeling of greater confidence in the validity and solidity of data deriving from its associated methods. But the chief point that is being made at this juncture is that the conflicts between the data (and the sources of their reconciliation) may be somewhat hidden from view in many instances.

This latter point strongly implies that we have few rules of thumb for dealing with research strategies which combine the two research traditions. The tendency to view the two traditions and their associated methods in 'either/or' terms has meant that when researchers have chosen to combine methods of data collection they have had few guidelines concerning the purposes and possible ramifications of a methodologically ecumenical strategy. It is generally accepted that textbooks on social research methods rarely convey the realities of social research and therefore do not always provide a particularly helpful guide to the actual conduct of research (Bryman, 1988), but, in the area of how, when and why different research methods might be combined, there are few if any pointers available. Rather, a 'case law' approach tends to have emerged, whereby (as in this chapter) a number of different experiences are assembled together and called upon as exemplars of particular practices.

It is striking that virtually all of the examples cited in this chapter have involved the use of the social survey or systematic observation as representatives of the tradition of quantitative research. Experimental research has hardly figured at all, except in one of the 'hybrid' studies cited above. This absence is slightly surprising since it might have been anticipated that field experiments in natural settings would have provided such an opportunity. Cronbach (1975, p. 125) has called for greater attention to 'intensive local observation' as an adjunct to the chief research designs in psychology, namely the experimental and correlational approaches, but his plea has had little effect on experimental research in the succeeding years.[4]

Notes

1 For this and all of the other points contained in this paragraph I am indebted to a personal communication from Richard Jenkins (23 June 1987) in connection with his book *Lads, Citizens and Ordinary Kids* (Jenkins, 1983).
2 However, the critics of such research draw attention to a number of other methodological weaknesses (e.g. A. Hargreaves, 1985, p. 27).
3 A number of other approaches to the integration of macro and micro levels have been suggested which do not involve the integration of quantitative and qualitative research to any substantial degree (Cicourel, 1981).
4 Much research within the field of cognitive social psychology uses experimental designs (Fiske and Taylor, 1984) and could be classified as 'hybrid' (see Chapter 5 for a brief elaboration of this point).

7

Comparing Quantitative and Qualitative Research

Can we genuinely combine the publications deriving from both quantitative and qualitative research, and so produce an overall view of a particular substantive area? This question is not confronted to the same degree as the issue of whether the two traditions can be combined in a single study, even though ostensibly it is just as important. Since the consumer of social research is very frequently confronted with substantive domains in which quantitative and qualitative research co-exist, the relationship between the output of the two approaches within a field is an important facet of the cumulative nature of knowledge within this field. The distinction between the epistemological and the technical versions of the debate about the two research traditions rears its head again in this context. It might be anticipated that the epistemological version would imply that the two sets of findings cannot be amalgamated since they are predicated on different views of the proper foundation of the social sciences. However, it is very unusual to see this point argued. For example, qualitative researchers are invariably quite prepared to show how pre-existing quantitative research influenced their research problem and how their own findings have implications for data emanating from the quantitative tradition.

Writers of textbooks in substantive areas usually ride roughshod over the possible epistemological issues which might be at stake when research based upon both quantitative and qualitative research is brought together and summarized. For example, in a text on industrial sociology, the following passage examines power and conflict in organizations:

> Dalton's view is that the social process of management within organizations amounts to 'a shifting set of contained and ongoing counter phases of action' (1959, p. 4). Conflict, of course, represents only one form of such action . . . Exchange, bargaining and conflict are all manifestations of management as a system of power . . . Crozier's study (1964) of French bureaucracy . . . pointed to uncertainty as having a critical role

in the retention of autonomy by departments which alone were able to cope with periodic and unexpected crises. The findings of Hinings *et al.* (1974) also suggest that the power of departmental managers derives from being able to cope with uncertainty, provided that what is done has some immediate benefit for the rest of the organization and that alternative ways of doing it are not readily available. (Parker *et al.*, 1977, pp. 123–4)

In this passage, the results deriving from a participant observation study (Dalton), a case study investigation in which semi-structured interviews produce both quantitative and qualitative data (Crozier), and a cross-sectional survey study of sub-units in seven organizations (Hinings *et al.*) are brought together to provide an overall statement on 'knowledge' in an area.

Most contexts in which the fruits of quantitative and qualitative research are combined implicitly adopt a technical version of the debate. The discussion in the previous chapter of the ways in which quantitative and qualitative research may be combined within a single project is relevant in this connection, because studies deriving from each of the two traditions can be merged in a similar manner. For example, if it is accepted that quantitative research is best suited to the elucidation of structural regularities in social life, while qualitative investigations provide access to processes, the combination of studies deriving from the two traditions can readily be envisioned: research on the correlates of organizational structure, like the Aston Studies (Pugh, 1988), can be integrated with qualitative case study explorations of the internal dynamics of organizations.

In this latter context, the dovetailing of the two types of research is possible because they are addressing different but complementary aspects of organizations. In like fashion, studies of delinquency might be brought together to provide a general picture of research in the area, with quantitative research emphasizing the causes of delinquency, and qualitative research providing details of delinquent life-styles and world-views. In these instances, the accumulation and integration of research stemming from the two traditions does not pose any difficulties to the technical version of the debate. The studies associated with the two approaches can be seen as pieces of a jigsaw.

Difficulties are more likely to be encountered when, within a single substantive area, quantitative and qualitative research address (or at least appear to address) the same issues. The technical version of the debate suggests that quantitative and qualitative research are each appropriate to different kinds of research problem. However, there is also a cluster of research problems to which the two traditions have both made contributions. A number of questions can be raised about empirical work within such domains, of which two will become a focus for this chapter. First, do quantitative and qualitative studies yield consistent findings? This question has some relevance to the issue of triangulation. Secondly, irrespective of whether results are consistent or inconsistent, are they *really* addressing the same issues?

Research on Mental Patients

The focus of this section is a review article by Weinstein (1979) of quantitative research on mental patients. Although primarily concerned with quantitative studies, Weinstein chose also to examine eleven qualitative studies of mental hospitalization. These qualitative studies between them employed a variety of methods of data collection, including unstructured interviews, observations on hospital wards, and participant observation by becoming a pseudopatient.The qualitative research portrays a consistent picture of mental patienthood. This portrayal will be familiar to readers of Goffman's *Asylums* (1961), which is one of the eleven studies. Together, the eleven studies convey a grim picture of what it is like to be a mental patient. Patients are portrayed as anxious about their commitment; as debased, worn down and moulded into pliancy by an oppressively authoritarian hospital regime which forces them to accept their illness; as betrayed by others and powerless to do anything about their situation; and as stigmatized by staff and the outside world.

The group of quantitative studies provides a different depiction of the mental patient's lot (Weinstein, 1979). This quantitative research was made up of two types of investigation. The first type comprised eighteen studies using 'objective tests to ascertain attitudes towards mental hospitalization' (p. 240). These investigations entailed the use of various quantitative techniques like sentence completion tests, multiple choice questions, and rating scales. Secondly, he examined questionnaire scale studies involving the administration of multi-item questionnaires. By and large, the quantitative studies suggest that mental patients have favourable attitudes towards their institutions, report some benefit from their hospitalization, do not object to the restrictions of hospital life, and even derive some enjoyment from the mental hospital.

The contrast between quantitative and qualitative research in this area of study can be illustrated by reference to a pair of investigations. Goldman, Bohr and Steinberg (1970) report the experiences of the second and third authors when they gained successful entry to different wards in a large metropolitan state hospital in the USA and so were able to serve as disguised observers. Both pseudo-patients experienced a pronounced fear of betrayal by their colleagues on admission to their wards, as well as an acute sensation of boredom. They also felt that the lack of stimulation within the wards created an apathy to the outside world among patients. Further, they argued that the structure of the hospital with its overworked attendants restricted the ability of patients to become self-determining agents once again. The contrasting study by Linn (1968) was conducted in a similar setting to Goldman *et al.*, but used what Weinstein calls an 'objective test' approach in that he employed a structured schedule with open-ended questions to interview 185 admissions. The chief finding deriving from this investigation is that the view of the mental hospital from the patient perspective is considerably more varied than the qualitative studies imply. For a sizeable proportion of mental patients, the mental hospital offers respite from an often distressing life outside. In Linn's view, while many mental hospitals are restrictive and authoritarian, as implied by the qualitative studies, the diverse experiences of mental patients prior to admission mean that they do not uniformly experience hospitalization in these terms.

One of the chief ways in which Weinstein accounts for the discrepancies between the two clusters of findings is to draw attention to a number of methodological weaknesses associated with the qualitative investigations: they focus on the effect of the hospital on the patients rather than the patients themselves; studies employing informal interviews did not test attitudes systematically but focused on what was mentioned spontaneously by respondents; 'samples' of patients interviewed were typically unrepresentative; and pseudopatient studies cannot genuinely report the experiences of mental patients since the investigators are not mentally ill. He also draws attention to what he perceives to be a number of biases in the qualitative studies which are associated with the theoretical predilections of social scientists who have conducted such research. In a comment on Weinstein's review, Essex *et al.* (1980) argue that he fails to adopt an even-handedness because the parallel limitations of the quantitative studies are not examined. The validity and reliability of the questionnaire scales used in the second of the two groups of quantitative studies *are* examined. However, the possibility of other kinds of methodological weakness in the questionnaire studies, of methodological shortcomings in the objective test investigations, and of theoretical biases affecting both sets of quantitative research on mental patients is largely untouched (Essex *et al.*, 1980; Weinstein, 1980).

These considerations would seem to imply that Weinstein was too predisposed to the quantitative research, although he denies any personal bias in this regard (Weinstein, 1980). Of further interest is a suggestion by Essex *et al.* that the quantitative and qualitative studies of mental patients were not in fact investigating the same thing. They argue that the qualitative studies were about the *experience* of being a mental patient, whereas the quantitative studies were concerned with mental patients' *attitudes*. The qualitative research points to negative experiences on the part of mental patients but, Essex *et al.* argue, this does not mean that they have negative attitudes; nor can it be assumed that negative experiences will lead to negative attitudes. Consequently, Weinstein's critics contend that the two groups of studies are not directly comparable. In response, Weinstein (1980) concedes that the qualitative studies emphasize the experience of being a mental patient, but maintains that many of the investigators within this tradition draw inferences about negative attitudes from their field-work.

Two points are of particular interest in this controversy. First, there is the suggestion that reviewers may not be entirely impartial when confronting research drawing on different traditions. Weinstein seems to be prepared to raise issues about the adequacy of the qualitative studies, which were not addressed in relation to the equivalent quantitative investigations. Secondly, the extent to which quantitative and qualitative studies are genuinely comparable in domains where they seem to be addressing the same issues is of particular interest. The crux of the criticism of Weinstein by Essex *et al.* is that he was not comparing the comparable. The strength of their comment in this regard can be underscored with a further observation about the quantitative and qualitative investigations: all of the latter studies are based on in-patients, whereas the majority of the objective test studies and nearly one-third of the questionnaire scale studies are based on data collected on admissions to or discharges from mental hospitals. The extent to which the differential location of mental patients may have influenced the contrast between the quantitative and qualitative groups of research is not examined by either Weinstein or his critics.

Further, because of Weinstein's disinclination to view the two clusters of studies as exploring different facets of mental patienthood, reconciliation between the two groups, and hence progress in this field, are not being promoted. The discovery of contrasting findings gleaned from different types of method is not unique to this area. For example, Hovland (1959) reviewed studies of attitude change and found that correlational, social survey research was considerably less likely than experimental research to find that people changed their attitudes subsequent to exposure to a communication. Hovland argued *inter alia* that in an experimental situation all subjects are fully exposed to the communication which is supposed to produce attitude change; in the social survey study there is an element of self-selection in that 'surveys primarily describe the effects produced on those already in favour of the view advocated in the communication' (p. 9). Hovland also pointed to other differences, such as the different time intervals used to evaluate the effects of a communication. In experiments the evaluation is usually much sooner than in the social survey context. Hovland also noted that the experimental and survey research differ in respect of the types of audience typically used and the kinds of communication issues utilized. Thus Hovland implicitly recognized that the experimental and survey studies were exploring different kinds of issues because of their divergent research strategies, and sought to develop ideas about how the insights deriving from each might be brought together to engender a better overall picture of knowledge in the field of attitude change. It is precisely these elements which are absent in Weinstein's review: insufficient attention is paid to the possibility that the similarities in focus between the quantitative and qualitative studies are more apparent than real and there is insufficient recognition that the differences can be used as a springboard for advancing the area of study.

Teacher Expectancies

The focus for this section is Rosenthal and Jacobson's (1968) often cited investigation of the effects of teachers' expectations on their pupils' school performance and ability. Rosenthal and Jacobson were not the first to explore this issue, but the striking results they obtained and certain unusual facets of their research strategy have attracted a great deal of attention to it. Their concern with teachers' expectations was part of a programme of research on the role of 'self-fulfilling prophecies' in a variety of settings. The idea of a self-fulfilling prophecy refers to the possibility that a person's expectations of another's behaviour may influence how the latter behaves. In the educational setting this idea suggested the possibility that teachers' expectations regarding their pupils' abilities may influence academic performance. The setting for the research was a school in a predominantly lower class area in the USA. A considerable proportion of the children were from minority group backgrounds (especially Mexican). In the spring of 1964 all children were administered a test which purported to be a means of establishing academic 'spurters' – pupils likely to show exceptional academic performance. At the beginning of the following academic year, each teacher was told the names of the children who had performed particularly well at the test, and who would excel.

Twenty per cent of pupils were identified in these terms. In fact, the test which had been administered was a conventional IQ test and the children who had been identified as 'spurters' had been selected randomly.

The focus of the research was to compare the academic performance of the 20 per cent of children identified as 'spurters' with the rest on a number of indicators. The investigation used an experimental design in that the 'spurters' constituted an experimental group, the rest made up the control group. Since the 'spurters' had been identified by a random process, the experimental and control groups were regarded as equivalent. Rosenthal and Jacobson's analysis suggests that significant gains were made by the experimental group relative to the control children in terms of such measures as reading performance and IQ. Such calculations were established by comparing pre- and post-experimental scores on these tests. There was a tendency for relative gains in academic performance to be strongest among earlier grades (especially first and second grades) in the school.

The study's striking results, and its clear relevance for the teaching profession, prompted many replications. In fact, there has not been an exact replication, but many researchers have sought to confirm or reject the general theme of the research. While a variety of research designs have been employed in such replications, two strategies are particularly in evidence. First, a number of investigators have sought to 'induce' teacher expectations in a manner similar to the original. One of the earliest replications was conducted by Clairborn (1969), who identified 'spurters' in a similar way to Rosenthal and Jacobson in three middle class suburban schools in New York State. Expectations were induced approximately one month into the second semester of the academic year. However, Clairborn could find very little evidence to confirm the Rosenthal and Jacobson study.

The second strategy is often called 'naturalistic' (e.g. Brophy and Good, 1974).[1] Research associated with this approach examines the effects of teachers' naturally occurring expectations (those which arise in the course of teaching a group of pupils) on pupil performance. An imaginative study within this approach is Palardy (1969). Two groups of five teachers were matched on a variety of characteristics and differed only in that Group A believed that first grade boys were as likely to be successful at learning to read as girls; Group B believed that they would be slower than girls. The pupils of the two groups of teachers were shown to be roughly equal in reading ability at the start of the academic year and there was no evidence of gender difference in reading ability; by March it was found that the reading achievement of Group A boys was considerably greater than that of the Group B boys, while there was no difference between the girls in the two groups. A somewhat different tack was taken to the naturalistic study of teacher expectations by Brophy and Good (1974), who developed a systematic observation schedule to record patterns of dyadic contact between teacher and each pupil in classrooms. The researchers were able to show that there were substantial differences in patterns of teacher–pupil interaction between those pupils identified by the teachers as likely to be 'high' achievers and those identified as 'low' achievers. The teachers' ratings had been established at a point in the school year at which there was no objective support for their beliefs about the differential capacities of their pupils. Brophy and Good found that there were distinct differences in the performance of the two groups of students. For example, the 'highs' showed a larger percentage of correct answers to teachers' questions followed by praise and a smaller percentage of wrong answers followed by criticism than the 'lows'.

All of the aforementioned investigations have been broadly within the tradition of quantitative research. However, one of the best-known studies of the role of teacher expectations was an ethnographic study by Rist (1970) of a group of black children in an urban ghetto school in the USA. Unlike the quantitative research in this field, Rist's study was concerned to examine the bases upon which differential teacher expectations are constructed and the ways in which expectations are manifested in the classroom. Rist observed the children over a period of two and a half years. Initially, he observed them during their kindergarten year and again in their second grade year. They were also briefly visited in their first grade year. Rist informally observed the classrooms and conducted interviews with the teachers. A major component of the kindergarten teacher's expression of her expectations of pupil behaviour was through the arrangement of the children into three tables, which was undertaken after the teacher had observed the children at work and play for eight days at the start of the school year. The children at the top table were better dressed and behaved and conformed more closely than the others to the teacher's 'mixed black–white, well-educated middle class' (p. 239) reference group. These children were deemed to be much more likely to achieve well at school and received much greater attention from the teacher than those at the other two tables. Ironically, Rist suggests, the children at the other two tables were not uninterested in school work and had developed their own patterns of learning among themselves. The pattern of differential seating and treatment observed in the kindergarten setting was carried over into the first and then the second grades. As Rist notes, in the second grade the seating arrangements were based on the past performance of the children rather than the teacher's expectations. Thus the initial seating pattern in the kindergarten, which derived from the teacher's beliefs and presuppositions, formed the basis for a system of stratification which was carried through into later grades and also for later differential treatment.

Rist's research allows the effect of teacher expectations to be shown in sharp relief. However, a study by Murphy (1974) in a British primary school produced results which appear to be inconsistent with Rist's findings. The author does not specify his methods of data collection very precisely, but observation and unstructured interviews were prominent. Murphy suggests that there was some evidence of the operation of self-fulfilling prophecies at work in the school, but argues that they are not as pervasive and as significant as Rosenthal and Jacobson and Rist imply. Further, they do not contribute to the underachievement of working class pupils, as Rist's research might have led one to anticipate.

Discussion

As this brief review of the voluminous literature on teacher expectations suggests, the findings from the various studies are not very consistent.[2] In contrast to the literature on mental patients in the previous section, the positive and negative findings relating to the effects of teacher expectations do not neatly coincide with quantitative and qualitative research. Qualitative research (Rist) seems to support the general tenor of Rosenthal and Jacobson's quantitative research, but Murphy's qualitative investigation is inconsistent with the Rist study. Further, the quantitative research is highly inconsistent in its support for the Rosenthal and Jacobson experiment. To some extent, this latter inconsistency can be attributed to the diversity of research methods and strategies adopted by investigators of teacher expectations within the quantitative tradition. For example, one of the most controversial aspects of the Rosenthal and Jacobson study was the implication that positive teacher expectations can enhance pupils' IQ. This possibility strikes at the very heart of the controversy about the extent to which IQ can be environmentally influenced (as implied by Rosenthal and Jacobson's findings) or is an inherited and invariant characteristic of the individual (Jensen, 1969). Indeed, the extent to which teacher expectations may affect pupils' IQ has proved to be one of the most difficult findings to replicate (Baker and Crist, 1971; Smith, 1980a). However, Raudenbush (1983) has shown that among 'induced expectancy' studies, the timing of the induction has an effect on whether expectations can be shown to have an effect on pupils' IQ. When the expectancy induction occurs at the start of the school year (as in Rosenthal and Jacobson, 1968) it is much more likely to have an effect on IQ than if it occurs one week or more into the school year (as in Clairborn, 1969). This conclusion may also have implications for the naturalistic and the ethnographic studies, since it might be anticipated that the timing of initial observations or measures may influence the findings of such research and hence may contribute towards the discrepant findings deriving from these other approaches.

This latter point reinforces the suggestion made in the context of the discussion of the mental patient studies that, in comparing different investigations, caution is always necessary in order to ensure that genuinely comparable items are being considered. Weinstein (1980) dismisses the possibility that the quantitative and qualitative research on mental patients may have been relating to different aspects of life in the mental hospital and tends to minimize the possible discrepancies *among* rather than between the quantitative and the qualitative studies. Clashes between the findings of different studies in a particular domain is a fairly common feature of the social sciences. Sometimes the clashes can be attributed to different findings being associated with particular research designs or methods of data collection, but on other occasions there is no obvious connection between results and methodology. As an example of the latter, research on the effects of participation in decision-making may be cited. In spite of considerable variety among studies which make up this vast literature on whether participation has positive effects on such dependent variables as job satisfaction and group productivity, a review by Locke and Schweiger (1979) could find no simple patterning in the degree to which particular types of findings were associated with particular research strategies (e.g. laboratory experiments versus field experiments versus correlational, survey studies).

If quantitative and qualitative research within a particular domain appear to be associated with incongruent findings, there should be a greater preparedness to search for the possibility that the two sets of findings may be only superficially comparable in that they may be addressing different facets of a topic. A more constructive approach would be to treat the two sets of results as indicative of different aspects of the phenomena in question and to search for hypotheses which would help to explain their inconsistency. In Weinstein's (1979, 1980) assessment of research on mental patients can be discerned a tendency to treat the quantitative research as unproblematic. A similar exercise has been conducted by Room (1984) in his analysis of ethnographic research on alcohol consumption and alcoholism in tribal and village cultures in developing societies (such as Latin America), as well as among North American Indians. The chief thrust of Room's examination is that the ethnographic literature 'deflates' (that is, minimizes) the extent to which there is a serious drinking problem in such cultures. When compared to the non-ethnographic literature on alcohol consumption (such as epidemiological research), he argues that there is 'a systematic bias in the modern ethnographic literature against the full recognition of alcohol problems in the cultures under study' (Room, 1984, p. 170). Room then proceeds to enumerate the chief causes and manifestations of this bias. He recognizes, for example, that the different methods of data collection may be a factor of some importance, when he writes:

> By design, ethnography is oriented to the study of the everyday, while epidemiology is oriented to the study of rare events . . . [T]he ethnographer is likely to witness all or most of the pleasures of drinking but to miss some of the problems – particularly the life-threatening problems that are the focus of attention of the epidemiologist. (Room, 1984, p. 172)

Room acknowledges that these different emphases mean that the two approaches can be 'useful correctives to each other' (p. 173), but this view sits uneasily with his suggestion that the ethnographic literature comprises a systematic bias. As one of his critics (Agar, 1984) observed, Room tends to use the epidemiological research as indicative of a 'true' position, a position which is itself debatable.

In Room's assessment can be discerned a similar stance to that of Weinstein, namely a tendency to view the qualitative research as biased and a posture which treats the quantitative research as unproblematic, although Room appears more sensitive to the possibility that the two research approaches may not be addressing precisely the same things. The implication that quantitative research can provide an objective standard is very difficult to sustain. Gergen (1973), for example, has cogently argued that the results of quantitative research in social psychology are affected by historical time periods. There is also a great deal of evidence which points to self-fulfilling prophecies in experimental research in psychology (Rosenthal and Rubin, 1978). An analysis by Eagly and Carli (1981) of research on gender differences in social influence has pointed to the possibility that the researcher's personal characteristics can affect study outcomes. Eagly and Carli examined seventy-five studies which sought to establish whether men or women are easier to influence. They found that male authors were more likely to obtain results which suggest that women are more influenceable than men. Clearly, considerable caution is necessary in deciding what such a finding means, but the possibility of gender bias would need to be on the agenda of potential explanations.

A further reason for caution when addressing domains in which quantitative and qualitative research appear to cover similar issues is the problem of 'publication bias'. The published material in any area in which quantitative research is used extensively is likely to be an unrepresentative sample of all quantitative research conducted within that field. Smith (1980b) reports ten instances in which investigators analysed the results of both published research and unpublished research in theses and dissertations. The ten topics were as diverse as the effects of television on anti-social behaviour and drug therapy in psychological disorders. In each case, the evidence in the published literature was more clear-cut than in the unpublished sources. Smith has examined in particular detail the literature relating to the extent to which there is a sex bias in counselling and psychotherapy against women (Smith 1980c). She found no evidence for such sex bias. However, in published research her review revealed that there is a small sex bias effect; when unpublished research was examined, a small sex bias effect was found *toward* women. Further confirmation of the effect of publication bias can be found in White's (1982) analysis of the literature on the relationship between socio-economic status (SES) and academic achievement. White conducted an exhaustive search of books, published articles, and unpublished theses and dissertations. He found the mean correlations between SES and achievement for these three sources to be .508, .343 and .292 respectively.

These findings imply that a good deal of caution is required when examining a cluster of studies conducted within the framework of quantitative research, if only published research is being examined (as in the cases of Weinstein and Room). The findings also invite a questioning of the reasons for discrepancies between published and unpublished research. The answers are bound to be a matter of conjecture, but an investigation by Greenwald (1975) sheds some light on the issue. He conducted a survey of both referees of articles and authors of articles submitted to the *Journal of Personality and Social Psychology*. Greenwald found that authors typically believe that they will be able to reject their null hypothesis (i.e that they will be able to come up with a positive finding) and that if they do not they are highly unlikely to submit their findings for publication. One likely reason for this pattern is that authors believe that their work is much less likely to be accepted for publication if the null hypothesis is not rejected.[3]

Finally, simply because the findings deriving from quantitative and qualitative studies appear consistent, the differences between them should not be neglected. In the section on teacher expectancies, the similarities between the results of Rosenthal and Jacobson (1968) and Rist (1970) were given considerable attention, but it is important not to lose sight of the differences in focus and emphasis among the two studies. The former study was concerned to demonstrate the existence of self-fulfilling prophecies in the classroom; Rist was concerned with the bases of differential teacher expectations and how they are revealed in the classroom. Thus, one of the particularly interesting features of this latter study is the use of data stemming from interviews with the teachers which address their biases. Such data allow Rist to locate these biases in the teachers' individual biographies. This element provided Rist with further access to the teachers' own perspectives on their work, so that he was able to interpret their actions in terms of their own frames of reference. A similar level of analysis can be perceived in the ethnographic study of 'typing' by teachers in two British schools by Hargreaves, Hester, and Mellor (1975), which is primarily concerned with the factors that are taken into account in the development of teacher expectations and the ways in which these are revised or maintained after their initial formulation. While the ethnographic studies such as those of Rist and Hargreaves *et al.* appear to be broadly consistent with Rosenthal and Jacobson's quantitative investigation, it is important not to lose sight of the additional empirical dimension that qualitative research offers.

The presence of publication bias in the quantitative research tradition invites caution when dealing with such material, but it is extremely difficult to know whether similar problems occur in regard to qualitative research. Since qualitative research is rarely guided by an explicit hypothesis, the issue of the failure to reject the null hypotheses is unlikely to be important in deciding what research gets published. It is likely that a general prejudice against qualitative research until relatively recently inhibited the publication of many investigations, especially in journals, because of their failure to manifest the desired attributes associated with quantitative research. It may be that the problems of finding outlets for published material in established academic journals in the social sciences prompted the founding of journals like *Urban Life and Culture*, *Qualitative Sociology* and *Anthropology and Education Quarterly* which emphasized qualitative material. While prejudice against qualitative research may have diminished, it still exists. For example, writing from the perspective of a journal referee in the field of organizational behaviour, Daft (1985, p. 201) has written: 'The single biggest problem I found with qualitative research was lack of theory.' However, as suggested in Chapter 2, in the view of many commentators the quantitative research tradition is frequently not explicitly guided by theoretical concerns, so that the suggestion that it is qualitative research in particular that is characterized by a lack of theory may be indicative of a degree of bias. These reflections relate to the possibility of publication bias against qualitative research and raise the possibility that articles which do get published may not be representative of all qualitative investigations in a particular field.

Conclusion

Quantitative and qualitative research can frequently be found together in particular substantive areas in the social sciences, be it delinquency, classroom studies, or whatever. By and large, the two research traditions can be viewed as contributing to the understanding of different aspects of the phenomenon in question. Thus quantitative studies of social mobility (e.g. Goldthorpe, 1980) can be viewed as contributing to an understanding of rates and patterns of social mobility, whereas school ethnographies (e.g. Ball, 1981) facilitate an understanding of the processes associated with the perpetuation of class in schools. Indeed, writers of textbooks in various substantive fields frequently combine the results of research deriving from both traditions in arriving at overall accounts of their chosen areas, with little regard to the different approaches to data collection which underpin them.

However, sometimes quantitative and qualitative research may address similar aspects of a certain field of investigation. In some instances, the two sets of results may appear discordant, as in the cases of research on mental patients and on alcoholism reviewed in this chapter; on other occasions, the results may appear to be highly consistent, as in the case of the research on teacher expectancies by Rosenthal and Jacobson (1968) and Rist (1970). When the data deriving from the two types of research appear to clash, it has been argued that it is necessary to ensure that one set of results is not artificially construed as providing a 'true' picture, since it is very rare that definitive rules of thumb can be found for making such a determination. Caution is also necessary in ensuring that the two sets of results are not in fact addressing different issues. The investigation of this possibility may provide a springboard for both a reconciliation of the incongruent findings and may also prompt a fresh agenda of substantive and methodological issues to be formulated. It is also necessary to be aware of the diverse findings which may exist *among*, as well as *between*, quantitative and qualitative research. In the case of the study of teacher expectancies, the inconsistencies are more pronounced among the studies deriving from each of the two traditions, rather than between them.

Even then, caution is necessary in viewing apparently compatible studies deriving from quantitative and qualitative research as mutually confirmatory, since they may have been conducted with somewhat different purposes in mind. Furthermore, the possibility of 'publication bias' renders comparisons of quantitative and qualitative studies somewhat problematic.

Notes

1   Note that 'naturalistic' means something quite different here from either of the two meanings previously encountered in Chapters 2 and 3.
2   For example, Rogers (1982, p. 37) concluded from an examination of studies relating to expectancy effects that 'they do not produce results that provide an immediately obvious and consistent picture'. However, Smith's (1980a) assessment was somewhat less pessimistic.
3   Many students do not appreciate that articles in most academic journals are assessed by at least two referees before publication. The process is usually a 'blind' one in that authors' names are not made known. Journals reject a very high proportion of articles sent to them. Major journals like *American Political Science Review*, *American Journal of Sociology*, *American Sociological Review*, *Administrative Science Quarterly*, and *Social Psychology Quarterly* accept only a small proportion of articles sent to them for publication (4 per cent, 14 per cent, 15 per cent, 9 per cent, and 8 per cent respectively in 1981). Even less-well-known journals like *Sociological Focus* accept less than one-third of all articles sent to them. Details of the acceptance rates of these and many other journals can be found in Huber (n.d.), from which the above percentages were extracted.

8

Conclusion

Probably the major theme to emerge from the preceding chapters is that many aspects of the debate about quantitative and qualitative research, which has been a prominent topic in discussions of social research methodology in recent years, are unsatisfactory. There are differences between quantitative and qualitative research, in terms of the kinds of data that each engenders and the levels of analysis at which each operates. Therefore, each has its own strengths and weaknesses. However, it is important not to minimize the importance of similarities between the two traditions. For example, there does not seem to be an obvious reason why qualitative research cannot be used in order to test theories in the manner typically associated with the model of the quantitative research process. A number of studies have used qualitative research to good effect in this respect. The suggestion that quantitative research is associated with the testing of theories, whilst qualitative research is associated with the generation of theories, can consequently be viewed as a convention that may have little to do with either the practices of many researchers within the two traditions or the potential of the methods of data collection themselves.

The tendency to talk about quantitative and qualitative research as though they are separate paradigms has produced ideal-type descriptions of each tradition with strong programmatic overtones, and consequently has obscured the areas of overlap, both actual and potential, between them. The conception of the two traditions as paradigms has been fuelled by the widespread view that they are underpinned by divergent and hence incompatible epistemological positions. Many writers tend to move uneasily back and forth between epistemological and technical versions of the debate. This very fact may be taken as indicative of some of the problems attaching to the epistemological version, for a theme in this book has been that the association of quantitative and qualitative research with different epistemological positions is largely assumed. There is much to suggest that the assumption is questionable when the practice of social research is examined. For example, a good deal of qualitative research shares an empiricist streak with quantitative research; much quantitative research shares a concern for subjects' interpretations, which is supposedly the province of the qualitative researcher.

Rather than the somewhat doctrinaire posturing of a great deal of the literature dealing with the epistemological leanings of quantitative and qualitative research, there should be a greater recognition in discussions of the general aspects of social research methodology of the need to generate good research. This injunction means attending to the full complexity of the social world such that methods are chosen in relation to the research problems posed. This is an old theme which harks back to Trow's (1957) rebuttal of Becker and Geer's (1957) view of participant observation. However, many of the studies cited in Chapter 6 are a testament to the advantages that can accrue when a non-doctrinaire stance is adopted and the two approaches to research are combined. Not all contexts lend themselves to such methodological integration, but this fact is consistent with the technical version of the debate about quantitative and qualitative research. If some research topics are more suited to a survey, while others would be better served by a qualitative approach, still others will be even better served by a marriage of the two traditions, whereas the integrated strategy may not fit some issues. The critical issue is to be aware of the appropriateness of particular methods (or combinations of methods) for particular issues. It may be that the debate about quantitative and qualitative research has sharpened our awareness of the advantages and limitations of particular methods. We are possibly more aware of the implications of choosing one method rather than another for the kinds of things we are likely to find. Above all, the debate has been associated with a growth in interest in qualitative research and a greater appreciation of its considerable strength as a method of social research. Qualitative research has a long way to go before it will have attained the same status as experimental and survey research, but it is no longer a Cinderella approach to social research. In particular, there is a greater preparedness to treat qualitative research as research in its own right, rather than as a source of hypotheses that need to be firmed up.

Precisely because quantitative and qualitative research have their respective strengths and weaknesses, it is necessary to adopt a cautious attitude when exploring substantive areas in the social sciences in which the two types of study appear to co-exist. In Chapter 7 it was argued that superficial similarities between quantitative and qualitative studies in a particular domain should be probed in order to see whether they are in fact addressing somewhat different issues. This conclusion can be viewed as a consequence of the suggestion that it is the practice of many researchers to tailor their research strategy to the problem at hand. If many researchers proceed in this manner, superficial similarities between studies may obscure deeper differences in the issues addressed. Above all, the artificial and often covert erection of quantitative research as a standard against which qualitative studies are judged (or vice versa) has to be guarded against.

This book is not meant as an invective against the introduction of philosophical ideas and reflection into the examination of social research. Rather it represents a view that such philosophical reflection should not lose sight of the practices of social researchers. Certain aspects of the debate about quantitative and qualitative research share with the philosophy of the social sciences an alarming disinterest in social research. Books on the philosophy of the social sciences often seem content to inveigh against the horrors of quantitative research on the basis of the deficiencies associated with exemplars (Durkheim's *Suicide* being one of the most frequently encountered) or with marginal figures who expressed immoderate views (such as Lundberg, 1939). Rarely is there a thoroughgoing attempt to address the practice of quantitative research as such. Equally, the debate about quantitative and qualitative research produced an idealized view of the latter by creating for it an epistemological rationale, in the form of such intellectual positions as phenomenology and *verstehen*. The application of philosophical ideas to social research must not lose touch with the practices and aims of social researchers.

Bibliography and Author Index

The bibliography incorporates an author index: page numbers in bold at the end of each entry indicate where the publication is referred to in this book.

Abel, T. F. (1948), 'The operation called *Verstehen*', *American Journal of Sociology*, vol. 54, no. 3, pp. 211–18. **57**

Abrams, P. (1984), 'Evaluating soft findings: some problems of measuring informal care', *Research, Policy and Planning*, vol. 2, no. 2, pp. 1–8. **79**

Adler, M., and Wozniak, E. (1981), *The Origins and Consequences of Default*, Research Report for the Scottish Law Commission No. 5, London: HMSO. **143**

Adler, P. A. (1985), *Wheeling and Dealing: An Ethnography of an Upper-Level Drug Dealing and Smuggling Community*, New York: Columbia University Press. **6, 7–10, 59, 63, 67, 96, 97, 100, 101, 102**

Adler, P., and Adler, P. A. (1985), 'From idealism to pragmatic detachment: the academic performance of college athletes', *Sociology of Education*, vol. 58, no. 4, pp. 241–50. **102**

Agar, M. H. (1984), 'Comment [on Room (1984)]', *Human Organization*, vol. 25, no. 2, p. 178. **167**

Aldrich, H. E. (1972), 'Technology and organizational structure: a re-examination of the findings of the Aston Group', *Administrative Science Quarterly*, vol. 17, no. 1, pp. 26–43. **43**

Alexander, J. C. (1982), *Theoretical Logic in Sociology. Volume 1: Positivism, Presuppositions, and Current Controversies*, London: Routledge & Kegan Paul. **16, 42**

Armistead, N. (1974), 'Introduction', in N. Armistead (ed.), *Reconstructing Social Psychology*, Harmondsworth, Middx: Penguin, pp. 7–27. **22**

Atkinson, J. M., and Drew, P. (1979), *Order in Court*, London: Macmillan. **71**

Atkinson, P. A. (1981), *The Clinical Experience*, Farnborough: Gower. **113**

Azumi, Y., and McMillan, C. J. (1973), 'Subjective and objective measures of organization structure: a preliminary analysis', paper presented at the annual meeting of the American Sociological Association, New York, August, **29, 43**

Babbie, E. R. (1979), *The Practice of Social Research*, 2nd edn, Belmont, Calif.: Wadsworth. **30, 42**

Baker, P. J., and Crist, J. L. (1971), 'Teacher expectancies: a review of the literature', in R. E. Snow and J. L. Elashoff (eds), *Pygmalion Reconsidered*, Worthington, Ohio: Charles A. Jones, pp. 48–64. **165**

Ball, S. J. (1981), *Beachside Comprehensive: A Case-Study of Secondary Schooling*, Cambridge: CUP. **66, 67, 73–4, 88, 109, 127, 140–1, 170**

Ball, S. J. (1984), 'Beachside reconsidered: reflections on a methodological apprenticeship', in R. G. Burgess (ed.) *The Research Process in Educational Settings: Ten Case Studies*, London: Falmer, pp. 69–96. **73, 78–9, 118**

Barker, E. (1984), *The Making of a Moonie: Choice or Brainwashing?*, Oxford: Basil Blackwell. **138–9, 140**

Barrett, S. R. (1976), 'The use of models in anthropological fieldwork', *Journal of Anthropological Research*, vol. 32, pp. 161–81. **99**

Beardsworth, A. D. (1980), 'Analysing press content: some technical and methodological issues', in H. Christian (ed.), *The Sociology of Journalism and the Press* (Sociological Review Monograph No. 29), Keele, Staffs.: University of Keele, pp. 371–95. **12**

Becker, H. S. (1958), 'Problems of inference and proof in participant observation', *American Sociological Review*, vol. 23, no. 6, pp. 652–60. **69, 112**

Becker, . H. S., and Geer, B. (1957), 'Participant observation and interviewing: a comparison', *Human Organization*, vol. 16, no. 3, pp. 28–32. **2, 107, 173**

Becker, H. S., Geer. B., and Hughes, E. C. (1968), *Making the Grade*, New York: Wiley. **87**

Becker, H. S., Geer, B., Hughes, E. C., and Strauss, A. L. (1961), *Boys in White: Student Culture in Medical School*, Chicago: University of Chicago Press. **56, 89**

Bell, C., and Newby, H. (1977) (eds), *Doing Sociological Research*, London: Allen & Unwin. **21**

Berkowitz, L., and Donnerstein, E. (1982), 'External validity is more than skin deep', *American Psychologist*, vol. 37, no. 3, pp. 245–57. **37**

Berreman, G. D. (1962), *Behind Many Masks: Ethnography and Impression Management in a Himalayan Village*, Ithaca, NY: Society for Applied Anthropology (Monograph no. 4). **77**

Bhaskar, R. (1975), *A Realist Theory of Science*, Leeds: Leeds Books. **34, 42**

Billig, M. (1977), 'The new social psychology and "fascism"', *European Journal of Social Psychology*, vol. 7, no. 4, pp. 393–432. **92**

Birkstead, I. K. (1976), 'School performance viewed from the boys', *Sociological Review*, vol. 24, no. 1, pp. 63–77. **72–3**

Bittner, E. (1967), 'The police on skid-row: a study of peace keeping', *American Sociological Review*, vol. 32, no. 5, pp. 699–715. **53**

Bittner, E. (1973), 'Objectivity and realism in sociology', in G. Psathas (ed.), *Phenomenological Sociology*, New York: Wiley, pp. 109–25. **76**

Blalock, H. M. (1964), *Causal Inferences in Nonexperimental Research*, Chapel Hill, NC: University of North Carolina Press. **31**

Blalock, H. M. (1970), *An Introduction to Social Research*, Englewood Cliffs, NJ: Prentice-Hall. **2, 38, 94**

Blau, P. M. (1955), *The Dynamics of Bureaucracy*, Chicago: University of Chicago Press. **12**

Blau, P. M. (1964), 'The research process in the study of *The Dynamics of Bureaucracy*', in P. E. Hammond (ed.), *Sociologists at Work*, New York: Basic Books, pp. 16–49. **117–18**

Blease, D., and Bryman, A. (1986), 'Research in schools and the case for methodological integration', *Quality and Quantity*, vol. 20, pp. 157–68. **141–2**

Bloor, M. (1978), 'On the analysis of observational data: a discussion of the worth and uses of inductive techniques and respondent validation', *Sociology*, vol. 12, no. 3, pp. 545–52. **67, 78–9, 81, 83**

Blumer, H. (1948), 'Public opinion and public opinion polling', *American Sociological Review*, vol. 13, no. 5, pp. 542–54. **39**

Blumer, H. (1954), 'What is wrong with social theory?', *American Sociological Review*, vol. 19, no. 1, pp. 3–10. **68**

Blumer, H. (1956), 'Sociological analysis and the "variable"', *American Sociological Review*, vol. 21, no. 6, pp. 683–90. **101**

Blumer, H. (1962), 'Society as symbolic interaction', in A. M. Rose (ed.), *Human Behavior and Social Processes*, London: Routledge & Kegan Paul, pp. 179–92. **55**

Blumer, H. (1969), *Symbolic Interactionism*, Englewood Cliffs, NJ: Prentice-Hall. **55, 56, 58, 96, 115**

Blumer, H. (1980), 'Comment: Mead and Blumer: The convergent methodological perspectives of social behaviorism and symbolic interactionism', *American Sociological Review*, vol. 45, no. 3, pp. 409–19. **56**

Bogdan, R., and Biklen, S. K. (1982), *Qualitative Research for Education: An Introduction to Theory and Methods*, Boston: Allyn & Bacon. **108**

Bogdan, R., and Taylor, S. J. (1975), *Introduction to Qualitative Research Methods: A Phenomenological Approach to the Social Sciences*, New York: Wiley. **4, 53, 54, 93**

Bresnen, M. (1988), 'Insights on site: research into construction project organizations', in A. Bryman (ed.), *Doing Research in Organizations*, London: Routledge & Kegan Paul, pp. 34–52. **99–100**

Bridgman, P. W. (1927), *The Logic of Modern Physics*, New York: Macmillan. **17**

Brophy, J. E., and Good, T. L. (1974), *Teacher–Student Relationships: Causes and Consequences*, New York: Holt, Rinehart & Winston. **163–4**

Brown, G. W., and Harris, T. W. (1978), *The Social Origins of Depression: A Study of Psychiatric Disorder in Women*, London: Tavistock. **121**

Bruyn, S. T. (1966), *The Human Perspective in Sociology: The Methodology of Participant Observation*, Englewood Cliffs, NJ: Prentice-Hall. **3**

Bryant, C. G. A. (1985), *Positivism in Social Theory and Research*, London: Macmillan. **14, 39, 41, 43, 44**

Bryman, A. (1986), *Leadership and Organizations*, London: Routledge & Kegan Paul. **33, 42, 43, 121–2**

Bryman, A. (1988), 'Introduction: "inside acounts" and social research in organizations', in A. Bryman (ed.), *Doing Research in Organizations*, London: Routledge & Kegan Paul, pp. 1–20. **99, 153, 155**

Bryman, A., Bytheway, B., Allatt, P., and Keil, T. (1987) (eds), *Rethinking the Life Cycle*, London: Macmillan. **32**

Buchanan, D., Boddy, D., and McCalman, J. (1988), 'Getting in, getting on, getting out, getting back', in A. Bryman (ed.), *Doing Research in Organizations*, London: Routledge & Kegan Paul, pp. 53–67. **78–9, 99**

Bucher, R. (1970), 'Social process and power in a medical school', in M. N. Zald (ed.), *Power in Organizations*, Nashville: Vanderbilt University Press, pp. 3–48. **69, 117**

Bulmer, M. (1979), 'Concepts in the analysis of qualitative data', *Sociological Review*, vol. 27, no. 4, pp. 651–77. **84–5**

Bulmer, M. (1982) (ed.), *Social Research Ethics*, London: Macmillan. **112**

Bulmer, M. (1986), 'The value of qualitative methods', in M. Bulmer (with K. G. Banting, S. S. Blume, M. Carley, and C. H. Weiss), *Social Science and Social Policy*, London: Allen & Unwin, pp. 180–203. **88**

Bulmer, M. and Burgess, R. G. (1986), 'Do concepts, variables and indicators interrelate?', in R. G. Burgess (ed.), *Key Variables in Social Investigation*, London: Routledge & Kegan Paul, pp. 246–65. **22**

Burgess, R. G. (1983), *Experiencing Comprehensive Education: A Study of Bishop McGregor School*, London: Methuen. **56, 63–4, 87, 88**

Burgess, R. G. (1984), *In the Field: An Introduction to Field Research*, London: Allen & Unwin. **49, 117**

Campbell, D. T. (1957), 'Factors relevant to the validity of experiments in social settings', *Psychological Bulletin*, vol. 54, pp. 297–312. **30, 36**

Campbell, D. T. (1979), ' "Degrees of freedom" and the case study', in T. D. Cook and C. R. Reichardt (eds) *Qualitative and Quantitative Methods in Evaluation Research*, Beverly Hills, Calif.: Sage, pp. 49–67. **122**

Campbell, D. T., and Fiske, D. W. (1959), 'Convergent and discriminant validation by the multitrait-multimethod matrix', *Psychological Bulletin*, vol. 56, no. 2, pp. 81–105. **29**

Carlin, J. E. (1966), *Lawyers' Ethics: A Survey of the New York City Bar*, New York: Russell Sage Foundation. **135**

Cavendish, R. (1982), *Women on the Line*, London: Routledge & Kegan Paul. **111**

Cicourel, A. V. (1964), *Method and Measurement in Sociology*, New York: Free Press. **29, 73**

Cicourel, A. V. (1968), *The Social Organization of Juvenile Justice*, New York: Wiley. **53**

Cicourel, A. V. (1981), 'Notes on the integration of micro- and macro-levels of analysis', in K. Knorr-Cetina and A. V. Cicourel (eds), *Advances in Social Theory and Methodology: Toward an Integration of*

Micro- and Macro-Sociologies, Boston: Routledge & Kegan Paul, pp. 51–80. **147, 156**

Cicourel, A. V. (1982), 'Interviews, surveys, and the problem of ecological validity', *American Sociologist*, vol. 17, no. 1, pp. 11–20. **97, 114**

Clairborn, W. L. (1969), 'Expectancy effects in the classroom: a failure to replicate', *Journal of Educational Psychology*, vol. 60, no. 5, pp. 377–83. **163, 166**

Clifford, J. (1986), 'On ethnographic allegory', in J. Clifford and G. E. Marcus (eds), *Writing Culture: The Poetics and Politics of Ethnography*, Berkeley: University of California Press, pp. 98–121. **80**

Clifford, J., and Marcus, G. E. (1986) (eds), *Writing Culture: The Poetics and Politics of Ethnography*, Berkeley: University of California Press. **80, 92**

Cohen, A. P. (1978), 'Ethnographic method in the real community', *Sociologia Ruralis*, vol. 18, no. 1, pp. 1–22. **64–5, 67–8, 99**

Cohen, P. S. (1980), 'Is positivism dead?', *Sociological Review*, vol. 28, no. 1, pp. 141–76. **13**

Coleman, J. S. (1958), 'Relational analysis: the study of social organization with survey methods', *Human Organization*, vol. 16, no. 4, pp. 28–36. **39**

Collins, H. M. (1985), *Changing Order: Replication and Induction in Scientific Practice*, London: Sage. **38**

Cook, J. A. (1984), 'Influence of gender on the problems of parents of fatally ill children', *Journal of Psychosocial Oncology*, vol. 2, no. 1, pp. 71–91. **132**

Cook, J. A., and Fonow, M. M. (1986), 'Knowledge and women's interests: issues of epistemology and methodology in feminist sociological research', *Sociological Inquiry*, vol. 56, no. 1, pp. 2–29. **132**

Cooley, C. H. (1902), *Human Nature and the Social Order*, New York: Charles Scribner's Sons. **55**

Crapanzano, V. (1986), 'Hermes' dilemma: the masking of subversion in ethnographic description', in J. Clifford and G. E. Marcus (eds), *Writing Culture: The Poetics and Politics of Ethnography*, Berkeley: University of California Press, pp. 51–76. **80**

Crompton, R., and Jones, G. (1988), 'Researching white collar organizations: why sociologists should not stop doing case studies', in A. Bryman (ed.), *Doing Research in Organizations*, London: Routledge & Kegan Paul, pp. 68–81. **48, 127**

Cronbach, L. J. (1975), 'Beyond the two disciplines of scientific psychology', *American Psychologist*, vol. 30, no. 1, pp. 116–27. **156**

Crozier, M. (1964), *The Bureaucratic Phenomenon*, Chicago: University of Chicago Press. **157–8**

Cunningham-Burley, S. (1985), 'Rules, roles and communicative performance in qualitative research interviews', *International Journal of Sociology and Social Policy*, vol. 5, no. 3, pp. 67–77. **115**

Daft, R. L. (1985), 'Why I recommend that your manuscript be rejected and what you can do about it', in L. L. Cummings and P. J. Frost (eds),

Publishing in the Organizational Sciences, Homewood, Ill.: Richard D. Irwin, pp. 193–209. **169**

Dalton, M. (1959), *Men Who Manage*, New York: Wiley. **45, 110, 157–8**

Daniel, W. W. (1968), *Racial Discrimination in England*, Harmondsworth, Middx: Penguin. **112**

Davies, H. (1972), *The Glory Game*, London: Weidenfeld & Nicholson. **113-14**

Davis, J. A. (1985), *The Logic of Causal Order*, Sage University Paper series on Quantitative Applications in the Social Sciences, series no. 55, Beverly Hills, Calif.: Sage. **30, 31, 32**

Delamont, S. (1976), 'Beyond Flanders' fields: the relationship of subject-matter and individuality to classroom style', in M. Stubbs and S. Delamont (eds), *Explorations in Classroom Observation*, Chichester: Wiley, pp. 101–31. **145–6**

Delamont, S. (1981), 'All too familiar? A decade of classroom research', *Educational Analysis*, vol. 3, no. 1, pp. 69–83. **86**

Delamont, S., and Atkinson, P. (1980), 'The two traditions in educational ethnography: sociology and anthropology compared', *British Journal of Sociology of Education*, vol. 1, no. 2, pp. 139–52. **119**

Delamont, S., and Hamilton, D. (1984), 'Revisiting classroom research: a continuing cautionary tale', in S. Delamont (ed.), *Readings on Interaction in the Classroom*, London: Methuen, pp. 3–24. **108**

Denzin, N. K. (1970), *The Research Act in Sociology*, Chicago: Aldine. **131**

Deutscher, I. (1966), 'Words and deeds: social science and social policy', *Social Problems*, vol. 13, pp. 235–54. **115**

Deutscher, I. (1973), *What We Say/What We Do*, Glenview: Scott, Foresman. **69**

Dipboye, R. L., and Flanagan, M. F. (1979), 'Research settings in industrial and organizational psychology: Are findings in the field more generalizable than in the laboratory?', *American Psychologist*, vol. 34, no. 2, pp. 141–50. **37**

Ditton, J. (1977), *Part-Time Crime: An Ethnography of Fiddling and Pilferage*, London: Macmillan. **67, 110**

Dodd, S. C. (1939), 'A system of operationally defined concepts for sociology', *American Sociological Review*, vol. 4, pp. 619–34. **22**

Douglas, J. D. (1972) (ed.), *Research on Deviance*, New York: Random House. **7**

Douglas, J. D. (1976), *Investigative Social Research*, Beverly Hills, Calif.: Sage. **4, 7, 89, 119**

Durkheim, E. (1952), *Suicide: A Study in Sociology*, London: Routledge & Kegan Paul. **12, 174**

Duster, T. (1981), 'Intermediate steps between micro- and macro-integration: the case of screening for inherited disorders', in K. Knorr-Cetina and A. V. Cicourel (eds), *Advances in Social Theory and Methodology: Toward an Integration of Micro- and Macro-Sociologies*, Boston: Routledge & Kegan Paul, pp. 109–35. **148–9**

Eagly, A. H., and Carli, L. L. (1981), 'Sex of researchers and sex-typed communications as determinants of sex differences in influenceability: a meta-analysis of social influence studies', *Psychological Bulletin*, vol. 90, no. 1, pp. 1–20. **167–8**

Essex, M., Estroff, S., Kane, S., McLanahan, S., Robbins, J., Dresser, R., and Diamond, R. (1980), 'On Weinstein's "Patient attitudes toward mental hospitalization: a review of quantitative research"', *Journal of Health and Social Behavior*, vol. 21, no. 4, pp. 393–6. **160–1**

Evered, R., and Louis, M. R. (1981), 'Alternative perspectives in the organizational sciences: "inquiry from the inside" and "inquiry from the outside"', *Academy of Management Review*, vol. 6, no. 3, pp. 385–95. **3**

Festinger, L., Riecken, H. W., and Schachter, S. (1956), *When Prophecy Fails*, New York: Harper & Row. **112, 122, 123**

Feyerabend, P. (1975), 'How to defend society against science', *Radical Philosophy*, no. 11 (Summer), pp. 3–8. **4**

Fiedler, F. E. (1967), *A Theory of Leadership Effectiveness*, New York: McGraw-Hill. **28**

Fielding, N. G., and Fielding, J. L. (1986), *Linking Data*, Sage University Paper series on Qualitative Research Methods (Vol. 2). Beverly Hills, Calif.: Sage. **146–7**

Filmer, P., Phillipson, M., Silverman, D., and Walsh, D. (1972), *New Directions in Sociological Theory*, London, Collier-Macmillan. **18, 104**

Filstead, W. J. (1970) (ed.), *Qualitative Methodology: Firsthand Involvement with the Social World*, Chicago: Markham. **3–4, 57**

Filstead, W. J. (1979), 'Qualitative methods: a needed perspective in evaluation research', in T. D. Cook and C. S. Reichardt (eds), *Qualitative and Quantitative Methods in Evaluation Research*, Beverly Hills, Calif.: Sage, pp. 33–48. **97, 98, 105, 106, 108**

Finch, J. (1986), *Research and Policy: The Uses of Qualitative Methods in Social and Educational Research*, London: Falmer Press. **66, 104**

Fiske, S. T., and Taylor, S. E. (1984), *Social Cognition*, New York: Random House. **121, 156**

Flanders, N. (1970), *Analyzing Teacher Behavior*, Reading, Mass.: Addison-Wesley. **12**

Fletcher, C. (1974), *Beneath the Surface*, London: Routledge & Kegan Paul. **4**

Ford, J., Keil, E. T., Beardsworth, A. D., and Bryman, A. (1982), 'How employers see the public employment service', *Employment Gazette*, vol. 91, no. 11, pp. 466–72. **128**

Freeman, D. (1983), *Margaret Mead and Samoa: the Making and Unmaking of an Anthropological Myth*, Cambridge, Mass.: Harvard University Press. **75–6, 80**

Freeman, J. (1986), 'Data quality and the development of organizational social science: an editorial essay', *Administrative Science Quarterly*, vol. 31, no. 2, pp. 298–303. **36, 101**

Fuller, M. (1984), 'Dimensions of gender in a school: reinventing the wheel', in R. G. Burgess (ed.), *The Research Process in Educational Settings: Ten Case Studies*, London: Falmer Press, pp. 97–115. **128–9**

Galton, M., and Delamont, S. (1985), 'Speaking with forked tongue? Two styles of observation in the ORACLE project', in R. G. Burgess (ed.), *Field Methods in the Study of Education*, London: Falmer Press, pp. 163–89. **89, 132, 153**

Galton, M., and Willcocks, J. (1983), *Moving from the Primary Classroom*, London: Routledge & Kegan Paul. **132**

Gans, H. J. (1962), *The Urban Villagers*, New York: Free Press. **45, 87, 89, 95, 96, 124, 137**

Gans, H. J. (1967), *The Levittowners*, London: Allen Lane. **48, 49, 113, 137–8, 140**

Gans, H. J. (1982), *The Urban Villagers*, 2nd edn, New York: Free Press. **95, 127**

Garfinkel, H. (1967), *Studies in Ethnomethodology*, Englewood Cliffs, NJ: Prentice-Hall. **53**

Garnica, O. K. (1981), 'Social dominance and social interaction – the Omega Child in the classroom', in J. L. Green and C. Wallat (eds), *Ethnography and Language in Educational Settings*, Norwood, NJ: Ablex, pp. 229–52. **141**

Gartrell, B. (1979), 'Is ethnography possible? A critique of *African Odyssey*', *Journal of Anthropological Research*, vol. 35, no. 4, pp. 426–46. **76–7**

Geertz, C. (1973), *The Interpretation of Cultures*, New York: Basic Books. **79**

Gergen, K. G. (1973), 'Social psychology as history', *Journal of Personality and Social Psychology*, vol. 26, no. 2, pp. 309–20. **167**

Giddens, A. (1974), 'Introduction', in A. Giddens (ed.), *Positivism and Sociology*, London: Heinemann, pp. 1–22. **13**

Giedymin, J. (1975), 'Antipositivism in contemporary philosophy of social science and humanities', *British Journal for the Philosophy of Science*, vol. 26, no. 4, pp. 275–301. **14, 42**

Glaser, B. G., and Strauss, A. L. (1967), *The Discovery of Grounded Theory*, Chicago: Aldine. **3, 83–5, 91, 117, 120, 132**

Goffman, E. (1961), *Asylums*, New York: Doubleday. **159**

Goldman, A. R., Bohr, R. H., and Steinberg, T. A. (1970), 'On posing as mental patients: reminiscences and recommendations', *Professional Psychology*, vol. 1, pp. 427–34. **159–60**

Goldthorpe, J. H. (with C. Llewellyn and C. Payne) (1980), *Social Mobility and Class Structure in Modern Britain*, Oxford: Clarendon Press. **109, 170**

Goldthorpe, J. H., Lockwood, D., Bechhofer, F., and Platt, J. (1968), *The Affluent Worker: Industrial Attitudes and Behaviour*, Cambridge: CUP. **26, 35, 121, 124**

Goode, W. J., and Hatt, P. K. (1952), *Methods in Social Research*, New York: McGraw-Hill. **1–2, 18**

Greenwald, A. G. (1975), 'Consequences of prejudice against the null hypothesis', *Psychological Bulletin*, vol. 82, no. 1, pp. 1–20. **168**

Gregory, J., and Monk, J. (1981), *Survey of Defenders in Debt Actions in Scotland*, Research Report for the Scottish Law Commission No. 6, London: HMSO. **142**

Griffin, C. (1985a), *Typical Girls? Young Women from School to the Job Market*, London: Routledge & Kegan Paul. **50, 111**

Griffin, C. (1985b), 'Qualitative methods and cultural analysis: young women and the transition from school to un/employment', in R. G. Burgess (ed.), *Field Methods in the Study of Education*, London: Falmer Press, pp. 97–113. **50**

Gross, N., Giacquinta, J. B., and Bernstein, M. (1971), *Implementing Organizational Innovations: A Sociological Analysis of Planned Educational Change*, New York: Basic Books. **149–51**

Guba, E. G. (1985), 'The context of emergent paradigm research', in Y. S. Lincoln (ed.), *Organizational Theory and Inquiry: The Paradigm Revolution*, Beverly Hills, Calif.: Sage, pp. 79–104. **18, 107–8**

Guba, E. G., and Lincoln, Y. S. (1982), 'Epistemological and methodological bases of naturalistic inquiry', *Educational Communication and Technology Journal*, vol. 30, no. 4, pp. 233–52. **3, 50**

Halfpenny, P. (1979), 'The analysis of qualitative data', *Sociological Review*, vol. 27, no. 4, pp. 799–825. **100**

Halfpenny, P. (1982), *Positivism and Sociology: Explaining Social Life*, London: Allen & Unwin. **14, 17, 42**

Hall, R. H. (1963), 'The concept of bureaucracy: an empirical assessment', *American Journal of Sociology*, vol. 69, no. 1, pp. 32–40. **29**

Hall, R. H. (1968), 'Professionalization and bureaucratization', *American Sociological Review*, vol. 33, no. 1, pp. 92–104. **29, 39**

Hall, R. H., Clark, J. P., Giordano, P. C., Johnson, P. V., and Van Roekel, M. (1977), 'Patterns of interorganizational relationships', *Administrative Science Quarterly*, vol. 22, no. 3, pp. 457–74. **39**

Hall, W. S., and Guthrie, L. F. (1981), 'Cultural and situational variation in language function and use – methods and procedures for research', in J. L. Green and C. Wallatt (eds), *Ethnography and Language in Educational Settings*, Norwood, NJ: Ablex, pp. 209–28. **151–2**

Halpin, A. W., and Winer, B. J. (1957), 'A factorial study of the leader behavior descriptions', in R. M. Stogdill and A. E. Coons (eds), *Leader Behavior: its Description and Measurement*, Columbus: Ohio State University, Bureau of Business Research, pp. 39–51. **27**

Halsey, A. H., Floud, J., and Martin, F. M. (1956), *Social Class and Educational Opportunity*, London: Heinemann. **74**

Hammersley, M. (1984), 'The researcher exposed: a natural history', in R. G. Burgess (ed.), *The Research Process in Educational Settings: Ten Case Studies*, London: Falmer Press, pp. 39–67. **63, 85, 118, 147**

Hammersley, M. (1985), 'From ethnography to theory: a programme and paradigm in the sociology of education', *Sociology*, vol. 19, no. 2, pp. 244–59. **86, 122**

Hammersley, M., and Atkinson, P. (1983), *Ethnography: Principles in Practice*, London: Tavistock. **45, 49**

Hammersley, M., Scarth, J., and Webb, S. (1985), 'Developing and testing theory: the case of research on pupil learning and examinations', in R. G. Burgess (ed.), *Issues in Educational Research: Qualitative Methods*, London: Falmer Press, pp. 48–66. **86–7, 122**

Hargreaves, A. (1985), 'The micro–macro problem in the sociology of education', in R. G. Burgess (ed.), *Issues in Educational Research: Qualitative Methods*, London: Falmer Press, pp. 21–47. **147, 156**

Hargreaves, D. H. (1967), *Social Relations in a Secondary School*, London: Routledge & Kegan Paul. **74**

Hargreaves, D. H. (1978), 'Whatever happened to symbolic interactionism?', in L. Barton and R. Meighan (eds), *Interpretations of Schooling and Classrooms*, Driffield, N. Humberside: Nafferton Books, pp. 7–22. **148**

Hargreaves, D. H., Hester, S. K., and Mellor, F. J. (1975), *Deviance in Classrooms*, London: Routledge & Kegan Paul. **169**

Harré, R. (1972), *The Philosophies of Science*, Oxford: OUP. **17, 34, 42**

Harré, R. (1974), 'Blueprint for a new science', in N. Armistead (ed.), *Reconstructing Social Psychology*, Harmondsworth: Penguin, pp. 240–59. **59**

Harré, R. (1979), *Social Being*, Oxford: Basil Blackwell. **59**

Harré, R. (1986), 'Ethogenics', in R. Harré and R. Lamb (eds.), *The Dictionary of Personality and Social Psychology*, Oxford: Basil Blackwell, pp. 102–5. **59–60**

Harré, R., Clark, D., and De Carlo, N. (1985), *Motives and Mechanisms*, London: Methuen. **40**

Harré, R., and Secord, P. F. (1972), *The Explanation of Social Behaviour*, Oxford: Basil Blackwell. **31, 34, 42, 59**

Heap, J. L., and Roth, P. A. (1973), 'On phenomenological sociology', *American Sociological Review*, vol. 38, no. 3, pp. 354–67. **52**

Heisenberg, W. (1975), 'The great tradition: end of an epoch?', *Encounter*, vol. 44, no. 3, pp. 52–8. **37, 38**

Hester, S. K. (1985), 'Ethnomethodology and the study of deviance in schools', in R. G. Burgess (ed.), *Strategies of Educational Research: Qualitative Methods*, London: Falmer Press, pp. 243–63. **78**

Hickson, D. J., and McMillan, C. J. (1981) (eds), *Organization and Nation: The Aston Programme IV*, Aldershot: Gower. **36**

Hilton, G. (1972), 'Causal inference analysis: a seductive process', *Administrative Science Quarterly*, vol. 17, no. 1, pp. 44–54. **32**

Hindelang, M. J. (1973), 'Causes of delinquency: a partial replication and extension', *Social Problems*, vol. 20, pp. 471–87. **7**

Hinings, C. R., Hickson, D. J., Pennings, J. M., and Schneck, R. E. (1974), 'Structural conditions of intraorganizational power', *Administrative Science Quarterly*, vol. 19, no. 1, pp. 22–44. **158**

Hirschi, T. (1969), *Causes of Delinquency*, Berkeley: University of California Press. **6–7, 9–10, 11, 19, 34, 35, 96, 97, 98–9, 100–101, 102, 110**

Hirschi, T., and Selvin, H. C. (1973), *Principles of Survey Analysis*, New York: Free Press (formerly published in 1967 as *Delinquency Research: An Appraisal of Analytic Methods*). **6**

Holmes, L. D. (1983), 'A tale of two studies', *American Anthropologist*, vol. 85, no. 4, pp. 929–35. **76**

Holmes, L. D. (1984), 'On the questioning of as many as six impossible things about Freeman's Samoa before breakfast', *Canberra Anthropology*, vol. 6, no. 1, pp. 1–16. **76**

Hovland, C. I. (1959), 'Reconciling conflicting results derived from experimental and survey studies of attitude change', *American Psychologist*, vol. 14, no. 1, pp. 8–17. **161–2**

Huber, B. J. (n.d.), *Publishing Options: An Author's Guide to Journals*, Washington, DC: American Sociological Association. **171**

Huberman, A. M., and Crandall, D. P. (1982), 'Fitting words to numbers: multisite/multimethod research in educational dissemination', *American Behavioral Scientist*, vol. 26, no. 1, pp. 62–83. **130, 133–4**

Hughes, J. A. (1976), *Sociological Analysis: Methods of Discovery*, London: Nelson. **31**

Husserl, E. (1927), 'Phenomenology', *Encyclopaedia Britannica*, 14th edn, pp. 699–702. **71**

Inkson, J. H. K., Pugh, D. S., and Hickson, D. J. (1970), 'Organization structure and context: an abbreviated replication', *Administrative Science Quarterly*, vol. 15, no. 3, pp. 318–29. **43**

Jenkins, R. (1983), *Lads, Citizens and Ordinary Kids: Working Class Youth Life-Styles in Belfast*, London: Routledge & Kegan Paul. **47, 62, 139–40, 156**

Jenkins, R. (1984), 'Bringing it all back home: an anthropologist in Belfast', in C. Bell and H. Roberts (eds) *Social Researching: Politics, Problems, Practice*, London: Routledge & Kegan Paul, pp. 147–64. **47–8**

Jensen, A. R. (1969), 'How much can we boost I.Q. and scholastic achievement?', *Harvard Educational Review*, vol. 39, no. 1, pp. 1–123. **165**

Kahl, J. A. (1953), 'Educational and occupational aspirations of "common man" boys', *Harvard Educational Review*, vol. 23, no. 2, pp. 186–203. **136–7, 145**

Keat, R. (1981), *The Politics of Social Theory: Habermas, Freud and the Critique of Positivism*, Oxford: Basil Blackwell. **15, 42**

Keat, R., and Urry, J. (1975), *Social Theory as Science*, London: Routledge & Kegan Paul. **12, 23, 42**

Keddie, N. (1971), 'Classroom knowledge', in M. F. D. Young (ed.), *Knowledge and Control: New Directions for the Sociology of Education*, London: Collier-Macmillan, pp. 133–60. **74, 77**

Kelly, G. A. (1955), *The Psychology of Personal Constructs*, London: Norton. **141**

Kennedy, M. M. (1979), 'Generalizing from single case studies', *Evaluation Quarterly*, vol. 3, no. 4, pp. 661–78. **90**

Kidder, L. H., and Judd, C. M. (1986), *Research Methods in Social Relations*, 5th edn, New York: Holt, Rinehart & Winston. **22, 38**

Kolakowski, L. (1972), *Positivist Philosophy: From Hume to the Vienna Circle*, Harmondsworth: Penguin. **15, 41, 42, 43–4, 120**

Kuhn, M. H. (1964), 'Major trends in symbolic interaction theory in the past twenty-five years', *Sociological Quarterly*, vol. 5, no. 1, pp. 61–84. **56, 125**

Kuhn, T. S. (1970), *The Structure of Scientific Revolutions*, 2nd edn, Chicago: University of Chicago Press (originally published in 1962). **4, 16, 45, 105, 108, 124**

Lacey, C. (1970), *Hightown Grammar: The School as a Social System*, Manchester: Manchester University Press. **74, 109, 131, 140**

Lacey, C. (1976), 'Problems of sociological fieldwork: a review of the methodology of *Hightown Grammar*', in M. Shipman (ed.), *The Organization and Impact of Social Research*, London: Routledge & Kegan Paul, pp. 63–88. **131**

LaPiere, R. T. (1934), 'Attitudes vs. actions', *Social Forces*, vol. 13, pp. 230–7. **115**

Lazarsfeld, P. F. (1958), 'Evidence and inference in social research', *Daedalus*, vol. 87, no. 4, pp. 99–130. **23–7**

LeCompte, M. D., and Goetz, J. P. (1982), 'Problems of reliability and validity in ethnographic research', *Review of Educational Research*, vol. 52, no. 1, pp. 31–60. **126**

Lewis, O. (1951), *Life in a Mexican Village: Tepoztlán Restudied*, Urbana, Ill.: University of Illinois Press. **75, 76, 135–6**

Lewis, O. (1961), *The Children of Sánchez*, New York: Vintage. **49**

Liebow, E. (1967), *Tally's Corner*, Boston, Mass.: Little, Brown. **100, 104**

Lindesmith, A. R. (1968), *Addiction and Opiates*, Chicago: Aldine (formerly published in 1947 as *Opiate Addiction*, Bloomington, Ind.: Principia Press). **81–3**

Linn, L. S. (1968), 'The mental hospital from the patient perspective', *Psychiatry*, vol. 31, pp. 213–23. **160**

Lipset, S. M. (1964), 'The biography of a research project: *Union Democracy*', in P. E. Hammond (ed.), *Sociologists at Work: Essays in the Craft of Social Research*, New York: Basic Books, pp. 96–120. **98, 134**

Lipset, S. M., Trow, M., and Coleman, J. S. (1956), *Union Democracy*, Glencoe: Free Press. **90, 97–8**

Locke, E. A. (1986) (ed.), *Generalizing from Laboratory to Field Settings*, Lexington: Lexington Books. **37**

Locke, E. A., and Schweiger, D. M. (1979), 'Participation in decision-making: one more look', in B. M. Staw (ed.), *Research in Organizational Behavior*, Vol. 1, Greenwich, Conn.: JAI Press, pp. 265–339. **166**

Lofland, J. (1967), 'Notes on naturalism', *Kansas Journal of Sociology*, vol. 3, no. 2, pp. 45–61. **58**

Lofland, J. (1971), *Analyzing Social Settings: A Guide to Qualitative Observation and Analysis*, Belmont, Calif.: Wadsworth. **4, 93**

Lofland, L. (1973), *A World of Strangers: Order and Action in Urban Public Space*, New York: Basic Books. **71**

Louis, K. S. (1982a), 'Multisite/multimethod studies: an introduction', *American Behavioral Scientist*, vol. 26, no. 1, pp. 6–22. **129**

Louis, K. S. (1982b), 'Sociologist as sleuth: integrating methods in the RDU study', *American Behavioral Scientist*, vol. 26, no. 1, pp. 101–20. **135**

Lundberg, G. A. (1939), 'Contemporary positivism in sociology', *American Sociological Review*, vol. 4, pp. 42–52. **22, 174**

Lupton, T. (1963), *On the Shop Floor*, Oxford: Pergamon. **45, 88, 124**

McCall, G. J. (1969), 'The problem of indicators in participant observation research', in G. J. McCall and J. L. Simmons (eds), *Issues in Participant Observation: A Text and Reader*, Reading, Mass.: Addison-Wesley, pp. 230–7. **122**

McCleary, R. (1977), 'How parole officers use records', *Social Problems*, vol. 24, no. 5, pp. 576–89. **120**

McDermott, R. P., Gospodinoff, K., and Aron, J. (1978), 'Criteria for an ethnographically adequate description of concerted activities and their contexts', *Semiotica*, vol. 24, nos 3–4, pp. 245–75. **78**

McNamara, D. R. (1980), 'The outsider's arrogance: the failure of participant observers to understand classroom events', *British Educational Research Journal*, vol. 6, no. 2, pp. 113–25. **74, 77**

McPhail, C., and Rexroat, C. (1979), 'Mead vs. Blumer: the divergent methodological perspectives of social behaviorism and symbolic interactionism', vol. 44, no. 3, pp. 449–67. **56, 125**

Magoon, A. J. (1977), 'Constructivist approaches in educational research', *Review of Educational Research*, vol. 47, no. 4, pp. 651–93. **3**

Marcus, G. E. (1986), 'Contemporary problems of ethnography in the modern world system', in J. Clifford and G. E. Marcus (eds), *Writing Culture: the Poetics and Politics of Ethnography*, Berkeley: University of California Press, pp. 165–93. **92**

Marcus, G. E., and Fischer, M. M. J. (1986), *Anthropology as Cultural Critique: An Experimental Moment in the Human Sciences*, Chicago: University of Chicago Press. **92**

Marsh, C. (1982), *The Survey Method: The Contribution of Surveys to Sociological Explanation*, London: Allen & Unwin. **121, 147**

Marsh, P., Rosser, E., and Harré, R. (1978), *The Rules of Disorder*, London: Routledge & Kegan Paul. **60–1**

Martin, J. (1981), 'A garbage can model of the psychological research process', *American Behavioral Scientist*, vol. 25, no. 2, pp. 131–51. **21**

Matza, D. (1969), *Becoming Deviant*, Englewood Cliffs, NJ: Prentice-Hall. **58–9, 110**

Mead, G. H. (1934), *Mind, Self and Society*, Chicago: University of Chicago Press. **54–5, 125**

Mead, M. (1928), *Coming of Age in Samoa: A Psychological Study of Primitive Youth for Western Civilization*, New York: William Morrow. **75–6, 80**

Measor, L. (1985), 'Interviewing: a strategy in qualitative research', in R. G. Burgess (ed.), *Strategies of Qualitative Research: Qualitative Methods*, London: Falmer Press, pp. 55–77. **46–7, 62–3**

Mehan, H. (1978), 'Structuring school structure', *Harvard Educational Review*, vol. 48, no. 1, pp. 32–64. **54, 78**

Merton, R. K. (1967), *On Theoretical Sociology*, New York: Free Press. **19**

Milgram, S. (1963), 'Behavioral study of obedience', *Journal of Abnormal and Social Psychology*, vol. 67, pp. 371–8. **95**

Mishler, E. G. (1986), *Research Interviewing: Context and Narrative*, Cambridge, Mass.: Harvard University Press. **116**

Mitchell, J. C. (1983), 'Case and situation analysis', *Sociological Review*, vol. 31, no. 2, pp. 186–211. **35, 90–1, 123**

Mook, D. G. (1983), 'In defense of external invalidity', *American Psychologist*, vol. 38, no. 4, pp. 379–87. **37**

Morse, N. C., and Weiss, R. S. (1955), 'The function and meaning of work and the job', *American Sociological Review*, vol. 20, no. 2, pp. 191–8. **121**

Mulkay, M., and Gilbert, G. N. (1986), 'Replication and mere replication', *Philosophy of the Social Sciences*, vol. 16, no. 1, pp. 21–37. **38**

Murphy, J. (1974), 'Teacher expectations and working-class under-achievement', *British Journal of Sociology*, vol. 25, no. 3, pp. 326–44. **165**

Nachmias, D., and Nachmias, C. (1976), *Research Methods in the Social Sciences*, London: Edward Arnold. **2**

Newby, H. (1977a), *The Deferential Worker*, London: Allen Lane. **154**

Newby, H. (1977b), 'In the field: reflections on the study of Suffolk farm workers', in C. Bell and H. Newby (eds), *Doing Sociological Research*, London: Allen & Unwin, pp. 108–29. **154–5**

Newby, H., Vogler, C., Rose, D., and Marshall, G. (1985), 'From class structure to class action: British working-class politics in the 1980s', in B. Roberts, R. Finnegan and D. Gallie (eds), *New Approaches to Economic Life*, Manchester: Manchester University Press, pp. 86–102. **36**

Nicholson, B. (1984), *Glory Glory: My Life with Spurs*, London: Macmillan. **113–4**

Oakley, A. (1981), 'Interviewing women: a contradiction in terms', in H. Roberts (ed.), *Doing Feminist Research*, London: Routledge & Kegan Paul, pp. 30–61. **111**

Oakley, A. (1984), *Taking It Like a Woman*, London: Cape. **96–7**

Okely, J. (1987), 'Fieldwork up the M1: policy and political aspects', in A. Jackson (ed.), *Anthropology at Home*, London: Tavistock, pp. 55–73. **103, 104**

Paget, M. A. (1983), 'Experience and knowledge', *Human Studies*, vol. 6, no. 1, pp. 67–90. **116**

Pahl, R. E. (1984), *Divisions of Labour*, Oxford: Basil Blackwell. **78**

Palardy, J. M. (1969), 'What teachers believe – what children achieve', *Elementary School Journal*, vol. 69, pp. 370–4. **163–4**

Parker, S., Brown, R. K., Child, J., and Smith, M. A. (1977), *The Sociology of Industry*, 3rd edn, London: Allen & Unwin. **157–8**

Patrick, J. (1973), *A Glasgow Gang Observed*, London: Eyre-Methuen. **110**

Patton, M. Q. (1975), *Alternative Evaluation Research Paradigm*, Grand Forks: University of North Dakota Press. **133**

Pennings, J. (1973), 'Measures of organizational structure: a methodological note', *American Journal of Sociology*, vol. 79, no. 3, pp. 686–704. **29, 43**

Phillips, B. S. (1966), *Social Research: Strategy and Tactics*, New York: Macmillan. **2, 18**

Platt, J. (1983), 'The development of the "participant observation" method in sociology', *Journal of the History of the Behavioral Sciences*, vol. 19, no. 4, pp. 379–93. **70**

Platt, J. (1985), 'Weber's *verstehen* and the history of qualitative research: the missing link', *British Journal of Sociology*, vol. 36, no. 3, pp. 448–66. **57**

Platt, J. (1986), 'Functionalism and the survey: the relation of theory and method', *Sociological Review*, vol. 34, no. 3, pp. 501–36. **19, 125**

Plummer, K. (1983), *Documents of Life: An Introduction to the Problems and Literature of a Humanistic Method*, London: Allen & Unwin. **71**

Pollert, A. (1981), *Girls, Wives, Factory Lives*, London: Macmillan. **111**

Polsky, N. (1969), *Hustlers, Beats and Others*, Harmondsworth, Middx: Penguin. **59**

Pugh, D. S. (1988), 'The Aston research programme', in A. Bryman (ed.), *Doing Research in Organizations*, London: Routledge & Kegan Paul, pp. 123–35. **42, 98, 103, 158**

Pugh, D. S., and Hickson, D. J. (1976), *Organizational Structure in its Context: The Aston Programme I*, Aldershot: Gower. **32, 36, 42, 103**

Pugh, D. S., Hickson, D. J., and Hinings, C. R. (1983), *Writers on Organizations*, 3rd edn, Harmondsworth, Middx: Penguin. **42**

Pugh, D. S., and Hinings, C. R. (1976) (eds), *Organizational Structure – Extensions and Replications: The Aston Programme II*, Aldershot: Gower. **36, 42**

Pugh, D. S., and Payne, R. L. (1977) (eds), *Organizational Behaviour in its Context: The Aston Programme III*, Aldershot: Gower. **103**

Randall, J. H. (1944), 'The nature of naturalism', in Y. H. Krikorian (ed.), *Naturalism and the Human Spirit*, New York: Columbia University Press, pp. 354–82. **58**

Ranson, S., Bryman, A., and Hinings, C. R. (1977), *Clergy, Ministers and Priests*, London: Routledge & Kegan Paul. **27**

Raudenbusch, S. W. (1983), 'Utilizing controversy as a source of hypotheses for meta-analysis: the case of teacher expectancy's effects on pupil IQ', in R. J. Light (ed.), *Evaluation Studies Review Annual*, Vol. 8, Beverly Hills, Calif.: Sage, pp. 303–25. **165–6**

Redfield, R. (1930), *Tepoztlán: A Mexican Village*, Chicago: University of Chicago Press. **75, 76, 135–6**

Redfield, R. (1955), *The Little Community*, Chicago: University of Chicago Press. **75**

Reichardt, C. S., and Cook, T. D. (1979), 'Beyond qualitative *versus* quantitative methods', in T. D. Cook and C. S. Reichardt (eds), *Qualitative and Quantitative Methods in Evaluation Research*, Beverly Hills, Calif.: Sage, pp. 7–32. **108**

Reicher, S., and Emler, N. (1986), 'Managing reputations in adolescence: the pursuit of delinquent and non-delinquent identities', in H. Beloff (ed.), *Getting into Life*, London: Methuen, pp. 13–42. **137**

Reiss, A. J. (1968), 'Stuff and nonsense about social surveys and participant observation', in H. S. Becker, B. Geer, D. Riesman, and R. S. Weiss (eds), *Institutions and the Person: Papers Presented to Everett C. Hughes*, Chicago: Aldine, pp. 351–67. **154**

Rist, R. C. (1970), 'Student social class and teacher expectations: the self-fulfilling prophecy in ghetto education', *Harvard Educational Review*, vol. 40, no. 3, pp. 411–50. **164–5, 169, 170**

Rist, R. C. (1977), 'On the relations among educational research paradigms: from disdain to detente', *Anthropology and Education Quarterly*, vol. 8, no. 2, pp. 42–9. **50, 105**

Rist, R. C. (1980), 'Blitzkrieg ethnography: on the transformation of a method into a movement', *Educational Researcher*, vol. 8, no. 2, pp. 8–10. **130, 154**

Rist, R. C. (1984), 'On the application of qualitative research to the policy process: an emergent linkage', in L. Barton and S. Walker (eds), *Social Crisis and Educational Research*, London: Croom Helm, pp. 153–70. **63, 87**

Ritzer, G. (1975), 'Sociology: a multiple paradigm science', *American Sociologist*, vol. 10, no. 3, pp. 156–67. **124**

Robbins, T., Anthony, D., and Curtis, T. E. (1973), 'The limits of symbolic realism: problems of empathetic field observation in a sectarian context', *Journal for the Scientific Study of Religion*, vol. 12, no. 3, pp. 259–71. **92**

Roberts, K., Cook, F. G., Clark, S. C., and Semeonoff, E. (1977), *The Fragmentary Class Structure*, London: Heinemann. **27, 35**

Robinson, W. S. (1951), 'The logical structure of analytic induction', *American Sociological Review*, vol. 16, no. 6, pp. 812–18. **81–2**

Rock, P. (1973), 'Phenomenalism and essentialism in the sociology of deviance', *Sociology*, vol. 7, no. 1, pp. 17–29. **85–6, 119**

Rock, P. (1979), *The Making of Symbolic Interactionism*, London: Macmillan. **55, 125**

Rogers, C. (1982), *A Social Psychology of Teaching*, London: Routledge & Kegan Paul. **171**

Room, R. (1984), 'Alcohol and ethnography: a case of problem deflation?', *Human Organization*, vol. 25, no. 2, pp. 169–78. **166–7, 168**

Rosenberg, M. (1968), *The Logic of Survey Analysis*, New York: Basic Books. **101, 145**

Rosenthal, R. (1966), *Experimenter Effects in Behavioral Research*, New York: Appleton-Century-Crofts. **112**

Rosenthal, R., and Jacobson, L. (1968), *Pygmalion in the Classroom:*

Teacher Expectation and Pupils' Intellectual Development, New York: Holt, Rinehart & Winston. **162–6, 169, 170**

Rosenthal, R., and Rosnow, R. L. (1969) (eds), *Artifact in Behavioral Research*, New York: Academic Press. **36**

Rosenthal, R., and Rubin, D. B. (1978), 'Interpersonal expectancy effects: the first 345 studies', *Behavioral and Brain Sciences*, vol. 3, pp. 377–415. **167**

Roy, D. (1960), 'Banana time: job satisfaction and informal interaction', *Human Organization*, vol. 18, no. 4, pp. 158–68. **45, 110**

Sayer, A. (1984), *Method in Social Science: A Realist Approach*, London: Hutchinson. **34, 42**

Scase, R., and Goffee, R. (1982), *The Entrepreneurial Middle Class*, London: Croom Helm. **106, 107**

Schatzman, L., and Strauss, A. L. (1973), *Field Research: Strategies for a Natural Sociology*, Englewood Cliffs, NJ: Prentice-Hall. **4**

Schutz, A. (1962), *Collected Papers I: The Problem of Social Reality*, The Hague: Martinus Nijhoff. **51**

Schutz, A. (1964), *Collected Papers II: Studies in Social Theory*, The Hague: Martinus Nijhoff. **52**

Schutz, A. (1967), *The Phenomenology of the Social World*, Evanston: Northwestern University Press. **51, 52**

Schwartz, H., and Jacobs, J. (1979), *Qualitative Sociology: A Method to the Madness*, New York: Free Press. **4, 54**

Seeman, M. (1967), 'On the personal consequences of alienation in work', *American Sociological Review*, vol. 32, no. 2, pp. 273–85. **25**

Serber, D. (1981), 'The masking of social reality: ethnographic fieldwork in a bureaucracy', in D. A. Messerschmidt (ed.), *Anthropologists at Home in North America: Methods and Issues in the Study of One's Own Society*, Cambridge: CUP, pp. 77–87. **111**

Shapiro, E. (1973), 'Educational evaluation: rethinking the criteria of competence', *School Review*, vol. 81, pp. 523–49. **132–3**

Sharp, R. and Green, A. (1975), *Education and Social Control: A Study in Progressive Primary Education*, London: Routledge & Kegan Paul. **125, 147–8**

Sieber, S. D. (1973), 'The integration of fieldwork and survey methods', *American Sociological Review*, vol. 78, no. 6, pp. 1335–59. **134–5**

Silverman, D. (1972), 'Methodology and meaning', in P. Filmer, M. Phillipson, D. Silverman, and D. Walsh, *New Directions in Sociological Theory*, London: Collier-Macmillan, pp. 183–200. **143**

Silverman, D. (1984), 'Going private: ceremonial forms in a private oncology clinic', *Sociology*, vol. 18, no. 2, pp. 191–204. **13, 144–5**

Silverman, D. (1985), *Qualitative Methodology and Sociology; Describing the Social World*, Aldershot: Gower. **13, 143–4**

Skolnick, J. H. (1966), *Justice without Trial: Law Enforcement in Democratic Society*, New York: Wiley. **88, 124**

Slater, M. K. (1976), *African Odyssey: An Anthropological Adventure*, Garden City, NY: Anchor. **76–7**

Smith, A. G., and Robbins, A. E. (1982), 'Structured ethnography: the study of parental involvement', *American Behavioral Scientist*, vol. 26, no. 1, pp. 45–61. **89, 129–30, 135**

Smith, J. K. (1983), 'Quantitative versus interpretive: the problem of conducting social inquiry', in E. R. House (ed.), *Philosophy of Evaluation*, San Francisco: Jossey-Bass, pp. 27–51. **3**

Smith, M. L. (1980a), 'Teacher expectations', *Evaluation in Education*, vol. 4, pp. 53–5. **165, 171**

Smith, M. L. (1980b), 'Publication bias and meta-analysis', *Evaluation in Education*, vol. 4, pp. 22–4. **168**

Smith, M. L. (1980c), 'Sex bias in counselling and psychotherapy', *Psychological Bulletin*, vol. 87, no. 2, pp. 392–407. **168**

Snizek, W. E. (1976), 'An empirical assessment of "Sociology: a multiple paradigm science"', *American Sociologist*, vol. 11, no. 4, pp. 217–19. **124**

Spindler, G. (1982), 'General introduction', in G. Spindler (ed.), *Doing the Ethnography of Schooling: Educational Anthropology in Action*, New York: Holt, Rinehart & Winston, pp. 1–13. **126**

Stanley, L., and Wise, S. (1983), *Breaking Out: Feminist Consciousness and Feminist Research*, London: Routledge & Kegan Paul. **111**

Stark, R., and Glock, C. Y. (1968), *American Piety*, Berkeley: University of California Press. **25**

Stewart, A., Prandy, K., and Blackburn, R. M. (1980), *Social Stratification and Occupations*, London: Macmillan. **121**

Stinchcombe, A. L. (1964), *Rebellion in a High School*, Chicago: Quadrangle. **134**

Strathern, M. (1987), 'The limits of auto-anthropology', in A. Jackson (ed.), *Anthropology at Home*, London: Tavistock, pp. 16–37, **79**

Strauss, A., Schatzman, L., Ehrlich, D., Bucher, R., and Sabshin, M. (1963), 'The hospital and its negotiated order', in E. Freidson (ed.), *The Hospital in Modern Society*, New York: Macmillan, pp. 147–69. **103**

Strong, P. (1977), 'Private practice for the masses: medical consultations in the NHS', Mimeo., MRC Medical Sociology Unit, Aberdeen (cited in Silverman, 1984). **144**

Sudnow, D. (1967), *Passing on: The Social Organization of Dying*, Englewood Cliffs, NJ: Prentice-Hall. **53**

Thomas, W. I. (1931), *The Unadjusted Girl*, Boston: Little, Brown. **54**

Thomas, W. I., and Znaniecki, F. (1918–20), *The Polish Peasant in Europe and America*, 5 vols., Chicago: University of Chicago Press. **49**

Took, L., and Ford, J. (1987), 'The impact of mortgage arrears on the housing careers of home owners', in A. Bryman, B. Bytheway, P. Allatt, and T. Keil (eds), *Rethinking the Life Cycle*, London: Macmillan, pp. 207–29. **115**

Trend, M. G. (1978), 'On the reconciliation of qualitative and quantitative analyses: a case study', *Human Organization*, vol. 37, no. 4, pp. 345–54. **134**

Trow, M. (1957), 'Comment on "Participant observation and interviewing: a comparison"', *Human Organization*, vol. 16, no. 3, pp. 33–5. **107, 173**

Turner, B. A. (1981), 'Some practical aspects of qualitative data analysis: one way of organising the cognitive processes associated with the generation of grounded theory', *Quality and Quantity*, vol. 15, pp. 225–47. **83–4**

Turner, B. A. (1988), 'Connoisseurship and the study of organizational cultures', in A. Bryman (ed.), *Doing Research in Organizations*, London: Routledge & Kegan Paul, pp. 108–22. **85**

Vidich, A. J., and Shapiro, G. (1955), 'A comparison of participant observation and survey data', *American Sociological Review*, vol. 20, no. 1, pp. 28–33. **2**

Wagner, R. (1981), *The Invention of Culture*, revised edn, Chicago: University of Chicago Press. **79**

Walker, R. (1985), 'An introduction to applied qualitative research', in R. Walker (ed.), *Applied Qualitative Research*, Aldershot: Gower, pp. 3–26. **106**

Wallace, W. (1969), *Sociological Theory*, London: Heinemann. **16**

Walsh, D. (1972), 'Sociology and the social world', in P. Filmer, M. Phillipson, D. Silverman, and D. Walsh, *New Directions in Sociological Theory*, London: Collier-Macmillan. **13, 40, 102–3**

Warshay, L. H. (1975), *The Current State of Sociological Theory: A Critical Interpretation*, New York: Macmillan. **21, 22**

Warwick, D. P., and Lininger, C. A. (1975), *The Sample Survey: Theory and Practice*, New York: McGraw-Hill. **109, 110, 115**

Webb, E. J., Campbell, D. T., Schwartz, R. D., and Sechrest, L. (1966), *Unobtrusive Measures: Nonreactive Research in the Social Sciences*, Chicago: Rand McNally. **36, 95, 112, 131**

Weber, M. (1947), *A Theory of Social and Economic Organization*, Chicago: Free Press. **26, 57, 147**

Weinstein, R. M. (1979), 'Patient attitudes toward mental hospitalization: a review of quantitative research', *Journal of Health and Behavior*, vol. 20, no. 3, pp. 237–58. **159–62, 166, 167, 168**

Weinstein, R. M. (1980), 'The favorableness of patients' attitudes toward mental hospitalization', *Journal of Health and Social Behavior*, vol. 21, no. 4, pp. 397–401. **160–1, 166**

West, W. G. (1984), 'Phenomenon and form in interactionist and neo-Marxist qualitative educational research', in L. Barton and S. Walker (eds), *Social Crisis and Educational Research*, London: Croom Helm, pp. 256–85. **148**

White, K. R. (1982), 'The relation between socioeconomic status and academic achievement', *Psychological Bulletin*, vol. 91, no. 3, pp. 461–81. **168**

Whyte, W. F. (1943), *Street Corner Society*, Chicago: University of Chicago Press. **35, 45**

Whyte, W. F. (1976), 'Research methods for the study of conflict and cooperation', *American Sociologist*, vol. 11, no. 4, pp. 208–16. **135–6**

Whyte, W. F. (1981), *Street Corner Society*, 3rd edn, Chicago: University of Chicago Press. **90**

Whyte, W. F. (1984), *Learning from the Field: A Guide from Experience*, Beverly Hills, Calif.: Sage. **99**

Wilkinson, L. C. (1981), 'Analysis of teacher–student interaction – expectations communicated by conversational structure', in J. L. Green and C. Wallatt (eds), *Ethnography and Language in Educational Settings*, Norwood, NJ: Ablex, pp. 253–68. **152**

Willer, D., and Willer, J. (1973), *Systematic Empiricism: A Critique of a Pseudoscience*, Englewood Cliffs, NJ: Prentice-Hall. **119**

Willis, P. (1977), *Learning to Labour*, Farnborough: Saxon House. **79, 87, 92, 119, 125**

Willis, P. (1980), 'Notes on method', in S. Hall, D. Hobson, A. Lowe, and P. Willis (eds), *Culture, Media, Language*, London: Hutchinson, pp. 88–95. **119**

Wolcott, H. (1975), 'Criteria for an ethnographic approach to research in schools', *Human Organization*, vol. 34, no. 2, pp. 111–27. **45**

Woods, P. (1979), *The Divided School*, London: Routledge & Kegan Paul. **47, 50, 62, 87, 88, 89–90, 107, 109, 127**

Woods, P. (1986), *Inside Schools: Ethnography in Educational Research*, London: Routledge & Kegan Paul. **47, 49, 98**

Woodward, J. (1965), *Industrial Organization: Theory and Practice*, London: OUP. **32**

Wright, E. O., and Perrone, L. (1977), 'Marxist class categories and income inequality', *American Sociological Review*, vol. 42, no. 1, pp. 32–55. **125**

von Wright, G. H. (1971), *Explanation and Understanding*, London: Routledge & Kegan Paul. **14**

Yin, R. K. (1984), *Case Study Research: Design and Methods*, Beverly Hills, Calif.: Sage. **35, 90–1, 123**

Znaniecki, F. (1934), *The Method of Sociology*, New York: Farrar & Rinehart. **81**

Subject Index